Cultural industries
A challenge for the future of culture

Cultural industries
A challenge
for the future
of culture

Published in 1982 by the United Nations
Educational, Scientific and Cultural Organization
7 place de Fontenoy, 75700 Paris
Typeset by Coupé S.A., 44880 Sautron
Printed by Imprimerie de la Manutention, Mayenne

ISBN 92-3-102 003-X
French edition: 92-3-202 003-3

Preface

The General Conference of Unesco, at its twentieth session, held in Paris from 24 October to 28 November 1978, approved the implementation of a comparative research programme on cultural industries.[1]

Unesco's Approved Programme and Budget for 1979–1980 thus stipulates in paragraph 4025 that 'comparative research will be carried out, in collaboration with national and international institutions, both public and private, on the place and role of cultural industries in the cultural development of societies'.

The execution of this programme was entrusted to the Division of Cultural Development, which, in collaboration with the Canadian National Commission for Unesco, organized a meeting of experts on 'The Place and Role of Cultural Industries in the Cultural Development of Societies'. This meeting was held in Montreal from 9 to 13 June 1980. Specialists in different fields of the social sciences and culture from various geocultural regions of the world were invited to help elucidate the problem of the cultural industries in the light of the studies published in the present work. These studies are here preceded by a foreword, prepared by Unesco.

The work itself, based on the papers presented at the Montreal meeting and the discussions to which they gave rise, bears witness to Unesco's efforts over the past ten years or so to update its thinking on culture.

In his opening address, Mr Makaminan Makagiansar, Assistant Director-General for Culture, pointed to the profound cultural changes taking place in the world today and stressed that these were the 'result of the mass production of messages and symbols, giving rise to what has been termed the new industrial revolution in culture'.[2]

The purpose of the texts gathered together in this publication is to set out the main problems involved in the definition of the term 'cultural industries', their scope, their mode of operation, some of their branches, their effect on social groups, the key problems of creative workers, phenomena of internationalization and the various forms of public and private intervention.

The Programme and Budget approved by the General Conference of Unesco at its twenty-first session, held in Belgrade in 1980, endorsed the idea of a publication on cultural industries and expected that this work, issued in English, French and Spanish, would be circulated on the occasion of the World Conference on Cultural Policies, to be organized in Mexico City in July 1982.[3]

The authors are responsible for the choice and the presentation of the facts contained in this book, and for the opinions expressed therein, which are not necessarily those of Unesco and do not commit the Organization.

NOTES

1. *Approved Programme and Budget for 1979-1980* (20C/5 Approved), Theme 4/3/05, pp. 409–10, paras. 4201 and 4205, Paris, Unesco, February 1979.
2. *Final Report of the Committee of Experts on 'The Place and Role of Cultural Industries in the Cultural Development of Societies'* (CC-80/CONF.629/COL.10).
3. *Approved Programme and Budget for 1981–1983* (21C/5 Approved), Theme 4/3.5/05, p. 421, para. 4170, Paris, Unesco, January 1981.

Contents

Foreword

'The stronger the positions of the culture industry, the more summarily it can deal with consumers' needs, producing them, controlling them, disciplining them, and even withdrawing amusement: no limits are set to cultural progress of this kind'.[1]

It was in these critical terms, taking primarily North America as their example, that the two best-known representatives of the Frankfurt school of philosophy, Max Horkheimer and Theodor W. Adorno, defined as far back as the mid-1940s what they considered to be the basic features of modern culture. In their view, culture today is characterized by the importance of its industrial dimension, the force of its political and economic impact, and the fact that, even if to begin with it originates from a small number of industrialized countries, it is disseminated throughout the world. In *Dialectic of Enlightenment* they argued that the methods of persuasion used by cultural industries were everywhere substantially the same, whether under dictatorships or liberal regimes.

Since the end of the Second World War, cultural industries have become increasingly important. New sectors of activity have emerged, such as television and the technologies stemming from it, computer science, video-recording and transmission techniques, and so on. The power of these industries and their international dimension are making themselves increasingly felt, thus decisively setting the future of culture at stake throughout the world.

All over the world, and taking the long-term view, the ways in which culture finds expression and the development of its content and role are seen to be increasingly determined—as they have been above all for the last forty years—by the industrialization of the systems of production and dissemination of cultural messages, whether in the form of products or of services.

Up to approximately the middle of the nineteenth century, all the world's cultures, whether popular or élitist, primarily reflected sets of symbols belonging to societies or religions; from the standpoint of their mode of production, their salient features were the pre-eminence of the single product, or one produced in a very small number of copies, and the continuity of craft techniques. This is still true of the dwindling number of societies that have had little or no experience of the industrial revolution. The development of industrial societies, first in Europe and then throughout the rest of the world, technological innovations following rapidly on each other, particularly in regard to communications, and above all the predominance of economic considerations since the advent of capitalism, have revolutionized the way in which all forms of cultural expression are produced and disseminated. In this respect the arrival of electronics and television represented a further 'qualitative leap'. This meant the gradual eclipse or marginalization of cultural messages that did not take the form of goods, primarily of value as marketable commodities, or that could not be used as a more or less sophisticated means of exerting pressure on public opinion.

The development of newspapers with a wide circulation, photography, the cinema, gramophone records, followed by other forms of sound recording, radio, and in particular, television and its derived video technologies, and more recently, a number of new and fast-developing uses of computer science, have produced at one and the same time new types of message, new relationships between 'transmitters' and 'receivers', and a new socio-economic and socio-cultural balance between those who hold power, whether political, economic or cultural, and the vast mass of those to whom the products of industrialized culture are distributed, either with a view to a short-term economic return (the population in terms of a market) or for purposes of social or political control (the population in terms of public opinion).

What is true for the industrialized countries is even more so for the developing nations. Here the untrammelled spread of cultural industries means, basically, not the development of endogenous activities matching identified needs, but the uncontrolled mass dissemination of messages which are in most cases culturally incompatible with local situations, either because they conflict with cultural identities, as in the case of pre-industrial cultures, or because access to them by the population, and by young people in particular, is dependent on the provision of suitable instruction, that is to say, a stage-by-stage assimilation process in regard to the radical innovations transmitted by cultural industries, especially in the field of mass media.

It would however be mistaken and unrealistic to confine oneself solely to the adverse effects of cultural industries, if the aim is to conduct an analysis which will be both scientifically rigorous and useful in defining response strategies. Admittedly, traditional cultural policies and, at a deeper level, education policies in all their forms, have to some extent given greater access to the products of the mind and cultural values. But above all, progress in communication techniques has increased, to a hitherto unimaginable extent, the range of cultural messages now available to mankind. It has also made possible a substantial reduction in production costs by comparison with non-industrial production standards, thus making the new cultural products both plentiful and economically accessible to nearly all members of the population, at least in the wealthiest countries.

The possibilities of access to the products of cultural industries are moreover not limited to the products of 'sophisticated' culture, which would constitute a somewhat doubtful result from the point of view of cultural democracy. Where certain favourable economic and political conditions exist, cultural industries can radically transform the exercise of artistic professions and creativity in general, enhance the contacts between creative artists and the population and, above all, give fresh impetus to educational action, whether in or out of school, and considerably strengthen effective participation by the people at large in the expression of their culture.

Here a number of specific examples can be quoted: the role of books, and that of educational radio and television broadcasting, which also cover the stage of literacy work, among young people in the developing countries; the revival of local languages for the less extensive cultural regions, particularly the smaller countries; recent or current experiments in 'two-way systems' in a number of countries, chiefly in North America; and the revitalization of local life by means of audio-visual techniques or rural communication in several African countries.

Lastly, it would be failing to recognize twentieth-century cultural reality if one overlooked the fact that the cinema, a major art for all types of public throughout the world, was to a great extent born of industrial systems, first in Europe and later in the United States. Similarly, it should not be forgotten that some great nineteenth-century novels in France, Great Britain and Russia were published in instalments with the use of a new system invented by the directors of the major contemporary daily newspapers to take advantage of the introduction of the rotary press, which gave them greatly increased printing capacity. (This is the first historically recognized case of the industrialization of a production system engendering a form of culture.)

This means that it is not possible to confine oneself to a purely critical analysis of cultural industries, particularly if the aim is to establish the discussion of cultural development on the basis of the material conditions governing the system of production of the most widely distributed cultural goods. Generally speaking, it can be said that a study of the ways and means of production, in this field as in others, coupled with a searching examination of the cultural dimension of the education system, environmental strategies, the social function of creation and the cultural impact of scientific and technological progress, is one of the key considerations in the whole set of problems involved in cultural development. How are cultural products conceived, selected, given form, manufactured, distributed, promoted and consumed? What is their situation in relation to all other forms of cultural communication? What is the relation between the economic and the symbolic values of industrially produced cultural messages? Such are the questions that must be asked if cultural industries are to be studied scientifically.

However, the defining of strategies in response to the worldwide challenge represented by the increasingly rapid spread of industrial combines of all kinds, and their growing international ascendancy, calls for an examination which will be more than purely descriptive in nature. How might it be possible to harness the power of cultural industries to the promotion of cultural development and, generally speaking, foster the mutual enhancement of cultures and the current process of universalization, while safeguarding the cultural identity of individual peoples and giving them the means of controlling their own development? Could the development of action at local level, and of small-scale production units, counterbalance the effects of the cultural standardization brought about by the mass media? What strategies could be effectively worked out at the purely national level, particularly in the developing countries, bearing in mind the urgent economic requirements these countries have to meet? If the responses are to be commensurate with the dimension of the challenges, should not they be sought at the level of international co-operation? These are all questions that necessarily form part of any thorough examination in preparation for action, if we really want to gain more accurate knowledge of the role played by the industries concerned with works of the imagination in world cultural trends as a whole, and tentatively to sketch out their prospects for the future.

It is already ten years since Unesco, moving away from the view of culture as something spontaneous and unconditioned, sought to give due recognition to the importance of analysis and critique of the nature, dimension and impact of mass culture, all issues which largely coincide with those raised by cultural industries.

At the regional conferences on cultural policies which followed the 1970 Venice Conference on Institutional, Administrative and Financial Aspects of Cultural Policies, and which were held in Helsinki in 1972 for Europe, Yogyakarta in 1973 for Asia, Accra in 1975 for the continent of Africa, and Bogotá in 1978 for Latin America and the Caribbean, and also at the regional conferences on communication policies held in San José (Costa Rica, 1976), Kuala Lumpur (Malaysia, 1976) and Yaoundé (United Republic of Cameroon, 1980), Unesco, in the context of its studies on the cultural dimension of development, showed its continuing concern with two basic aspects of culture.

In the first place, there is the relation between cultural development, economic growth and technological development, particularly as regards the application of the latter to the mass media, and in the second place, the growing and increasingly firm awareness that works reflecting the cultural values of a given society are the result of a specific and rational production process, which has to be known if its impact on the content of these works and the values they transmit is to be measured.

Accordingly, at the Conference on Cultural Policies in Latin America and the Caribbean (Bogotá, 1978) the Director-General of Unesco closely associated culture and communication in his opening address, so as clearly to highlight the interrelation between them. He stated that

the mass media that have become one of the basic supports of cultural dissemination transmit messages that are not culturally neutral. They reflect the thinking, the ideas, the values, in short, the vision of the world of those who use them. When they serve as the channel for transmitting to a given region value systems or ways of life which are foreign to the peoples of that region, they cannot be prevented in the end from wiping out the specific values of those peoples, thus becoming, even if unintentionally, instruments of cultural alienation. . . .

The important thing, no doubt, is to recognize this fact and to seek ways of safeguarding the cultural identity of each people without jeopardizing the necessary continuation of exchanges among different cultural areas, or the indispensable mutual enrichment of cultures, since it is also important, for the life and development of each culture, to avoid the other extreme, that is to say the isolation which can also be harmful.

Thus the interdependence of different human societies and the key importance of cultural and communication policies for endogenous development find one of their most striking reflections in the problems raised by cultural industries. In its Draft Programme and Budget for 1981–1983, as discussed and approved at the General Conference of Unesco at its twenty-first session, held in Belgrade in 1980, the Organization accordingly set itself the aim of continuing and intensifying its programme relating to cultural industries, with a view to elucidating more clearly the difficulties and critical areas, particularly as they affect decision-makers.

The problems that appear to require special study are those that concern the impact on cultural development of cultural messages and goods that are industrially produced, disseminated and stocked, particularly in the audio-visual field.

The vast quantity of messages showered on receivers by cultural industries can be analysed not only from the point of view of the content of these messages (which do no more than 'universalize' certain conceptions of the world), but also from that of their impact on the dialectic of access and participation. An abundance of messages of exogenous origin, while promoting access by the receiving populations to certain cultural goods and services, tends at the same time to frustrate or place more and more difficulties in the way of local aspirations to active participation in the form of programme design.

For example, television programmes purchased abroad for a few hundred dollars an hour, which can count on commercial acceptance or sponsorship from the outset, are a standing invitation to a local station to avoid running the risk of national production, which would cost more and would be less sure of acceptance. The result for the public is greater access to programmes of foreign origin, and hence dwindling participation at the local level in the production of messages.

In order to throw light on some of these problems and provide the international community with sufficiently detailed documentation and information to facilitate decision-making, Unesco has undertaken a whole series of studies bearing *inter alia* on the collection and analysis of economic data relating to the structures of cultural industries and the strategies they follow; the good and bad effects of the mass production and distribution of certain cultural products on national, regional and, in particular, rural cultures; the expectations of various social groups, especially young people, women and the elderly, in respect of cultural industries; the socio-cultural effects of technological innovations on the use of leisure, and possible new forms of leisure pursuits and tourism; the evaluation of original experiments in the use of light-weight audio-visual equipment by local communities, and ways and means of encouraging such experiments. Case-studies are also being carried out on the impact of the internationalization of cultural products in the developing countries. Lastly, the relationship between creative artists, intellectuals and those professionally employed by the media, on the one hand, and the cultural industries, on the other, will be discussed at an international symposium; at the same time representatives of cultural industries and their organizations will be made aware, at their own meetings, of the importance of the role of creative workers, intellectuals and artists in the design and production of cultural messages.

But Unesco's part in this process of reflection on the question of cultural industries is not confined to its programmes of studies concerned with culture. The Division of Free Flow of Information and Communication Policies has chosen to study, during the same period, the main features of the international flow of information today: its principal currents, nature, mechanisms, different forms, effects, and the scope and influence of the messages conveyed. Also under study is the impact of advertising—a decisive factor in the analysis of the economic conditions affecting the mass media—in particular its repercussions on the content of messages and the management of national media, special attention being paid to the forms of interdependence between the advertising industry and certain communication industries, and to the specific financial conditions under which information organs operate. Exhaustive scientific studies are also being conducted on the concentration of the industrialized production of messages designed for the press, radio, cinema and television, and on its consequences for programme distribution.

The essential nature of this work of investigation and study of the question of cultural industries, particularly as regards mass communication, in association with the current study of information issues, was fully recognized and agreed by the participants at the last session of the General Conference of Unesco, since a large number of delegates stressed the importance to be attached to research in connection with cultural industries. Congratulating the Unesco Secretariat on the action it had taken in this field, they hoped that its activities would be intensified and developed, and they considered that the question was a vital one, both for the development and for the preservation of endogenous activities, having regard, naturally, to the ambiguous role of cultural industries in this respect. The latter point appeared to require clarification so that the consequences for both industrialized and developing countries might be ascertained. It also appeared necessary to study cultural industries and the mass media in conjunction, since the latter represent one of the most important aspects of these industries taken as a whole.

The need to seek a balanced approach to study and appraisal of the role of the cultural industries was also voiced during the discussions of the General Conference of Unesco, for while some participants emphasized the possible adverse effects of these industries, others, on the contrary, stressed that they offered the hope—and the means—of bringing about the desired democratization of culture. Similarly, while some held the opinion that the mass media might constitute an attack on endogenous cultures and attitudes to life, others considered that they represented a means of cultural dialogue, which is unanimously recognized as the foundation for peace. The aim therefore should be to define the prerequisites for a balanced and pluralistic development of cultural industries, in the light of each society's specific characteristics and needs. However, suitable responses commensurate within the dimension of the problems can be determined only when these problems are better known. Here international co-operation has an important part to play.

It was as part of this broad, diversified and, we would stress, medium-term study process, that an expert committee, convened by Unesco in co-operation with the Canadian National Commission for Unesco, met in Montreal (Canada) from 9 to 13 June 1980, to examine the place and role of cultural industries in the cultural development of societies. It is only against this background that a full appraisal can be made of the statements and arguments advanced by the participants, who came from a great variety of countries and whose experience thus prepared them for a proper understanding of the diversity and complexity of the problems involved.

First of all, taking as their basic a brief historical account of the concept of cultural industries, and a tentative definition and description of their scope, the experts attempted to elucidate the following points: (a) the impact on the public of traditional means of cultural dissemination as compared with those of cultural industries; (b) the respective importance of the different production and marketing processes according to the different media: likely predominance of one or other of these processes; and (c) the place of cultural industries in the light of creativity, cultural identity and the cultural influence of a country: alternatives to the functioning of cultural industries.

Next on the agenda of the meeting came consideration of the mode of production and content of the products of cultural industries. The first task was to analyse the actual functioning of cultural industries at the various stages of the production and distribution process, such as the creation of the product and the production, distribution, marketing and storage networks, and to attempt to determine the influence of the method of production on the content of the product.

Next, an attempt was made to describe the commercial environment within which cultural industries operated, financing, profitability, degree of competition, in particular the share of the market under national control, the relationship between the nationality of the owner and that of the product, the trend towards concentration and internationalization, the role of public, semi-public or private ownership, and so on. This analysis should make it possible, it was considered, to determine whether or not cultural industries favoured the development of a national culture or a multinational culture, a special study being made of the role of multinational enterprises in establishing the framework and fixing the limits within which national cultural efforts were exercised; it should also be possible to gauge the influence of technology on the cultural development of societies.

An important question examined at the meeting was the place of artists, creative workers and performers, who constitute the cornerstone of cultural industries and whose creative or performing ability largely determines the production of these industries. Special consideration was called for in respect of: (a) the strains that existed between art (creativity and talent) and industry (mass production), and between culture and trade; (b) the strains inherent in the process of collective creation; (c) the protection of artists, creative workers and performers; and (d) the influence of technology on their freedom and creativity. Stress was laid on the need for not only an economic but also a sociological approach in order to gain a better insight into the reality of the relationship between artists and cultural industries, bearing in mind their respective characteristics.

In this connection it should be noted that some months after this expert meeting had been held, the General Conference of Unesco, at its twenty-first session, held in Belgrade from 23 September to 28 October 1980, unanimously approved the Recommendation concerning the Status of the Artist, a large part of which deals with the safeguarding of the artistic and professional interests of creative artists and performers *vis-à-vis* the production systems of cultural industries. Section VI, paragraph 6 of the Recommendation reads as follows:

Recognizing in general that national and international legislation concerning the status of artists is lagging behind the general advances in technology, the development of the media of mass communication, the means of mechanical reproduction of works of art and of performances, the education of the public, and the decisive part played by the cultural industries, Member States are invited to take, wherever necessary, appropriate measures to:

(a) ensure that the artist is remunerated for the distribution and commercial exploitation of his work and provide for the artist to maintain control of his work against unauthorized exploitation, modification or distribution;

(b) provide, to the extent possible, for a system guaranteeing the exclusive moral and material rights of artists in respect of any prejudice connected with the technical development of new communication and reproduction media, and of cultural industries; this means, in particular, establishing rights for performers, including circus and variety artists, and puppeteers; in doing so, it would be appropriate to take account of the provisions of the Rome Convention and, with reference to problems arising from the introduction of cable diffusion and videograms, of the Recommendation adopted by the Intergovernmental Committee of the Rome Convention in 1979;

(c) compensate any prejudice artists might suffer in consequence of the technical development of new communication and reproduction media and of cultural industries by favouring, for example, publicity for and dissemination of their works, and the creation of posts;

(d) ensure that cultural industries benefiting from technological changes, including radio and television organizations and mechanical reproduction undertakings, play their part in the effort to encourage and stimulate artistic creation, for instance by providing new employment opportunities, by publicity, by the dissemination of works, payment of royalties or by any other means judged equitable for artists;

(e) assist artists and organizations of artists to remedy, when they exist, the prejudicial effects on their employment or work opportunities of new technologies.

More detailed consideration was then given to a particular industry, namely the book industry. The aim was to throw light on factors such as the internal structures of publishing firms, concentration of publishing and foreign influences in this field, the various methods of distribution and dissemination, publishers' strategies according to their markets and the type of work they publish, particularly as regards the definition of products and price fixing, and the influence of the media on book production and consumption.

Here attention was drawn to the fact that, given the fragile nature of all the other supporting media commonly used by cultural industries (film, plastics, magnetic tapes, etc.), which in the present stage of the art are not guaranteed to last more than a century, books continue to be the most reliable medium on account of their durability, which makes it possible to pass on knowledge. This conclusion incidentally raises the serious problem of the ephemeral nature of almost all the reproduction systems used today by cultural industries.

As regards the impact of cultural industries, special attention was paid to the audio-visual field, on the basis of case-studies concerning the socio-cultural behaviour of young people and women in a number of countries. Here consideration was given to the impact of practices in television, radio and the cinema on traditional values, the expectations of various social and cultural groups, including age-groups, the problems of representation and training, and the influence of cultural industries (with their causes), whether making for standardization or otherwise, on individual or collective strategies.

The last question examined, a vital one from the point of view of defining national strategies for cultural industries, concerned the various possible ways in which a balance could be struck between the public authorities and the private sector in this field. What are the options open to governments as regards support for cultural industries? What means of support are available to the state, what are the objectives and the limits of its action in this field by comparison with the private sector? Can countries formulate and apply national cultural policies which would enable cultural industries to play a constructive role in keeping with the aim to develop endogenous cultural creation, while taking sufficient account of the need for contacts between cultures and the reality of the international scene? Can international agreements help to counterbalance the spread of standardized international mass culture?

Such were the questions that served as a basis for the discussion by the expert committee which met in Montreal, and for the papers presented at that meeting. As reproduced here, the papers do not, of course, cover all the points briefly listed above; they define, either globally or by means of particular examples, the general problem posed by cultural industries, and describe their impact, trends and possible future development. They also outline possible forms of action, and attempt to fit together the main components of an integrated strategy in respect of cultural industries within the context of cultural development. They do, in fact, link up with the statement of the problem set out above and it is basically in relation to this statement that they should be considered, whether they are papers providing general food for thought or recording specific experiments whose diversity obviously reflects the remarkable variety of national situations.

NOTE

1. M. Horkheimer and T. W. Adorno, *Dialectic of Enlightenment,* p. 144, New York, Herder & Herder, 1972.

Part One

General statement of the problem and definitions

Though the term 'culture industry' (in the singular) was coined, as noted above, by Adorno and Horkheimer in one of the chapters of the *Dialectic of Enlightenment,* there is still some doubt as to the type of activities it is supposed to cover (for example, photography, computer science in general, or the manufacture of all the equipment and installations used in the production and dissemination of messages: film and television cameras, radio or television receivers, photographic apparatus, record players of all kinds, video-tape recorders, and so on—and even tourism and advertising). Depending on the activity included, and the hardware or software involved, the economic factors vary considerably in scale, and the transparency of the interrelationship between industries also varies.

Generally speaking, a cultural industry is held to exist when cultural goods and services are produced, reproduced, stored or distributed on industrial and commercial lines, that is to say on a large scale and in accordance with a strategy based on economic considerations rather than any concern for cultural development. There are various types of cultural industry, for example, those in which a created work, still in most cases the work of a craftsman, is reproduced on a large scale with the use of machines and by industrial processes. Cases in point are gramophone records, books and art reproductions. There are increasing signs, moreover, all pointing the same way, of a radical change in the conditions of creation within cultural industries of this type, for example in the case of music. In other types of cultural industry, particularly the cinema and television, but also in certain areas of 'pop' music, the actual creative process requires from the outset complex equipment and installations, thus bringing about marked imbalances in the build-up of production costs, and entailing the collective use of facilities.

Given these technological and economic developments and their effects on the production methods of cultural industries, the basic problem appears increasingly to be that of the ownership and control of the means of production and of distribution circuits, the trend towards the concentration and internationalization of the most representative firms, and the subordination of creative artists to market forces or to more or less overtly dictated consumer demand. It is open to question whether, in order to obtain an accurate portrayal of the system of forces at work in the cultural industries, the assumed symmetry of classical communication theories should not be replaced by a firmly asymmetrical view, reflecting the predominant influence of the industrial producer of the messages (or the interests backing him), who in the end dictates the choice of channel, the content and even the consumer's taste, in the interests of economic or ideological control.

Hence the lively controversy between those, whose feelings towards cultural industries are those of fundamental and outright distrust, and those for whom cultural industries are the key to cultural democracy and the vehicle for putting it effectively into practice. The former consider that emphasis should be laid on the adverse effects stemming from the very abundance of products and their extremely rapid turnover, linked to the logic of the market. In particular they stress what is to all intents and purposes the supremacy of a standardized form of production, based on the commonplace, the ephemeral and the impoverishment of content, in which hackneyed expressions of all kind predominate. Just as, in the field of information, the effect of the constant bombardment of news reports is that the most dramatic real-life events tend to become purely and simply a form of entertainment, so the pace set by producers or distributors for the market for cultural goods and services tends to militate against a questioning attitude, and turn the user into a consumer avid for novelty. The same difficulties apply to creative workers and performers, particularly in the world of records and television, where they do not really receive their due, and where agreeable mediocrity is sometimes preferred to genuinely creative talent, quite apart from the question of the dangers that certain cultural industries entail for intellectual property in general. It is, finally, just as if at the international level, there were a distribution of tasks between the countries producing messages (the industrialized countries) and the countries receiving them (small or developing countries), which have no real say in the matter.

In answer to this criticism, the defenders of cultural industries emphasize the plentiful supply of inexpensive cultural products, which are sufficiently diversified to offer the public much greater opportunities of contact with a wealth of works and, as regards the mass media, to provide on a continuing basis a vast amount of cultural information and knowledge from most of the world's major cultural areas. They stress that, for the first time in the history of mankind, it is possible to have virtually instantaneous knowledge of significant events throughout the world and, hence, to have a greater awareness of the world's cultural, socio-economic and ideological diversity. Some even add that, in a market economy, it is the producers who conform to the consumer's taste, not the other way round, and that it has never been possible to impose a type of cultural product or service on users against their will. Furthermore, in the view of other experts, cultural industries, far from threatening the status of the artist, represent both for creative artists and for performers (and intellectuals in general) a tremendous extension of the possibilities of reaching their public, and also a guarantee of substantial resources, at a time when public expenditure on culture is being seriously cut back. Lastly, it is stressed that, used carefully and realistically, cultural industries, particularly books and radio, can provide developing countries with a very efficient means of cultural 'take-off'.

It is with this twofold approach in mind that the following three studies should be read. That by the Canadian economist Albert Breton portrays and staunchly defends a liberal economy in the field of the cultural industries, as they appear in Canada and the North American context. It is in lively contrast with the Marxist type of critique presented by Armand Mattelart and Jean-Marie Piemme, who go back to the very origins of the concept of cultural industry in relation to its underlying reality. Augustin Girard notes the uncertainties and inevitable pitfalls of all kinds bound up with industrial mechanisms in the cultural field, as elsewhere, and attempts to determine whether, under certain conditions, cultural industries may provide a new opportunity for cultural development and cultural democracy.

1   Cultural industries: a handicap or a new opportunity for cultural development?

Augustin Girard

Professeur Agrégé de l'Université,
Lecturer at the Panthéon-Sorbonne, Paris

Recent studies on the cultural life of the population as a whole (statistics on cultural practices and household consumption, semiotic studies and sociological surveys) bring out more and more clearly the importance of industrially manufactured cultural products giving access for the greatest number of people to culture.

It is true to say that 'cultural machines' have produced more sweeping changes in the cultural life of the vast majority of the population—excluding intellectuals—during the last thirty years than in the hundred years before. In January 1978, a performance one evening of Beethoven's Ninth Symphony by the Berlin Philharmonic Orchestra was heard by 120 million listeners throughout Europe. Every year some books, films and records succeed in winning over a million readers, viewers or listeners. Every evening in every country, thanks to television, audiences of several millions are reached by a film or a dramatic, musical or even literary work.

Yet the study of cultural policies carried out over the last ten years has related almost exclusively to the effort made by the public authorities through a limited number of institutions, and has overlooked what is nevertheless the considerable growth of the market sector of culture.

The cultural scene today is thus made up of two phenomena existing alongside each other, in parallel, without ever meeting: on the one hand a cultural 'explosion', the cultural life of the various strata of the population, which has been extensively—perhaps even profoundly—changed, in terms of time spent, the 'cultural' equipment of households, and the consumption of 'cultural' products; and on the other, an awareness by the public authorities of the need to spell out or implement more rational cultural policies.

The reason these two phenomena never converge is that the thinking behind cultural policies has been focused mainly on traditional methods of dissemination and has been directed towards the democratization of institutions previously reserved for an élite; the very important simultaneous development of the industries concerned with works of the imagination and of cultural 'consumption' by a very widespread public has virtually been disregarded.

Thus for twenty years cultural policies have been curiously lopsided, the result being a clear lack of relevance to the reality of cultural life, and a deep-rooted need for renewal.

Today, discussion is not only inevitable but also highly desirable, and it should be held at all levels, from the smallest dwelling in each locality to important centres of cultural policy-making, including all intellectual circles. Fresh consideration must be given to the interrelation between cultural policies and cultural industries, particularly in view of the fact that the latter are only beginning to develop.

But this process of reflection cannot advance, or even be embarked on seriously, unless it is based on information and facts that make it possible to get away from the antithesis of business and culture, or art and industry, which is as false as it is facile. Before passing judgement or condemning out of hand, one must first look at the facts.

THE NEW CONDITIONS FOR CULTURAL DEMOCRATIZATION

The past fifteen years have seen the emergence of three concomitant phenomena: (a) a two-, five- or ten-fold increase, according to the country, of public spending on culture; (b) despite the increased spending, stagnation in the use made by the public of cultural institutions; and (c) a twenty-, hundred- or thousand-fold increase in public contact with artistic works as a result of industrial cultural products.

The three simultaneous phenomena present a problem to those who are responsible for culture, for all cultural policies throughout the world are aimed at broadening the access of the general public to culture: democratization and decentralization are the two watchwords wherever an explicit cultural policy is pursued by government authorities.

Curiously, although Adorno and Horkheimer observed the phenomenon and used the term 'culture industry' as far back as 1947,[1] and attention was drawn to cultural industries again in 1972,[2] those responsible for cultural policies have persistently turned a blind eye to the growing importance of the products of these industries in people's leisure time. And yet they have affected children and adults alike, including the older generation; they are an intrusive, obvious phenomenon of which everyone has some experience. The figures are impressive: several hours a day, in other words most of people's available leisure time, are spent in the company of cultural machines. George Bernard Shaw was right when he said that evidence is the most difficult thing in the world to see.

MAKING CULTURE ACCESSIBLE TO MORE PEOPLE

The conclusion that inevitably springs from this observation is that far more is being done to democratize and decentralize culture with the industrial products available on the market than with the 'products' subsidized by the public authorities.

It will be argued that such distinctions in terms of quantity are unwarranted, that a cultural product that is transmitted or reproduced does not have the same 'cultural'[3] value as a work communicated directly, at a live performance, for instance. Moreover, distinctions must be made between the various areas of cultural activity: theatre, film, music, debates or exhibitions.

But what exactly is the difference in 'cultural effect' between a film seen in a cinema and the same film watched at home on a television screen (which before long will be the same size as a cinema screen)? How many music lovers now prefer to listen to a quartet in the peaceful atmosphere of their homes, with the range of sound that can be produced with their hi-fi equipment, rather than in a concert hall with all its distractions, distortions and disturbances of all kinds? When in Poland or the United Kingdom 60 per cent of the population sits at home once a week watching a first-rate play, does it not have a closer contact with the theatre than when only just over 15 per cent of the population sees one of those plays once a year in a theatre? To find the answers to questions of this kind, very detailed studies must be carried out, independent of any considerations that smack of intellectual snobbery.

After several years of deliberate policies to develop culture in a great many countries, it has become clear that cultural institutions have succeeded only marginally in expanding the audience for artistic works, while at the same time public preference has gone to works produced industrially. In the space of ten years, gramophone records have more than doubled their audience among nearly all sectors of the population while the concert-going public has stagnated and concerts have remained the preserve of an élite. And yet cultural institutions, too, have had recourse to marketing procedures, at often considerable expense. As with education or health, there comes a time when institutions are spending increasingly large sums of money for a smaller and smaller return.

PSYCHOLOGICALLY, WHICH ARE THE MESSAGES THAT IN PRACTICE REACH THE BROADEST PUBLIC?

A second reason, qualitative rather than quantitative this time, for considering the network of cultural institutions to be inadequate and for turning to cultural industries is that after ten or fifteen years of institutional policy it is found that the cultural message is not 'getting across'; it comes up against a kind of resistance from the bulk of the people—for whom it is primarily intended—whereas those very people are receptive to other messages affecting their life—styles and consumption patterns. It is passive resistance akin to indifference and bordering on apathy, but it goes deep. This has implications in terms of cultural policy: while almost everywhere the most vigorous cultural policies are contriving to set up institutions which, it is gradually becoming clear, serve only to give a little more to those who are already the 'haves' as regards culture and money, and merely make it easier for them to avail themselves of forms of culture which they already command, at the same time among the less privileged sectors of the population there is what might be termed an 'explosion of cultural life' but in the shape of consumption sustained by cultural industries.

How cultural policies have misfired

By a curious combination of factors, in their concern for democratization, some cultural policies have spectacularly misfired. State involvement, which has increased by 100, 200 and 300 per cent and has been designed to benefit the most deprived sectors of the population living furthest away from the capital cities, has both worked to the advantage of those whom high culture benefits most and resulted in the expansion of central institutions to the point of ossification, while the people themselves have lost interest in public facilities, have equipped their homes with cultural apparatus and have been consuming the products of mass culture at home.

　　This whole sequence could conceivably be reversed and the balance rectified by working out a policy that would take into account the technical, economic and sociological factors of the last five years, and would seek to ally cultural values (those which the public authorities are trying to promote) with the tools whereby they are transmitted (which enjoy favour with the public, who will also more readily accept the financial outlay involved). New relationships between artistic creation and the public should be devised so as to establish contact between the public and the higher-quality works; in order to do this, the role of the institutions and of the professional people working in them should be reviewed and their goals and working methods re-examined. At the same time, those responsible for cultural industries should be induced to work towards cultural ends in fulfilling their functions, to make radical improvements in the quality of the programmes they have to offer and to give more consideration to the opportunities for cultural learning afforded by programmes carefully conceived in terms of potential public response.

Cultural industries afford one of the only possible ways out of the economic deadlock of live entertainment today

A third reason for a thorough investigation of the potential and the functioning of cultural industries is the critical state of live entertainment. The well-known analyses of Baumol and Bowen demonstrated that live entertainment was doomed financially because of the fact that costs were increasing along with professional salaries without any chance of greater productivity. The fact is that unless there are compensating subsidies, companies are faced with losses that are aggravated as their activities develop. Opera, for instance, costs more as its repertoire and public expand.

　　The theatre today is faced with the same difficulties, and studies are being carried out in all countries to try to overcome the 'economic dilemma' described by Baumol and Bowen, either through the market or by state assistance. But it always comes down to the fable of the water-carrier who sells each glass at a loss, hoping to make it up on the quantity sold.

For opera and the theatre, there is a way out of the economic deadlock, perhaps the only one, and that is a link-up with cultural industries. Video recording means that performances can reach millions of spectators, be retransmitted for the amateurs and stored in archives for the specialists. Such a link-up does, of course, have difficulties, because the rapport between the stage and the audience, all-important in a theatrical production, cannot be transposed to a television screen, but it is absolutely necessary not only because the retransmission of a play—or a new presentation of it for television—pays back production costs in a single evening, but also because the audience it reaches, a hundred times greater than at a live performance, at last lives up to the playwright's ambitions. Recourse to cultural industries is justified not only from the economic point of view but also from the point of view of cultural development.

THE DECENTRALIZATION OF INSTITUTIONS CANNOT KEEP PACE WITH CULTURAL DEMAND

Even if the structural inadequacy of cultural institutions (theatre companies, orchestras, cultural centres) did not preclude it, the number of such institutions could not be increased fast enough to meet the public demand created by education and the mass media in all parts of the country. Small and large towns alike are now demanding the same facilities as the capital cities. The role of the mass media in disseminating economic and social models and needs is applicable also to cultural patterns and needs.

In the face of a growing demand that is also more exacting with respect to quality, one may well ask if there is enough talent that is up to what might be termed national standard for so many decentralized institutions. This view may seem Malthusian when one considers the rampant unemployment in the artistic world, but there is a paradox that stems from the very existence of cultural industries and it must be borne in mind. Before, in the days when there was no electronic communication, a local company could put on *Tosca* to the great enjoyment of small-town audiences, using artists who were altogether worthy but not as talented as those who would perform in the capital, or were not of what is called today 'international standard'. Now that the same public can hear on records or on the radio or see on television the best actors in the world in their best roles, second-rate local productions do not bear comparison and are not viable economically. The theatres no longer draw full houses and the public is no longer satisfied.[4]

The problem of satisfying greater local demand can no longer be solved, then, by merely increasing the number of cultural institutions and local companies, but only through some form of cultural industry, possibly a new one that has yet to be invented.[5]

ENHANCING THE STATUS OF THE CREATIVE ARTIST

The fifth reason for endeavouring to understand and control the expansion of cultural industries is that, contrary to widespread belief, those industries will make it possible to approach the problem of the status of the artist and creative work in contemporary society on a far more constructive basis. Since the system of cultural production must inevitably keep pace with the fast-moving development of communication, and the media and the cultural industries create a considerable demand for cultural products in a context of keener competition, the artist—whether creator or performer—will be assigned a role which paradoxically he never acquired in the system of high bourgeois culture.

In the Victorian and Edwardian eras, the artist had to consider himself satisfied if his works were read, heard or exhibited at all. His rewards were chiefly psychological, since royalties were slow in coming and were regarded almost as a bonus. Even today, there is the residual subconscious conviction among the general public and hence among many political and administrative authorities that the mere fact of giving an artist a chance to be known is doing a lot for him. The idea that he may be entitled to regular annual remuneration like any other citizen, like the inventor of a new industrial product or a scientist,[6] is one that is far from being generally accepted. The prevailing attitude, even surreptitiously among those who claim to love the arts, is that either the artist is a star earning a fabulous amount of money as if by magic, or else penury is the price he has to pay for being fortunate enough to live 'the life of an artist' and do exactly as he pleases.

Is it not conceivable that with the increased demand for cultural products as part of a vast, profit-making economic process, a premium should increasingly be put on creative work, which should command its true price, and that relationships between authors, publishers and programmers—at a time when one and the same creative idea can be processed by several media (television, cinema, books, cassettes) and in more than one country—should be governed by contracts negotiated on a more equitable basis and, in commercial terms, in what is ultimately a greater spirit of fair dealing? Will it not then be found that intellectual and artistic creation has not been assessed at its true value, just as oil used not to be? That in terms of the amount of time and energy spent and risks taken, creative work is underpaid to the tune of not two times less than what it is worth, but ten times? That whereas industrial design work is properly remunerated in the research department, the composer of a symphony is compelled against his will to rely on patronage?

Enhancing the status of the artist will mean promoting the 'long-seller' as well as the best-seller, and it is to be hoped that a more prosperous system of cultural production in a more active market will enable publishers and programmers to give a chance to a larger number of artists, take more risks and finance works that will not become part and parcel of the system of cultural industries with its inevitable negative sides. In that way, there could always be scope for renewed creativity, experimental work and exploration, where creation would remain a solitary act with its 'impenetrable core of darkness'.

SAFEGUARDING NATIONAL CULTURAL IDENTITY

The last but not the least of the reasons for dealing with the question of cultural industries has to do with their international character. Where equipment is concerned, the international division of labour operates on a global scale, production and distribution being shared between a few big 'multinational' corporations with their headquarters in Japan, the Netherlands, the United States or the Federal Republic of Germany but with factories and retail outlets in every country. With regard to the programmes feeding these millions of machines (400 million receivers in the world in 1978, 800 million in 1985, 5,000 television stations), the world of culture—artists, publishers and programmers—can no longer be kept within national boundaries or language areas, which are too narrow for production to be economically viable. Within the space of a year, an artist's fame crosses frontiers, and publishers have to take part in international 'fairs' on a world market.

And just as the structure of supply, with the technology and economics involved, necessarily becomes worldwide in scope, so the demand for 'programmes', cultural contents, fiction or music by the public the world over is very often directed towards international products. Broadcasting time doubles every five years and the rate of increase will accelerate with the launching of broadcasting satellites; programme demand will increase at the same rate, just as the consumption of recorded music has risen by 30 per cent annually over the past decade.

Each country's share in this rapidly expanding market will be proportionate to the vitality of its cultural industries and the quality of its cultural products. This may provide the opportunity for each country or each region of the world to extend the sphere of influence of the most universal elements of its culture—which may well be those that are most specific to the culture or nation concerned, most deeply human (one need only think of Ingmar Bergman). Or, on the contrary, it may mean greater dependence by countries with a low production capacity on those with powerful production capabilities.

It would of course be absurd to speak of cultural self-sufficiency at the end of the twentieth century. Even if it were desirable, which it is not (cultures have always been transnational and have always nurtured one another), self-sufficiency would not be possible, for whatever the extent to which programmes are jammed or literature is censured, young and old alike will always succeed in procuring the literary or musical messages they want or need. What one has to speak of, however, is cultural non-dependence, in other words a country's ability both to restrict superfluous imports and ensure competitive national production. Today only flourishing, appropriate cultural industries can enable countries to take up this challenge.

NEW WAYS OF SPREADING CULTURAL INFLUENCE

The cultural influence of a country in 1980–2000 can no longer be seen in the same terms as at the beginning of the twentieth century or even at the time when Unesco was first set up. Artistic exchanges used to be based on contacts between people—lecturers, soloists, theatre companies, or exhibitions. The new era for the spread of cultural influence was ushered in by American films after the Second World War. The massive export of American films to the rest of the world, at prices that were low because the films had already paid their way on the American market, coincided with the massive increase in film demand in the period between 1950 and 1970. Since then television has taken over from the cinema, and cinema films have been replaced by television film series, but the effect is the same as far as cultural influence is concerned. The world of the imagination is a powerful vector of ethical, ideological and practical models whose political influence is far-reaching.

Whereas artistic exchanges and traditional 'cultural relations' used to cater for narrowly circumscribed intellectual circles—and not even the intelligentsia as a whole, including students and teachers, but just the élite whose culture was already international—the import and export of the products of cultural industries affect not only a new, very much broader intelligentsia (major foreign authors are published in paperback editions) but all young people, through gramophone records (multiplied by the effect of promotion on the radio). The electronics industry, in which costs are dropping, can now provide the entire population with television series that are ten to a hundred times cheaper to import than to produce in the country.

The perfectly natural phenomenon of easier cultural exchanges through industrial products may be considered beneficial or detrimental. It is detrimental if the consumption of imported products is at variance with the cultural models the education system is endeavouring to foster, if it inhibits and paralyses national production, which becomes too expensive or is unable to produce anything as attractive as that produced elsewhere at considerable expense (in the audio-visual media, the appeal of a product is largely proportionate to the financial input). The northern European countries with their limited linguistic areas are well aware of the problem of the need to resist the baser products of industrial culture.

But the phenomenon can be turned to account if appropriate national or international measures are adopted to bring the national system of cultural production up to the standard of international competition. If this is done, the products of cultural industries become powerful factors in spreading a country's cultural influence. Van Gogh (through reproductions of his works rather than just by exhibitions) and Ingmar Bergman (through his films) have done more for the cultural influence of the Netherlands and Sweden than all the painstaking labours of embassy cultural attachés.

Television film libraries, record libraries and film archives are more important today in cultural institutes abroad than the holding of exhibitions of works by great painters: negotiating a contract for a hundred hours of television broadcasting on a foreign network has a far greater impact than a series of a hundred lectures given by a visiting academician.

So far, very little has been done to foster co-productions within the main regions of the world, and interregional broadcasting agreements are still few and far between. What would be better, however, where anything to do with fiction, music or variety shows is concerned, would be to broadcast the best of what a region has to offer over the various national networks, rather than uninspired national productions or imported programmes whose only merit is that they are cheap.

CULTURAL INDUSTRIES: WHAT ARE THEY
AND HOW SHOULD THEY BE DEALT WITH?

Much has been written about mass culture, whether from the aesthetic, semiotic or humanistic point of view. There is no lack of theory either, and passions run high, since values are at stake; but so far there has been little close investigation into cultural production using economic tools.

Despite their diversity (books, records, radio, television, cinema) the common denominator of the communication and broadcasting media is that they are at the junction of two worlds. One is the world of creative work, which, even if it is less and less the product of a single person, still makes for a unique relationship between creative artists and those for whom their works are specifically intended. The other world is that of the means of reproduction and dissemination, which, from the technological point of view, are developing apace and are devised and operated by enterprises with the power to reach millions of people.

Creation-dissemination is the tandem that throughout the ages has enabled art to emerge within society. For centuries creative work and the means of its communication were on a small scale. Dissemination then became massive, and hence industrial, thanks to Gutenberg for the written word and Edison for sound. And now even creative work is based on industrial processes.

The distinction can accordingly be made between various types of cultural industry. There are those in which what is basically a small-scale creative activity is subsequently reproduced in a large number of copies (books, art reproductions, records) by means of industrial processes: these are the publishing industries. In others, the actual act of creating something implies from the outset a substantial industrial input (cinema, television): these are sometimes termed programme industries. Lastly, there is photography, and here we have a complex industrially produced object, the camera with its built-in electronic technology, which enables a large number of people to enjoy individual creative freedom, to play with light and colour so as to re-create for themselves the world around them, even if it means subsequently relying on other machines to develop and print the film.

Adorno denounced the progression of the reign of the commercial product and predicted the regression of culture and the arts. He could not have been more wrong as far as literature and music are concerned. By replacing the manuscript, the book industry has done an immense service to literary creation. Complementing live concerts, records have had a tremendous effect in stimulating a taste for music; with the renewed interest in listening to music, there is evidence that more and more people are taking up music and singing, and enrolment in music schools has never been so high.

Between these various degrees of industrialization, forms of co-existence and interaction already exist and are developing rapidly. In order to understand them better and see them in their proper context, possibly even control them, it is necessary to know what they are and to make them known.

What precisely are the constraints that these techniques entail? Do they inevitably present a threat to creative activity? Experience in the case of books has proved to be successful for 400 years and with records for almost a hundred years, but it was impossible to foresee their development at the outset. It is natural that new products should give rise to a debate on cultural policy. Will their development be determined by the tastes of the public? By developments in technology? By business decisions? Should the government intervene? These questions are all-important for the future of the cultural life of the people, far more so than the amount of a subsidy granted to the national opera. They call for meticulous socio-economic, historical and political studies as a matter of urgency.

It seems difficult however to make a study of cultural industries, owing to the fact that the symbolic and aesthetic value of their products so clearly eclipse their market value, and the way in which it is constituted, in the usual type of analysis. Critics in the arts usually approach the subject from the aesthetic point of view and refer to the readers' or listeners' values or pleasure and not to the way a work is manufactured or marketed. The publisher—or the record producer, art dealer or television programmer—is not seen as a business man producing and selling goods, but as a prestigious intermediary between the talent of the creative artist and the enjoyment of the public, as a sort of patron to the artist and benefactor to the user. His 'aura' is akin to that of the university or the teaching profession, the places and modes of transmitting knowledge and the cultural heritage of mankind.

Cultural policy-makers will have to look beyond this aura in making their analysis and attempt to gauge the economic factors involved at each stage in the production and marketing process, determining the exact role of the participants in this economic process—those who control the capital, business men, authors and creative artists, art directors, promoters, distributors or salesmen. By going deeper into the analysis of the various stages in this vast production process, it will be possible to detect the strong points on which to base policy and the weak points which need consolidating. The weaknesses may lie at the initial stages of the production-marketing cycle—creative workers, artists or the conditions in which they work—or at the end—the export of their products to the rest of the world—or, again, at some intermediate stage of the economic process. For instance, in book production the retail trade may be at fault, in videogram production the weakness may lie at the publishing stage, and in the press the actual production process or local distribution may be in difficulty.

The various forms of horizontal or vertical concentration and integration must be closely watched if certain forms of expression and creation are to be prevented from disappearing altogether for the simple reason that they are not profitable.

Cultural industries must on no account, then, be considered as a single entity but must be broken down by sectors. The breakdown must be done in two ways, making the distinction on the one hand between the various stages in the production and marketing process and on the other, as these various stages are not the same in each of the media, between the media themselves, each of which is governed by a production and marketing rationale of its own.

TABLE 1. Cultural industries: branches of activity and stages in the production and marketing process

Branches \ Stages	Total (Value, volume, personnel)	01 Creative work	02 Publishing, production	03 Manufacture, reproduction	04 Promotion	05 Wholesale distribution	06 Retailing	07 Imports	08 Exports	09 Archives
1. Books	E1	11	12	13	14	15	16	17	18	19
2. Newspapers, magazines	E2	21	22	23	24	25	26	27	28	29
3. Records	E3	31	32	33	34	35	36	37	38	39
4. Radio	E4	41	42	43	44	45	46	47	48	49
5. Television	E5	51	52	53	54	55	56	57	58	59
6. Cinema	E6	61	62	63	64	65	66	67	68	69
7. New audio-visual products, services	E7	71	72	73	74	75	76	77	78	79
8. Photography	E8	81	82	83	84	85	86	87	88	89
9. Art reproductions	E9	91	92	93	94	95	96	97	98	99
10. Advertising	E10	101	102	103	104	105	106	107	108	109

This grid can be used either for making a critical assessment of the situation or for planning measures or studies. The boxes can be completed with figures representing either the value (turnover of the branch, in terms of production or consumption) or the volume, i.e. titles, number of copies, broadcasting time, number of users, the personnel employed in the branch, or, again, the percentage of national capital in relation to foreign capital or the percentage of public investment in relation to private funding.

THE VARIOUS STAGES IN PRODUCTION AND MARKETING

The distinction between the various stages in the production and marketing process set out in Table 1 was based as much on theoretical reflection as on practical necessity for the purposes of analysis, for when it comes to making a critical appraisal of a particular branch of activity, ascertaining exactly where the problems or difficulties lie, and accordingly finding out where state assistance may be needed, the entire process must inevitably be split up.

It is true to say that only two actual stages can be singled out: namely production, including the creative artist's work, the publisher's or programmer's responsibility and the actual manufacturing process; and marketing, including promoting the product (advertising, creating public demand), wholesale distribution and retailing.

This breakdown into two stages does not, however, make for a diagnosis or indicate what steps should be taken. In the film industry for example the shortcomings may not be on the creative side but on the production side. In the press, the situation may be perfectly healthy from the editorial angle, but there may be problems on the publishing side and a critical situation with the modernization of manufacturing and printing procedures.

On the distribution side wholesale activities may be efficient (as in the case of records for example), but there may be shortcomings at the retailing end. With regard to the cinema, the distributors may be in a very strong position, whereas exhibitors may be experiencing serious difficulties.

Table 1 includes three additional items, since they also have a bearing on the state of health of each branch of activity. They are exports and imports, which govern the strength of a product's influence abroad, or, on the contrary, the country's cultural dependence, and lastly the keeping of archives, which can be seen to pay dividends only in the long term but may be vital to the development of any one branch: for example, the video-disc can develop only if it has a well-stocked and varied film library behind it.

IDENTIFYING THE SCOPE OF CULTURAL INDUSTRIES: THE VARIOUS BRANCHES OF ACTIVITY

In Table 1 cultural industries have been divided into ten categories: books, newspapers and magazines, records, radio, television, cinema, new audio-visual products and services, photography, art reproductions, and advertising. Each of them alone affords vast scope for study. But taken as a whole they are nevertheless closely and strongly interrelated.

When it comes to planning the part to be played by the public authorities in any given country, a judicious approach is of course to proceed pragmatically and to broaden the field of study or action only as the need arises. Attention, then, will be paid to any particular means of expression or branch of industry which may be in difficulties at some stage of the production and marketing process. Other sectors of primary importance for national cultural life may subsequently be incorporated because they require action, and each area will be dealt with separately according to the situation peculiar to each country. But the underlying unity and the close links (financial, human, professional, market) between all these industries will be quickly realized. There are already large corporations which have interests in all the different sectors, with major companies like Warner in the United States or distribution specialists like Hachette in France attacking simultaneously on all fronts.

PRODUCTS MAY ALSO BE CLASSIFIED ACCORDING TO MANUFACTURING METHODS...

There are few identification problems where books, records or the film industry are concerned, for they are the oldest industries and follow a strictly conventional pattern as far as the various stages in production and marketing are concerned.

More difficult to pinpoint, however, are radio, television and the new audio-visual products and services, which involve several modes of expression (literary, musical, cinematographic, etc.) and several branches of industry, with even more massive-scale distribution and a very substantial turnover. They constitute networks that on the face of it are 'neutral' with regard to the nature of the cultural products disseminated, but the power relations between the various agents—financiers, programmers, authors and performers—must be ascertained with precision and caution, for their influence is culturally decisive. The respective roles of the public authorities and the private sector, particularly in advertising, are more difficult to analyse here and their operational and promotional relationships with the publishing industries of the first group are more complex.

Taking the criterion of the manufacturing procedure, a distinction can be drawn, as it has been above, between a first group of cultural industries in which an initially small-scale and personal piece of creative work is then multiplied by means of industrial techniques (books, art reproductions, records), and a second group in which the creative activity itself presupposes considerable technical input from the outset (cinema, television) and in which distribution is of a collective nature.

Photography and home movies offer an interesting combination of manufacturing processes. The user buys an industrial product on the market, but what he is buying is in fact the raw material, and with it he expresses his personality through an activity that is to a greater or lesser extent creative; he then hands on the exposed film to another industry, which returns to him a 'developed' picture that is both unique and reproducible and in any case personal.

... OR ACCORDING TO THE WAYS IN WHICH THEY ARE USED

A distinction may also be drawn between two groups of industries according to cultural and not just economic criteria. Books, phonograms and videograms enable the user to make an active choice between very different products. These three items are acquired by the user as durable goods, and his attachment to them is strong and lasting. He uses them as and when he sees fit, lends, borrows, copies and reuses them. As far as the supply of this first category of products is concerned, the personality of the publisher plays a more important part. Supply still takes precedence over demand, whereas in mass cultural industries demand takes precedence over supply. Items that are not immediately profitable (poetry, philosophy and early or contemporary music) are still being produced. In this case the publishing function is less dominated by the distribution function. Such industries may be termed publishing industries.

With regard to films, radio and television, on the other hand, the audiences may be from one thousand to ten thousand times greater, but the choice open to them every evening is limited and hence more passive, and it cannot be reproduced (as long as video recorders are not in widespread use). Production is more akin to that of the products of ephemeral, rapidly obsolescent mass-consumption related through advertising to the rest of the consumption of non-cultural goods. For the purposes of the analysis, it might be more apt to term them 'services' rather than cultural goods.

It should not be forgotten, however, that radio and television use the products of the more noble publishing industries and those of live entertainment as a 'cultural reservoir' and inevitably promote them. As a result, radio and television are gradually becoming the driving force in cultural production as a whole, in both its 'live' and reproduced forms.

'CULTURAL INDUSTRIES' DOES NOT MEAN THE INDUSTRIALIZATION OF CULTURE

To avoid any misunderstanding, it should be specified that the use of the term 'cultural industries' does not necessarily mean the industrialization of culture in the sense in which the term is used for the building industry, for instance. One can speak of industrialization when referring to goods produced by assembling mass-produced parts on a site or in a factory.

This acceptation of the word 'industrial' does not apply to cultural industries, even if certain techniques are reminiscent of it. The division of labour in the production of strip cartoons, the repeated use of certain simplistic, commonplace themes in films, collections of reproductions in art books published in several languages, the adoption by song writers of the latest trends in rhythm ('disco', for instance) will not automatically produce a work that will pay its way, let alone a best seller. The talent of the creative artist, his rapport with the public, both of which are unique and cannot be reproduced, are essential for the success of a cultural product. There is something in cultural production and even mass production that has to do with the very essence of culture and means that it cannot be industrialized.

Even if the cultural product is a marketable item from the point of view of its promotion and distribution and the methods used to sell it, it is not like other goods, and the laws of capital accumulation do not operate in the same way as elsewhere when culture is at issue. This has been amply demonstrated by historical analyses of the record and film markets.

'CULTURAL' INDUSTRIES ARE NOW ALL... CULTURAL

Although books, records, films, art reproductions, radio and television form part of cultural industries from the economic standpoint, distinctions can be drawn within these branches when they are viewed from the specifically cultural angle. The information function of television and radio (which accounts for up to one-third of broadcasting time but under a third of costs), the purely educational function of school textbooks (a large market) and company (or advertising) films may or may not be considered to meet the aims of cultural policies. Distinctions of this kind are reflected in practice when one considers various forms of state assistance: for example, subsidies may be granted to books of poetry but not to practical guidebooks. The same considerations will be taken into account when it comes to deciding whether or not newspapers and magazines should be included in cultural industries. The first point to make is that the cultural influence of these mass media on all sectors of the population is considerable (cultural sections in magazines and newspapers, the promotion of books, records and films through reviews, guidance to the listener in his choice of radio and television programmes in television magazines). The next point to note is that the personnel employed is largely the same and, it will be found, shares the same resources (advertising resources on the one hand and household leisure budgets on the other). Newspapers and magazines can therefore justifiably be included within the scope of cultural industries.

A similar problem arises where advertising is concerned. Advertising finances the mass media, takes up a large proportion of publishing space and broadcasting time, is necessary for the products of the publishing industry, employs to some extent the same personnel (audio-visual producers and technicians, graphic artists) and exerts a cultural influence on the public, on people's imagination and their way of perceiving pictures and language. Any far-reaching conception of 'cultural industries' should therefore include advertising, which has a very large turnover in some countries.

Lastly, the development of new audio-visual products, services and networks (videograms, satellites and all the techniques that will stem from the linking of computer technology, the telephone and the television screen) must be followed closely, for they will in the short- or long-term dictate the future of all other cultural products.

The scope of cultural industries will, then, be defined, limited or extended in each country according to whether emphasis is placed on an economic, technical or cultural approach. The approach will be chosen according to the end in view. Those dealing with the theory of economics or the mass media will not apply the same criteria as those responsible for the future of a particular branch (professional film- or book-industry unions, for example) or those responsible for decision-making in government cultural policy.

By considering the various stages of the production and marketing process within each branch of cultural industries separately, it will be easier to ascertain not only the trouble spots in the individual branch but also exactly where strategic decisions are made for the whole of the branch and where there is concentration.

The word 'strategic' will be construed differently by those responsible for the commercial side and by government representatives. From a business man's point of view, by identifying the strategic nerve-centre of the branch—often distribution—he will be able to see where he stands, conclude agreements with his competitors and seek to gain a commanding position. Marketing techniques, which are well known, will then enable him to modify his production, i.e. the type of cultural product he publishes or programmes, in terms of the rest of the system. The inevitable concomitants of such a system—which is no longer that of the individual bookseller or publisher of yesteryear who would print the books he liked, but that of the industrialist producing over a thousand titles a year—are well known: stardom, best sellers rather than 'long-sellers', a foothold in the international market, media integration.

NOTES

1. M. Horkheimer and T. W. Adorno, *Dialectik der Aufklärung,* Amsterdam, 1947 (translated into English under the title *Dialectic of Enlightenment,* New York, Herder & Herder, 1972).
2. A. Girard, *Cultural Development: Experience and Policies,* pp. 27–42, Paris, Unesco, 1972.
3. 'Cultural' both in the aesthetic sense and in the sense of cultivating one's sensitivity and creativity.
4. Even in one of the most affluent cities of the world, New York, the recent attempt by a brave director of the Metropolitan Opera to reduce costs by engaging national artists rather than great international stars was not well received by either the public or the critics.
5. An example is the current move to use the now underutilized network of cinemas to project national cultural (and sporting) events promoted by the mass media on full-size screens for the general public.
6. In Pasteur's time, scientific research had the status of a pastime indulged in by the scientist on his own responsibility, and not of an occupation recognized as being socially useful.

2 Introduction to an economics of culture: a liberal approach

Albert Breton

Professor, Department of Political Economy, and Research
Associate, Institute for Policy Analysis, University of Toronto

What may be labelled the economics of culture—the description and analysis of
the observable characteristics of demand and supply as well as those of their
interrelationship in the various 'industries' that make up the cultural sector—must
inevitably accord considerable attention to those features of the sector that are
peculiar to it and which, if not absolutely unique, at the very least are combined
in a singular fashion.

There are many such features. Without being exhaustive and for the sole
purpose of illustration, one may mention the star system, the predominance of
suppliers over consumer preferences for many categories of product, the
prevalence of tying-in contracts, as manifested in book- or record-of-the-month
clubs and film 'packages' in cinemas, the high degree of vertical integration, the
importance of 'older' over 'newer' forms of output (classical v. modern music,
painting, sculpture, etc.) the relative inaccessibility of quality products, the
volatile nature of the cultural product cycle and many others.

In the following pages I should like to suggest a model based on a certain
specification of the demand for, and the supply of, cultural output, in which the
features of the cultural sector listed above, and possibly others, are all seen to be
responses to the same basic economic forces. The hypothesis is formulated in the
methodology of neoclassical economics in the very fundamental sense that
production responses, which are the primary object of analysis here, are seen to
be adjustments to demand conditions and to changes in them. The point is of some
importance, because it has often been assumed that the 'industries' of the cultural
sector are under the control, management, inspiration or influence of producers
(artists) and are unresponsive to consumers. Many of the problems encountered
by governmental regulators stem from that fact.

But, before turning to demand considerations and the production problems
that are particular to the cultural sector, it is important to be clear about the nature
and characteristics of the products of that sector. Cultural products are indeed
different in many respects from other goods and services marketed in
contemporary economies, and the fact that they have often not been defined with
sufficient care has meant that many of the puzzles of their production have

remained unresolved. Consequently, it seems appropriate first of all to give a definition and a specification of some essential characteristics which cultural products seem to possess in relatively large amounts.

VARIABILITY IN CULTURAL PRODUCTS: VOLATILITY OF CONSUMPTION OR MARKETING WEAPON?

The set of all products which can be called cultural is not homogeneous. At the outset, one distinction is essential, namely that between cultural consumer products of a durable nature and the services flowing from these durables. The distinction is based on the fact that consumers use capital assets (radios, television sets, video cassettes, record players, cameras, etc.) as equipment, instruments, or means of production, combined with the contributions of other products, to produce flows of services—called cultural products—which are then consumed. This paper is not concerned with the production and use of consumers' cultural capital, but with the production economics of the flow of services—the true cultural products. These include radio and television programmes, sound recordings, magazine and newspaper articles, attendance at concerts, plays, operas, etc. The distinction between the stock of capital and the flow of services derived from that stock, which is clear and precise in some instances, is fuzzier in others. For example, between a book and the messages it contains, between a record and the sounds registered on it and between a film and the images imprinted on it, there may be only a subtle difference, but the practical difficulties of distinguishing between stocks and flows are resolvable and, indeed, resolved in one way or the other in such exercises as the construction of national accounts. The distinction is, however, so important for clear thinking, that whatever the practical difficulties involved, it must be made.

Given the distinction, one of the most essential aspects of cultural products from the point of view of the consumer is that, for many of them, consumption cannot be repeated, and for virtually all of them, it cannot be repeated very many times. One can, of course, be inclined to read Edward Gibbon's *Decline and Fall* two or even three times but, without intending injury to Gibbon's memory, one feels that diminishing returns would set in quite sharply after that! The same can be said of Mahler's Fourth Symphony after repeated performances and even of Picasso's *Guernica*. But these illustrations are hardly to the point. Who would want to read this morning's newspaper, listen to yesterday's radio programme or view television's extravaganza of last night again today?

The distinction between a classical or enduring work of art and another less important, less famous one is, it would seem, based on the greater capacity of the former to bear repetition. Unlike food, clothing, transportation, heating, lighting, etc., which can be and are demanded repetitively over decades by the same consumers, cultural products are not and cannot be demanded in that way. Variety, diversification, dissimilarity, variation (possibly on a theme, but variation) and multiplicity are essential attributes of cultural products. This fact, it seems, is one of the main reasons why the consumption of cultural products has sometimes been (erroneously?) associated with the use of leisure or simply with recreation and entertainment.

Cultural products are not the only commodities purchased by consumers which display the property of not lending themselves to repeated usage. Another typical example is fashions, especially in clothes, but also in interior designing, furniture, automobiles, etc. The economics of production related to fashion has some resemblance to that related to culture, but in the former instance it has been associated with the notion of styling.

Styling is nothing but a technique used by producers and suppliers seeking to control the volatility of consumption which is associated with fashions. It has, of course, sometimes been used as a marketing weapon,[1] especially in products such as motor-cars where design is only one attribute of the product, and not an essentially important one at that, but it has also been used in an effort to dominate or control the vagaries associated with the fact that certain attributes of products cannot be consumed repeatedly.

Considered as products, clothes, furniture and automobiles are different from culture in that the former fulfil basic or primary functions associated with warmth, storage and transportation, while the basic function of culture is more difficult to define or at least more difficult to verify empirically. But though the difference between the two types of product is real, it is a matter of degree, not of kind.

Before looking at certain properties of the demand for cultural products *per se,* one should note that because of the fundamental non-repetitive feature just described, the elasticity of demand for cultural products by each individual will tend to be very small for all prices over a wide range. The larger elasticity displayed by market demand functions will, therefore, be the result of variations in the size of the market, as the price varies more than individual adjustment.

THE ECONOMIC DEMAND FOR CULTURAL PRODUCTS: A HOMOGENIZING OR DIVERSIFYING PROCESS?

Imagine that as the income of a group of individuals or of a society decreased, we observed that the amount of certain goods bought by consumers did not change or changed only by a very small amount, while the quantity purchased of others decreased by a large amount, possibly to zero. We could then use that observation to classify commodities. Such a classification would, of course, be arbitrary in that the boundaries between classes of goods could change as the tastes of people changed or as living patterns varied.[2] But such arbitrariness need not hinder the classificatory scheme's usefulness. We, therefore, put commodities into three classes: the first, called necessities, would include goods whose consumption varied very little when income varied; the second, called normal, would be intermediate; and, the third would be luxuries, namely those that varied much with income.

Using such a classification, one would have to classify most, if not all cultural products, as super-luxuries, that is, as luxuries at the upper end of the luxury class. This, at least, would seem to be the conclusion imposed by the available evidence.[3] In other words, relatively small changes in income levels lead to relatively large changes in the demand for cultural products.

But cultural products are super-luxuries in a different sense also, associated with non-repeatedness in demand. At high income levels, the demand for cultural products is relatively large, but the composition of demand is constatly shifting because of that phenomenon. The volatility of demand does not manifest itself only between product types, but even within types. In other words, non-repeatedness in demand leads to volatility between types of cultural products such as television programmes, films, sound recordings, museum attendance, etc., but also within a product type between one kind of film and another, one kind of recorded music and another, etc.

One need not emphasize that this great volatility of demand, related to high income (or wealth) and to product attributes, creates great problems for suppliers. Indeed, it implies that the production of cultural products is inherently a very risky business, that is, one in which the risks of success or failure are higher than in most other endeavours. In a large class of phenomena when risks are high, human beings are induced to respond and often those responses articulate themselves in institutions. For example, in the face of risks of loss from fire, theft, death, etc., one response has been insurance companies and insurance; in the face of the risks of loss through bankruptcy, one response has been limited liability and the modern corporation. Other illustrations could be given.

In the cultural sector, in the face of the high risks briefly outlined, there have also been individual and institutional responses on the part of producers and suppliers.

It may now seem appropriate to speculate briefly on the social forces at work which, given income levels and product attributes, tend to make for the degree of (economic) volatility of the demand for cultural products which we observe.

The necessity to supply an ever-growing volume of diversity and variability in culture, as incomes rise and the amount of free time increases, implies that 'local' reservoirs of symbols, myths, images and messages cannot satisfy the demands placed on them. It becomes impossible for entrepreneurs in the cultural sector not to tap larger and larger reservoirs, so that effectively all sources are used at once.[4] One implication of this phenomenon is that messages, images and symbols possess less and less of a 'local' content, significance and resonance and consequently are unable to appeal to local emotions and sentiments. This phenomenon does not describe a vicious circle, but a dynamic process whereby the need to supply an ever larger demand for cultural artefacts of all types brings about a homogenization and standardization of the basic materials to which the creative mind can appeal in an effort to produce these artefacts. That homogenization in turn accelerates the demand for diversity and change by not being able to satisfy fundamental needs for identification with profound and meaningful symbolism, mythologies and imageries.

That phenomenon is further accelerated because of the incapacity of the cultural élites to breathe new meaning and significance into the older materials of symbolic expression, transformation and creativity. The question of whether true creativity requires 'local' roots is still very much an open one, but the phenomenon often described as the internalization of culture reflects the view that the 'new' cultural artefacts to a large extent are world artefacts. If that is the case, the risks attendant on the production of cultural products are going to increase still further and some of the behaviours and institutions analysed below will become ever more important.

THE SUPPLY OF CULTURAL PRODUCTS: 'STABILIZING' THE DEMAND

The production economics of culture must not be examined as a phenomenon in itself, but as the response of producers and suppliers to the great volatility of demand which, of course, makes the profitability of cultural production very risky.[5] The various responses which can be identified with concrete and particular historical behaviour are to be found in different forms or manifestations whenever the risks to producers are of the type encountered in the cultural sector.

Two examples: the layout of newspapers and the television and film industry's star system illustrate the adjustment to the production risk consequent on product demand volatility. These are two extreme or polar cases. But a little bit of what one finds in the laying-out of newspapers and in the star system can be found in the organization of art galleries, in the programming of film festivals, in the stocking of bookshops and in the distribution of records. This means that, even if they are particular cases, they are general enough to provide an introduction to a production economics of cultural output.

The layout of newspapers

One does not have to go back many years to observe that even national newspapers—though on a global scale these were fewer in number—were fairly specialized products, geared to the service of a particular market. Even today there are still many newspapers that are to a very large extent oriented towards particular markets. This specialization implies that well-defined and stable markets exist and can be identified. That, in turn, means that demand is also stable and predictable. Under these circumstances, the risks of publishing a fairly specialized newspaper—whether specializing in politics, religion, sports, the arts, etc.—though positive, are not large enough to elicit a compensating or corrective response.

But the newspapers that have to compete with other media in their coverage of events and that cannot identify a stable market, because that market is too volatile, abandon specialization for diversification. Indeed, the great national newspapers are like supermarkets, with coverage of public affairs, the arts, books, fashions, sports, comics, business and editorials.

Editorials are, indeed, a fascinating feature of large daily newspapers. It is reported that only about 2 per cent of buyers read them; it is acknowledged that they influence virtually no one's positions on controversial issues, yet they continue to be written and published. Why? Simply because there is 'out there', difficult to identify and permanently changing in composition, a group of individuals who have to read something to convince themselves that the truths to which they hold are shared by some one else!

Diversification is, of course, a standard way of dealing with risk, since pooling risks, if they are uncorrelated with each other, reduces the aggregate. A newspaper that specialized in editorials, or in business news,[6] or in sports, not only would not have a large readership—that may or may not be a problem—but it would have a volatile one—a great source of difficulty. The best way of looking at the large dailies is to compare them to supermarkets. Large newspapers are effectively marketing exercises with write-ups on everything under the sun, but also within 'product-areas', with different 'brands': different reporters on the same item, different agency columns, etc. The purpose is to stabilize demand.

It has often been argued that the increasing concentration in newspapers—essentially a tendency towards one paper per city—is caused by large economies of scale in production. The existence of a very large number of profitable specialized newspapers sheds no doubt on that view. The phenomenon of 'one-stop shopping' described above seems a better explanation of this tendency towards concentration.

Tying-in arrangements

There are many instances in modern economies of what is technically known as full-line forcing, namely the requirement that to be able to purchase one product, a consumer must also purchase another. Breakfast cereals are often sold with a 'gift', hotel rooms are sold with television sets, razor blades are sometimes sold with a 'free' razor and inexpensive cameras are sold in packages including a film. But, in no area, it would seem, is the phenomenon more widespread than in the cultural sector. But, because the institutional form it takes is often at variance with technical full-line forcing, one can use the terminology of 'tying-in contractual arrangements'.

Examples are not difficult to supply. Books and records of every type and variety are often sold through arrangements which in one form or other resemble the pioneering book-of-the-month-club formula. In these schemes, a big inducement is given to join the club; it is then theoretically possible to drop membership after a number of purchases have been effected, but the difficulties of doing so are only truly appreciated by those who have tried. Film producers use 'block-booking' extensively. This is a formula whereby operators of cinemas must buy the use of a number of films as a 'block'; they cannot buy one film in the block and not others. Blocks take various forms: the requirement to buy the use of films over a period; the requirement to buy the use of 'shorts' or 'documentaries' for every showing; or the requirement to buy the use of two (or more) 'tied' feature films per showing. Theatre, opera, symphony and dance companies seek very actively to sell season tickets, often at a lower price than if each of the performances were bought separately, and thus seek to tie the sale of their product.

There are many other examples. The point, however, is that each one of these is a tying-in contract aimed at stabilizing a volatile demand. If a supplier is successful in selling such arrangements, he at the same time reduces the variance of his profit stream and thus reduces the risk of his operation. There is a difference in institutional and legal form between the various tying-in contracts described in this subsection and the one-stop shopping contrived in the layout of newspapers, but from the economic point of view the difference is more one of degree. These institutional and legal forms are all responses to the high volatility of demand. Their presence reduces that volatility and thus reduces the risk attendant on the supply of these cultural products.

The star system

Augustin Girard has already associated the institutional phenomenon of the 'star system' and risk.[7] What he did not sufficiently emphasize, in my view, is that the star system is a response to the presence of risk due to the volatility of demand and serves to tie in or attach consumers indirectly—that is, through the building of an affective and emotive link with one or more stars—to certain classes of product.

It is important to realize that if the image of Hollywood automatically springs to mind at the use of the expression star system, it is only because Hollywood has been able to develop that system further than other cultural sectors. But a star system of sorts exists and is cultivated in virtually all cultural-product markets. Such is certainly the case in opera, ballet, music and live theatre; it is also the case in painting, sculpture and the other visual arts; and it is the case with authors of books. Its importance in films, records and other mass-market products need not be underscored.

As noted earlier, the star system exists to stabilize a volatile demand and since volatility is to a degree related positively to the level of income, one expects the star system to be more important in wealthier countries than in poorer ones. The operation of the star system is a simple one. Suppliers do not know and cannot know if a new product will be successful, because they do not know the tastes or preferences of consumers. But if consumers develop an emotive attachment of sorts to certain performers, it is then easier to forecast demand, because that demand is more stable.

Girard correctly stressed that stars are not created by producers and suppliers. But if a performer elicits a response from consumers, then the producer marshals all he can to build that performer into a star. This proposition is easily verified by observing the time pattern of advertising expenditures for the promotion of stars. These expenditures do not begin before, but only after, a performer or a performance is successful. I will come back to this in the discussion of vertical integration.

Again, one should note that there is a great resemblance between how newspapers are laid out, how consumers get tied in to certain consumption packages and the operation of the star system, which requires them to consume certain products in order to have access to their favourite performer, even if those particular products are known not to be attractive.

Prototypes

Anyone who has reflected on the structure of standard television and radio programmes, films, and even that of some books, plays and musical compositions cannot but be impressed by the extent to which they seem to be produced according to a blueprint or recipe. Indeed, it is possible to argue that the production pattern of many cultural products is done according to prototypes. The idea is not that all output follows a given standard prototype, but the more interesting notion that if a product—a film, record, book, etc.—is successful, it then serves as a model, a prototype, for the production of a stream of other products—of other films, records, books, etc. The success of a product serves as a signal that it can be used as a prototype for the fabrication of others.

Prototypes play at their own level the same role or function as stars. They are not, any more than stars, foisted on the public, but if a product is successful it is sure to become a prototype for the fabrication of others. Prototypes are to products what stars are to performers.

One could argue that prototypes exist because they permit lower production costs, since the use of prototypes implies to some extent production by combination of modules and therefore a form of mechanical production. One cannot rationalize the use of prototypes by their effects on costs, since sustained use of a prototype is, in general, made at increasing cost. These data do not suffice to prove that prototype usage serves to stabilize demand, but they certainly lay to rest the notion that cultural prototypes are like dies, casts or stamps used in manufacturing, to reduce production costs.

The view that prototypes serve to stabilize demand can be supported by the available evidence we have to the effect that, after a point at least, the rate of return on investment in them begins to fall. Although there is no evidence on stars, one suspects, from casual observation, that the same is also true for them. This implies that stabilizing volatile demand is an economic activity which is costly. To put it differently, just as individuals can stabilize their income stream against the ill effects of uncertain events by buying insurance, so firms can stabilize their income streams by the expenditure of resources on prototypes, on stars, on tying-in contracts and on 'one-stop buying' activities.

Vertical integration

It has been known for a long time that some classes of mergers and business consolidations, especially those that go backward to a 'primary' supplier, are made in an effort to combat uncertainty.[8] But in the cultural sector, some vertical consolidations are undertaken with a different immediate objective.

There can be little doubt that in the cultural sector, as elsewhere in modern economies, vertical integration serves a number of purposes. Without prejudging the relative importance of each factor one can list the following: (a) integration, by consolidating sales and hence profits with different and unpredictable variance time streams, reduces aggregate variance so long as these streams are uncorrelated; (b) integration allows the placement of funds in opportunities whose parameters are better known to entrepreneurs, since these opportunities are similar to the activities in which these entrepreneurs are already engaged; and (c) integration permits the exploitation of lowest-cost sources of supply, especially in periods of disturbances and unrest.

But integration also permits the rapid and correct monitoring of the sales of products whose appeal is unknown. For example, there has been a tendency in the gramophone record industry for producers to purchase down to the retail level and if not that far at least down to the wholesale level. The rationale for such integration has simply been that producers must know immediately if a record is being sold. When a new record is released, jobbers or retailers convey sales information daily to producers. If sales are moving briskly, they engage in large advertising campaigns; if sales are slow, advertising is kept at a low level. In this case integration is a means to rapid and reliable information. That information, in turn, is needed because producers do not know whether a record will be successful or not.

In this connection, it is interesting to speculate on the existence of an institution which at one time was widespread and which is rumoured to be still important, namely the institution of payola. Payola, among other things, refers to the granting of side-payments to disc jockeys in exchange for the promotion of certain records. The institution did (does?) characterize the record industry in a particular fashion, but there is no reason to believe that it was (is?) restricted to that industry. Furthermore, if one is not bogged down by legal niceties and, consequently does not limit the notion of side-payments to transfers of cash, but is willing to incorporate, as necessary, transfers in kind, including promotions, recommendation, attendance at international conferences, etc., then payola may in some areas be a dominant form of market organization.

In the present context, payola could very well be the outcome of public restriction imposed on vertical integration. To put it differently, if integration plays a crucial role in the monitoring and promotion of certain products and if that integration is curtailed by law, then the curtailment creates an opportunity for profit. The exploitation of that opportunity gives rise to payola. It is not certain that the foregoing speculations are based in facts. If they are, however, they should not be used to exonerate payola, but instead, as a measure of the size of the problem that producers face because of the volatility of demand. In a way, the sums transferred as payola are an index of the cost of stabilizing demand.

The 'old' versus the 'new'

It is not difficult to prove that in theatre, ballet, music and other forms of live artistic expression, it is often much easier to gain access to works that have been produced in the past than to current production. That is not the case with all cultural products. In painting, sculpture, architecture, for example, modern forms of expression, though they may have had a very difficult time in piercing through at the outset, have found a much larger audience.

To some extent that phenomenon can be explained with the help of the apparatus used in this chapter. Note that one of the important differences between the two types of art forms mentioned in the last paragraph is that in one case—music, ballet and theatre—a large audience is required if even moderate success is to be achieved. In the second case—sculpture, painting and architecture—it suffices, at the limit, that one person, one client, be sufficiently interested to guarantee some success. Of course, if one or a number of wealthy patrons are not available, it will not be easier for this second kind of art form; but it would seem reasonable to assume, that one or a few patrons are more easy to find than a large audience.

However, even if large audiences could be found for dance, music and plays, the difficulty of ascertaining preferences for new productions would be an incentive to supply older and more tried expressions. To put it differently, the risks associated with an older production may be substantial, but they are known, whereas for newer output these risks are unknown and therefore subjectively greater. One way for suppliers to sell new productions is to 'tie' them to older forms, but that will only be successful if such tying in does not adversely affect the sales (of season tickets, for example).

The greater supply of older and tried productions is thus seen to be a response to the greater uncertainty that attaches to newer forms of expression. In this connection, one should note that the average art critic will tend to be much more critical of newer forms than of older ones, for the same reasons that suppliers give preferences to the older expressions. In addition, art critics in newspapers must criticize in directions that will be appreciated by their readers. If the readers, on the whole, do not like new art forms, one can bet good money at favourable odds that the critics will condemn the new forms!

Inaccessible quality

It has often been noted that many television programmes are of poor quality. It is to describe that phenomenon that the expression 'wastelands' was used by President John F. Kennedy. What is less often noted is that the poor quality of television programming is repeated in other areas of the cultural sector. It is very difficult to buy a book, a periodical, or a record of good quality in standard bookshops, periodical stands, or record shops. That at least is true if we define quality as the property of departing from the mean of a distribution.

One need not labour the point that this clustering of products round an average represents a way of dealing with volatile demand by the simple device of catering primarily, if not exclusively, for that portion of the demand that is stable in the sense of not deviating from the mean.

To conclude this chapter, it must be once more emphasized that many of the production idiosyncrasies of the cultural sector are essentially responses to the very high risks which are, in turn, associated with a highly volatile demand, so that these idiosyncrasies are best understood as institutional efforts to stabilize demand or part of it. Whenever such stabilization is not possible output will simply not be forthcoming.

The high volatility of the demand for cultural products is associated with two factors: intrinsic properties of cultural goods, which make repeated consumption uninteresting (technically, which make marginal utility fall rapidly), and high income or wealth which allows people to indulge their taste for variety and diversity. The ability to satisfy variety soon empties cultural products of local content and the disappearance of local content re-inforces the desire for diversity and change. It would be interesting to model this dynamic process, but the modelling of stable dynamic processes is not at all a simple matter. It is surely not an accident that very many dynamic models are either implosive or explosive and hence uninteresting.

The foregoing is a purely analytic exercise but the reader should be aware that it has a number of important policy implications. To illustrate, let us consider briefly the question of national or local content in cultural products. Many countries are preoccupied with national content; to be more specific, many countries desire and seek ways of increasing the fraction of cultural goods produced locally. However, in a world in which demand is volatile such an exercise is a very delicate one. Indeed, if national content is defined in terms that do not allow producers to deal with volatile demand, that demand will simply spill over to other, possibly, non-national markets. An efficient policy of national content must recognize the characteristics of demand in a world of wealthy and fitful consumers.

NOTES

1. J. A. Menge, 'Style Change Costs as a Market Weapon', *Quarterly Journal of Economics*, Vol. LXXVI, No. 4, November, 1962.
2. Note 'as living patterns varied' and not 'as culture varied'; indeed in a paper on the 'economics of culture', one must distinguish sharply between artefacts, symbols and representations on the one hand, and patterns of life, social conventions and modes of social interaction on the other. The literature on culture in the first sense is full of *non sequiturs* because of the confusion between these two orders of concepts and realities.
3. S. J. Prais and H. S. Houthakker, *The Analysis of Family Budgets*, 2nd ed., Cambridge, Cambridge University Press, 1971.
4. For a more detailed discussion of this phenomenon, the reader is referred to the excellent paper by K. E. Boulding; a paper which, however, does not always avoid the pitfall of moving from one definition of culture to another. K. E. Boulding, 'The Emerging Superculture', in K. Baier and N. Rescher (eds.), *Values and the Future*, New York, The Free Press, 1969.
5. Whether the expectation (in the mathematical sense) of profit is positive has been questioned, but in a neo-classical model it must be assumed, at least, that the expectation of the stream of benefits (both monetary and non-monetary) is positive.
6. Even the *Wall Street Journal* and the *Financial Times* of London, which are aimed at a specialized market, must and do diversify to stabilize readership.
7. A. Girard, 'Industries culturelles', *Futuribles*, September–October, 1978.
8. See, for example, F. M. Scherer, *Industrial Market Structure and Economic Performance*, Chicago, Rand McNally, 1970.

3 Cultural industries: the origin of an idea

Armand Mattelart and Jean-Marie Piemme

We are well aware of the fact that concepts do not exist in their own right, but refer to very real problems and tell us about a particular place and time. To trace the concept of 'cultural industry/industries' to its origins in order to discover the attitudes to reality underlying it is already to take the first step towards inquiring into the workings of such an industry or industries.

THE CULTURAL INDUSTRY AS DEFINED BY THE FRANKFURT SCHOOL

We had to wait nearly twenty years in France for a readily available translation of the key work by Max Horkheimer and Theodor W. Adorno on the cultural industry.[1] This delay was not due to chance or oversight. The work has been deliberately ignored. Why translate a book whose general analysis of the problem departed radically from French research on the media at the time? In discussions of the media in France between 1950 and 1970, the idea of culture as an industry did not really take hold. Not that the fact was denied, but quite simply the proper questions were not asked and so no inferences were drawn from it. Nowadays, when the concept of the media as cultural industries has become eminently respectable, we are permitted to read Adorno and Horkheimer. Even so, there is an unbridgeable gulf between their analysis and present-day reality. Nevertheless their work is part of the genealogy of the concept, and it is vital to read it, whatever criticism it may require.

Here, then, is a piece of writing by two men who fled to the United States to escape Nazism. They speak of the developments they have seen in that country: the power of radio, the power of the cinema and the emergent power of television. Horkheimer and Adorno are, first and foremost, philosophers, and it is as philosophers that they tackle the subject that concerns us. The essay published in French under the title La production industrielle des biens culturels is a meaningful unit in itself. However, the full meaning of that unit is impossible to grasp unless the work is placed in the context of the overall philosophy of its two authers. It marks a stage in the development of that philosophy. It belongs specifically to the general discussion of the future of culture, which was one of the major concerns of those two authors.

In their view, the cultural industry is a clear illustration of the breakdown of culture and its degeneration into commerce. To place a monetary value on a cultural act is to destroy its critical impact and to rob it of all traces of authentic experience. The reign of pseudo-individuality, which began with the rise of the middle class, is arrogantly and ostentatiously expanding to absorb the culture of the people at large. 'That which is individual finds itself subject to the capacity of the general to stamp the accidental with such a strong imprint that it will be accepted as such. It is precisely the obstinate reserve or elegant appearance of the individual brought to prominence that is being mass produced—like Yale safety locks, differing from one another by fractions of a millimetre.'[2]

Even if we take no definite stand on this interpretation of culture and its breakdown, we find that the general theory of Horkheimer and Adorno can, to some extent, convey both the value and the limitations of their views on the effects of the new communication technologies as these took shape in the 1940s. This is particularly apparent in the chosen subject of the two theorists, namely the cultural industry. The importance of the links that have been forged between technology, culture, government and the economy will be lost on nobody: we are invited to explore a complex whole. But the use of the singular (industry rather than industries) also raises questions. What is implied by this curtailment, this limitation to oneness?

We may, of course, reply that it is the outcome of a desire to be comprehensive, and that it designates an overall movement of the production of culture as a commodity. But the generality sought is itself much less a characteristic of a practical analysis of the machinery of present-day capitalism, and much more a feature of the philosophical postulates of these two Frankfurt School theorists. If the link between the cultural industry and capitalism needs to be studied, the reason is not so much to clarify a particular juncture of capitalism as to prove the deterioration of the philosophical and existential role of culture. Horkheimer and Adorno refer to the economy and to power structures only for the sake of such proof. The most obvious result of this approach is the paradox that, in order to discuss the industrial production of cultural goods, it is by no means necessary to view that production as a diversified and contradictory collection of specific economic components occupying a given place in the economy. Similarly, in order to discuss the relations between that particular culture and government, it is by no means necessary to construct a model of those relations involving, for example, the type of institutionalization implicit in such production.

From these somewhat sweeping references to the economy and to government, one inference may be drawn: the real subject of Horkheimer's and Adorno's analyses is not cultural industry, but its presumed product, namely, mass culture.[3] In the last analysis, it is this concept that underlies all their thinking, while the concept of cultural industry is there only to lend it extra support. It is the setting for the former, so to speak, but is not itself subjected to scrutiny. For the rest, the best descriptions are of the effects of cultural industry on actual products. Through an industrial type of production, a mass culture is obtained that consists of a series of objects bearing the clear stamp of the cultural industry: serialization, standardization and division of labour. It is this that concentrates the two authors' full attention, for it is here that the breakdown of culture is most apparent.

However, with hindsight, it seems possible that the thesis of Horkheimer and Adorno seeks to be unduly universal. The mere existence of an industrial form of production leads them to lump together jazz and comic strips, radio and cinema. Ultimately, one might be inclined to think that it is not so much the effect of capitalism on culture that is under attack but rather the industrial production of cultural goods. Nowadays, we are well aware that jazz is not on the same plane as soap opera, and that the financial influence of Hollywood is not a threat to the legitimacy of the cinema as such. However perspicacious Horkheimer and Adorno may have been in their analysis of cultural phenomena, it would seem that they have glimpsed only one aspect—a fundamental one admittedly—of the bond between art and technology, and that their rather over-reverent attitude to art as a catalyst of revolution has prevented them from seeing all the other aspects of that bond.

To be convinced of this, one need only return to Walter Benjamin's essay entitled 'L'œuvre d'art à l'ère de sa reproductibilité technique',[4] which anticipates the Frankfurt philosophers by more than ten years. In it, Benjamin shows how the very principle of reproduction (and he demonstrates clearly how an art like the cinema has no *raison d'être* except by virtue of reproduction, not a single production) renders obsolete an older view of art that he calls 'pious'. The question arises how far Adorno and Horkheimer also stigmatize mass culture because the process of its manufacture can scarcely inspire the reverence in which art has been traditionally held.

In fact, more generally, it is difficult not to read between the lines in Adorno and Horkheimer and discover a strong protest by the literate against the intrusion of technology into the world of culture. The fly in the ointment certainly seems to be the reproducibility of a cultural object by the technical processes of which Benjamin writes. We have no desire to whitewash the cultural industries by denying the standardization that they threaten to impose on cultural products for the sake of financial profit and ideological control, or to maintain that culture is not endangered by commercialization. But it must be acknowledged that, in some cases, legitimate criticism of the cultural industry is too closely connected with nostalgia for a cultural experience untainted by technology. There is, as it were, a Jansenism of the written word, which confidently and systematically condemns all other means of communication (especially pictures) as works of the Devil. It is as if the written word, which preserves the original, were also by that very fact a guarantee of the authenticity and wisdom of communication. Images, on the other hand, lending themselves directly to reproducibility, are always pregnant with undesirable un-wisdom.

Curiously, this kind of value judgement underlies politically incompatible approaches to the media. It is to be found as much in Ortega y Gasset as in Adorno: in these cases, the cultural heritage overdetermines the system of political and philosophical values. And, nearer home, we may inquire whether the same 'literary suspicion' has not infiltrated the pointed criticism that Régis Debray levels at the media in *Le pouvoir intellectuel en France*. We may certainly agree with Debray that nowadays communication has become the dominant ideological tool of the state. But should we therefore share his implicit and underlying idea, wholly secondary to his main thesis, that the written word is ultimately more reliable than the image?

Be this as it may, it is important at this stage to point out that the spurious conceptual reality of the idea of a cultural industry (spurious because not discussed in its own right) opens the door to exploitation of these German philosophers' arguments by cultural snobs. Edgar Morin, for example, in a book which, to be sure, has more to offer than this, spoke of the spirit of the age when describing a set of values that were current in the mass culture of the 1950s and 1960s. But in his book, even more than in Adorno's and Horkheimer's, the reference to economics and politics forms only a general background to the analysis. It is more symbolic than useful.

THE MATERIAL WORLD AND MATERIALISM

The offerings of the Frankfurt School were only an interlude. Magnified by Morin, modified by the Italians and taken over by certain Third World philosophers, the concept of 'cultural industry' rapidly became threadbare. On the other side of the Atlantic it was, admittedly, commented upon and discussed in some academic circles, but the Americans, less prone to philosophical and moral punditry, at least in this respect, inclined from 1966 onwards towards a concept that is both more pragmatic and more comprehensive. This is the concept of the 'knowledge industry', devised by the economist F. Machlup, who was more concerned to assess the participation of this new branch of industry in the national product than to vituperate against the vulgarization of culture and the end of the reign of the intellectuals.[5] 'Knowledge industry' was the umbrella concept under which some thinkers, feeling the need for an economic rather than a materialist approach, placed the many different machines used to produce knowledge, including machines used for communication.

Some three years later, another German philosopher, H. M. Enzensberger, completed the trilogy by fashioning the concept of the 'consciousness industry';[6] this time, the aim was not to analyse, but, as the new broadcasting technologies began to arrive, to condemn the failure of the left to make use of the electronic media and to criticize its imprisonment in the Gutenberg galaxy. For nearly ten years, this piece of writing was to be the manifesto of the left as it castigated its own inertia. It should be noted that in France the book was virtually unknown and was not even translated.

With the association of computers, telephones, television, cable and satellites, and with the advent of telematics networks, a newcomer, the 'information industry', seems likely to oust the 'knowledge industry' (and perhaps, eventually, all the other concepts). This concept, introduced by the economists of Stanford University, encompasses both basic information (all kinds of data banks, financial, commercial and scientific information, etc.) and so-called cultural information (films, serials, books, newspapers, magazines, news bulletins, etc.) and also the whole area of know-how, i.e. patents, valuation, counselling, management, etc. This field of investigation is limitless, since the aim is no longer merely to define a section of industrial activities or to establish the frontiers of a scientific discipline, but in point of fact to determine a new form of society, namely 'the information society', which is the successor to the industrial era. If the Americans do it so much honour, it is probably because they intend thereby to make the new status of information and knowledge a leading factor in production, and above all, as a new power system, a new tool of government.[7]

The 'cultural industry' will not produce the practical analyses that it seemed to portend. Through not having seized the process of communication as it actually operates, it will leave the door wide open to all kinds of beliefs, illusions and myths, and as we have now begun to realize, the media are a particularly fertile soil for the nurturing of myths and ideologies. The ubiquitous nebula of 'standardization' has clouded our vision of the exact part played by each national reality in these grand concerts of the media. We do not wish to imply that each instance should be made into a special case or sealed off from outside influence as though its whole meaning were contained within itself, but rather that the type of communication that each country produces should remain attached to its natural roots. In our obsession with the 'global village', feared and rejected by some, desired and welcomed by others, we have lost sight of the fact that Canada is not France and that the United States may be quite different from Italy. We have forgotten that while mass communication and culture may indeed be a message, they are also an accumulation of ideas, technologies, customs, laws, institutions and power relationships. And we have also forgotten that the global village is a machine in which the various institutions concerned in a particular mode of production of communication are linked together.

Credit is none the less due to Adorno and Horkheimer for having had the courage to assert that, at one time or another, in one way or another, the material always overtakes the immaterial. In the 1950s and 1960s and at the beginning of the 1970s, this was no easy matter. Most European countries were not at all inclined to espouse a view that ran counter to idealism. In 1947, the French publisher of a book by P. Bachlin, a Swiss-German Marxist historian of the cinema, dealing with the emergence and evolution of the American and European film industry, changed the original title *Films as Commodities (Der Film als Ware)* to *The Economic History of the Cinema*. Doubtless he hoped in this way to avoid offending eyes and ears accustomed to a more aesthetic perception of the seventh art. Of course, Malraux's little dictum: 'The cinema is an art, but it is also an industry' will serve as a catchword for some time to come, but it still does not say where the art begins and the industry ends. And yet the cinema has always been one of those rare places where, more than anywhere else, it was possible to glimpse how a large-scale communication medium operated in actual practice. On the other hand, the questions it raised have rarely been applicable to the other media.

Nowadays, however, the scene is changing, on both the right and the left. The change has come about during the past ten years, and not only in Europe. From the point of view of criticism, the break has occurred in many parts of the world, e.g. the United Kingdom, Italy, Finland, France, the United States, Latin America and numerous other places. There is no doubt that a current of critical research is developing under highly varied conditions of production, so that the resulting conceptual structures also show great diversity. The terms used vary from the political economy of communication and culture to analysis of the media as an apparatus or analysis of cultural industries.[8]

Although they start from their own specific tenets, these approaches converge in their concern both to understand how the media culture actually works—leaning sometimes towards political analysis, sometimes towards economic analysis or a combination of the two—and to break with functional positivism and with the theoretical bias of a certain Marxist approach or the formalism of the analytical dissection of messages. This current of criticism, still weak and confined to a minority in some countries yet already well established and with majority support in others, will doubtless take some time to formulate a global theory encompassing an analysis of the communication apparatus as a producer of attitudes and aesthetic views, as an industrial sector and as a generator of consent, not to mention the need for a theory of the reception of messages. But it goes virtually without saying that these theories will eventually materialize.

The factors that led to the formation of this critical fringe among researchers vary from country to country. In the case of Italy, for instance, there is no denying the major role played by the inquiry into the functioning of the public television monopoly and the institution of an alternative network. We would learn as much from tracing the genealogy of each of these separate currents of opinion as from an analysis of the mechanism through which media culture is produced. For instance, the motives behind the first attempts in France to analyse the ever-increasing tendency for capital to be directed towards the production of cultural goods and to apply an economic approach to the concept of 'cultural industries' are evident to anyone who looks at the direction taken by a particular branch of French critical research.

The emergence of new ideas is bringing about a quiet transition to a materialization of the cultural sphere. These new ideas should enable humanist culture, which has always had trouble in accepting technology and the market-place within its field of vision, to hold its head up and adapt itself to the requirements of the new national and world economy. Take, for example, the collocation 'technical culture', two words that we are unused to seeing side by side and a combination that some may find objectionable. And yet how are we to make people realize that the industrial era, with its men, buildings, machines and products, with its glorious achievements and its base distortions, constitutes an important cultural reality and that to lose track of it amounts to maintaining its blemishes? It is essential to keep our technical memory alive and to make the most of our industrial heritage so as to throw light on its successes, or even its failures, in order to create a productive environment where critical thinking about the phenomenon can develop. If the aim of science is knowledge, that of technology is action and know-how; and indeed, in the last few years, the principle of innovation, or the introduction of novelty into the status quo, has aroused widespread enthusiasm. We must combat the sin of pride, a particular failing of the Latin countries, and acknowledge that beyond the realm of philosophic, literary or scientific culture, the importance of which we have no intention of belittling, we must proceed, contrary to custom and, putting it bluntly, to human self-respect, to raise the status of technical culture, among professionals of course, but also among amateurs and the general public, as is already the practice in English-speaking countries. Our first care must be to preserve the object as such, since it is often an essential link in the forward movement of the technological system. It must be discovered, recorded and possessed in order to save it from certain destruction or from an unexpected transformation such as that whereby the eighteenth-century Leyden jar degenerated into an electric lamp stand.[9]

The new technology clearly needs a history and a memory, a memory that undergoes a significant shift of emphasis and henceforth no longer serves just to draw up the inventories called for by the celebration of 'heritage year'. Factories are shut down by the crisis. So 'industrial museums' are set up to salvage the remains. The technological memory and industrial heritage are preserved in the name of preserving the popular memory!

Not everyone can be a materialist. The concept of 'cultural industries' in the plural, while improving matters by setting the whole question of the mass media firmly within a framework that was only alluded to by Adorno and Horkheimer, may also, if insufficient care is taken, lead to the taking of a backward step. One kind of approach to the study of cultural industries based on a vulgar materialism, while raising a series of new questions, may at the same time cloak them in obscurity. The risk of obscurity stems from at least three sources.

First, can it not be said that the declared aim of studies of this kind ('if the public authorities want to take action in full knowledge of what is involved, they must know how the industries function'), however laudable it may be, is fraught with pitfalls from the start? The public authorities—or, to spell it out, the state—are regarded as an arbiter. It is assumed that of the two parties involved, one—the state—is invariable. What is left unsaid is that there may be a dialectical relationship between the state and cultural industries. What if that state were affected by the same process of commercialization as culture? To ask this question is also to ask whether cultural industries are not directly involved in the restructuring of the state. Surely the questions asked about state monopoly and the barrage of criticism against it all over Europe are evidence of this osmosis between the function of the state and the function of industry? Are they not indicative of the proliferation of power delegation that is a necessary fact of life at this precise moment is history?

Second, can the idea that the products of cultural industries are the means of making cultural goods accessible to the greatest number, of contributing to democratization, be accepted unreservedly? Is democracy not seen here as an ahistorical, absolute phenomenon, as though this process of democratization were not reversible? Does it not mean believing uncritically in the notion of mass culture as a means of reducing social inequalities? Is it not forgetting too hastily that mass culture is not only a means of disseminating culture but also a means of social control that can take different forms according to the system's ability to meet the demand of the various classes and social groups? Many things conspire against this 'brave new world', ranging from the pronouncements by the leaders of the major industrial sections claiming democracy to be in a state of crisis to the proliferation of emergency laws in the free world. Can the whole apparatus of culture remain unaffected by the great ideological changes brought about by the new needs created by the international accumulation of capital? In order to keep in step with the growing tendency for national economies to be encompassed in a world pattern and with the new distribution of power and hegemony evident in North–South and East–West tensions, the nation-states are led to seek other ways of ensuring cohesion between the various social classes and groups. The new consensus must link up the 'national' with the 'global'. Cultural industries play a pivotal role in this ideological redeployment as the generators of the new spirit of shared purpose, very much a rare commodity. Might it not be argued that the process of commercialization of the state to which we have already referred, particularly in connection with the introduction of new communication techno-logy, is the tribute which the nation-state, that legacy of the nineteenth century, has to pay to the movement towards the multinationalization of economies? With the fortunes of the welfare state at low ebb, any steps it might take to support cultural industries will certainly not be in the form of state patronage of the arts, even if the belief may subsist in some quarters that culture may be the last bastion of resistance to globalization.[10]

Why deny what, as time passes, can be seen as the facts? The theorists (American or otherwise) of the restructuring of the state in Western societies provide the sticks with which to beat the protagonists of culture theory. A NATO consultant—who can scarcely be suspected of subversive sympathies—puts things in the proper perspective, after his own fashion, in the *NATO Review*[11] even if in doing so he reinforces the myths (for instance, decentralizing power towards hypothetical local authorities, the old dream cherished by multinational corporations in their attempt to polarize the world between their macroscopic sphere of influence and microscopic local entities) that will legitimate the smooth transition towards that new state; that it will cease to be liberal is deliberately left unsaid. What he says in effect is that prevailing values are being swept away by what is to all intents and purposes a tidal wave, and the main obstacles to the conversion of the new values into policies and institutions are neither the limitations of material or intellectual resources, but the limitations of the government. The political leaders put on a brave face but we are increasingly aware of their inability to make decisions. Centralized economic planning, which has spread across the whole globe, partly at the hands of the industrial democracies who would not dream of applying it themselves, is floundering nearly everywhere. The new migratory proletariat swarms across frontiers, whether national immigration laws allow it or not. Ethnic and religious rivalries and separatist movements threaten the integrity of long-established nations: the Republic of South Africa, Nigeria, Ethiopia, Jordan, Lebanon, the United Kingdom and Canada are the most recent examples. Power is slipping away from national governments in three directions: into the hands of local communities who want more discretionary power, non-governmental enterprises that can act more swiftly and more flexibly than the government authorities, and the international agencies that have to try in some way or another to manage the new technologies that cut across national jurisdiction. In short, government institutions are the relics of an era for which they were created—an era of blind growth in which the many and varied forms of growth were independent of one another. In a statement made during a week of discussions on the subject of the 'Computer and Society' held in Paris in the autumn of 1979, another American sociologist, Daniel Bell, expressed himself in rather more laconic terms in drawing attention to this localist-versus-universalist trend when he said: 'What is happening today is that for many societies the national state is becoming too big for the small problems of life and too small for the big problems of life.'[12]

We are a long way here from the therapeutic—indeed one might say orthopaedic—view of the relationship between the public authorities and cultural industries which carefully obliterates the political function of the mass communication apparatus and, more generally speaking, of the new information system, and calls upon the state only in so far as it is in a position to grant special tax measures, selective aid and subsidies, to place orders or specify standards.

The main point of the first two remarks is to demonstrate that although one must guard against viewing the state as a monolithic entity free of conflict, it must not be hallowed as neutral ground either. There may be no such thing as a ghetto state, but neither is there such a thing as a state open to all influences.

Finally, it is difficult to take stock of cultural industries as though they could be seen in equivalent terms or as though they were compartmentalized with no dialectical relationship between them. Cultural industries are a part of a system, they are a system and within that system there are some that are at the centre and others on the periphery, and their fate is largely determined by the changes taking place at that centre. When cultural industries are viewed from the non-political angle, they are seen as a non-hierarchical succession of channels, concealing the fact that within that sequence (television, press, radio, cinema, etc.) there are some that contain within themselves the matrices that to a great extent determine how the others develop, and that from this point of view, some channels, some cultural industries, are hegemonic, imposing their own rules on the others. All these channels are part of a system that has its pace-setters, pace-setters that may not even figure among the leading cultural industries concerned. Advertising (whose role in this respect is soon to be taken over by computer technology) is a case in point, and the fact that it is not included in the list of cultural industries is evidence that there is mystification afoot, to say the least. We must give credit again to Adorno and Horkheimer for having taken it into account.

But in playing the sorcerer's apprentice, one cannot get away scot-free. One day an analysis will have to be made of how this official acceptance of cultural industries has enabled considerable headway to be made in the critical apprehension of the workings of the power of communication.[13] This goes to show that concepts, too, are stakes in the game.

NOTES

1. M. Horkheimer and T. W. Adorno, *Dialektik der Aufklärung*, Amsterdam, 1947. Translation into French under the title *La dialectique de la raison. Fragments philosophiques*, Paris, Gallimard, 1974.
2. Ibid.
3. See in particular T. W. Adorno, 'Television and the Pattern of Mass Culture', in W. Schramm (ed.), *Mass Communications*, Urbana, Ill., University of Illinois, 1960. See also T. W. Adorno and H. Eisler, *Komposition für der Film*, Munich, Rogner und Bernhard, 1969.
4. W. Benjamin, 'L'œuvre d'art à l'ère de sa productibilité technique', *L'homme, le langage et la culture*, Paris, Denoel/Gonthier, 1971.
5. F. Machlup, *The Production and Distribution of Knowledge in the United States*, Princeton University Press, 1966. For an excellent analysis of this concept, see G. Barile, 'Analisi economiche della produzione di conoscenza: una rassegna', *Ikon*, Milan, Institut Agostina Gemelli, January 1979.
6. H. M. Enzensberger, *The Consciousness Industry*, New York, Seabury, 1974.
7. Z. Brzezinski, *La révolution technétronique*, Paris, Calmann-Lévy, 1971.
8. All over Western Europe research groups are springing up, their object being to evolve a materialistic theory of communication, as attested by the emergence of reviews such as *Ikon* (new series) in Italy, and *Media, Culture and Society* in the United Kingdom. See in this connection N. Garnham, 'Contribution to a Political Economy of Mass Communication', *Media, Culture and Society* (London, Academic Press), Vol. 1, No. 2, April 1979; and G. Cesareo, 'The Form of the Apparatus in the Mass Media', ibid., Vol. 1, No. 3, July 1979. In France, see as an example the study by Lefèbvre, A. Huet, J. Ion, B. Minge and R. Peron, *Capitalisme et industries culturelles*, Grenoble, Presses Universitaires de Grenoble, 1978; A. and M. Mattelart, *De l'usage des média en temps de crise*, Paris, Éditions Alain Moreau, 1979, preceded by A. Mattelart, *Multinationales et systèmes de communication*, Paris, Anthropos, 1976; P. Flichy, *Les industries de l'imaginaire*, Grenoble, Presses Universitaires de Grenoble, 1980.
9. M. Magnien (director of studies and research at EDF, President of the Centre de Recherche sur la Culture Technique), Preface to the first issue of *Technique et Culture* (Paris), 1979.
10. For a global analysis of ideological redeployment, see A. and M. Mattelart, op. cit. See also, Université de Paris VIII-Vincennes, various authors, *Le nouvel ordre intérieur*, Paris, Alain Moreau, 1980.
11. H. Cleveland 'La trosième phase de l'alliance', *Revue de l'OTAN*, No. 6, December 1978.
12. Quoted in G. Soulier et al., *Actualité de la question nationale* (studies collected by Cao-Huy Thuan), Paris, Presses Universitaires de France, 1980.
13. If only by giving institutional sanction to a field of research. One last point should be made: even if there is no doubt that many European governments have selected cultural industries as the concept to be used henceforth in speaking about their cultural policies, it is not so certain that they have all considered its full implications, even from their own restricted point of view. There is a patent inability to put intentions and proclaimed ideas to practical effect. All too often in Europe 'cultural industries' are used simply as a means of barter or an export item in international forums. Things can change rapidly, however. The international debate on cultural industries, which is still confined to the European areas, should become more lively once organizations like Unesco join in. As we know, Unesco intends to include the question of cultural industries in its programme for the next five years. There is every likelihood that the conflicting North–South positions that emerged from the debate on the 'new international information order' will not fail to come to the forefront again here, with particular virulence, since it is no longer just a matter of looking into imbalances in information but of dealing with a whole mode of communication based on unequal exchange. A new conflict will no doubt arise, namely between East and West. The countries of the

socialist bloc will no doubt be reluctant to accept this ecumenical notion of cultural industries which in their view does not adequately reflect the functioning of the cultural apparatus of their states. Another point that often causes problems (as shown by the statements at the meeting on 'the place and role of cultural industries in the cultural development of societies' organized by Unesco in Montreal in June 1980) is that of defining the scope of the concept 'cultural industries'. On the one hand, if cultural industries are associated with the media (cinema, radio, television, etc.), this leaves out industries such as tourism, which, as was pointed out by several participants at the meeting, could legitimately call itself a cultural industry. On the other hand, associating cultural industries too exclusively with leisure means overlooking the strong tendency to merge education with entertainment. This tendency is reflected both in the merging of education industries and leisure industries (e.g. ITT, RCA, CBS and many others) and in the infiltration of media-based patterns into educational material (e.g. series like *Sesame Street*).

Part Two

The impact of cultural industries

Considered from the standpoint of their cultural impact, the cultural industries which exert most influence over all sectors of the population are undoubtedly, in descending order, television programmes and to a lesser extent radio programmes, the daily press and magazines, followed by records, films and books. In terms of their economic importance, the order would no doubt be somewhat different, since records and books can sometimes produce very high cost-benefit ratios. However, we cannot legitimately consider this aspect only of the functioning of cultural industries, or take advantage of the new opportunities they afford for the developing countries, without going into the effects of the products of these industries on the various social groups and on different cultures.

How can the cultural repercussions of the intrusion on a massive scale of transnational industries on traditional societies be gauged, especially when it comes to the gradual breakdown of interpersonal communications and certain forms of community life, and the stifling of former practices and scales of values, especially in areas with small populations or among linguistic minorities? It is, however, important in this respect to guard against excessive idealism. Whereas it is true that everything must be done to prevent cultural differences from being stamped out by a massive-scale spread of universally applicable standards, there is no doubt either that some moves to safeguard identity in fact conceal attempts to marginalize certain social groups.

For some time now, Unesco has been particularly concerned with investigating the impact of the audio-visual media on the socio-cultural behaviour of young people and women. At the Intergovernmental Conference on Communication Policies in Asia and Oceania, the Director-General of Unesco pointed out that 'mass media, and above all television and radio, have such an impact on the population in general and young people in particular that their conditioning power makes them potential sources of cultural alienation, and even of social deviation'. As far as women are concerned, the media usually portray them in stereotyped roles that even the numerous and significant contributions by women to modern life cannot offset. Much remains to be done, therefore, to enable women to play a greater part in the media and to be portrayed in the media as they really are.

The question of the cultural impact of cultural industries has very far-reaching implications and raises a series of problems as yet unsolved. Do they really make the public more receptive and more sensitive to the arts or do they just satisfy the more superficial drives? By what ways and means might these industries instil genuinely new values in the users, instead of plunging them into the conditioned reflexes and apparent apathy that they do today? How can a genuine dialogue be set up, and not just the very limited tentative exchanges between those who produce messages and the people at large? How can users participate in the choice of the products to be disseminated when, as we know, such choices are determined by market forces or by considerations of political expedience? How can people's need to take part in the exchange of messages be stimulated? What steps should be taken to enable all social groups to understand and control cultural industries so as to ensure their own development? Can consumer-protection movements conceivably be launched in the field of cultural industries for the purpose of safeguarding the diversity of the products proposed, in other words freedom of choice, as well as public access to all types of message, while keeping up the standards of such products? It is clear that the questions that have not yet found a theoretical solution in this area are many and varied, and are extremely important. The authors of several of the papers submitted to the Montreal meeting touched on several aspects of these problems. The two papers concerned with the impact of cultural industries on various social groups focused specifically, however, on the problem of young people and women. The Polish sociologist Krzysztof Przeclawski dealt particularly with the effects of audio-visual media on the value systems and socio-cultural behaviour of youth, in the light of their particular subculture. For her part, the Irish sociologist Margaret Gallagher analysed the relation of women to the media, either as consumers of media messages or as participants in their functioning, or again as they are portrayed by the media.

4 The impact of cultural industries in the field of audio-visual media on the socio-cultural behaviour of youth

Krzysztof Przeclawski

Assistant Director,
Institute of Social Prevention and Resocialization,
Warsaw University

CHARACTERISTIC FEATURES OF THE CULTURAL INDUSTRY

In some countries the cultural industry is, above all, an instrument applied in the competitive political and ideological struggle. It is used by various pressure groups. In other countries it constitutes, essentially, a source of profit for its owners and therefore is mainly of a commercial nature. Finally, in some countries it is principally a tool of ideological impact monopolized by the state.

L. Althusser considers that the cultural industry can be treated as the 'ideological state apparatus'. Some hold the view that for many, television represents a mythicized 'natural force' in the sense that everything shown on the television screen is being received as objectively existing. Thus, television reflects practically 'the natural world order'. In reality the actions of the mass media are intended actions subordinated to the ideological system which they serve. Therefore, contrary to certain suggestions, the mass media are not a 'public service', but rather an instrument of 'control over the public'—a tool which serves in many countries, above all, to consolidate the existing socio-political order.[1]

The cultural industry creates a new market for creative work; it leads to the emergence of groups of specialists concentrated in closed professional centres, thereby attracting creative workers from smaller, provincial centres. On the other hand, it injects into the general circuit and makes known to the general public people who hitherto had only access to a limited audience.[2]

In some countries the cultural industry constitutes a source of great profit and the struggle for these profits determines the form and contents of the transmitted programmes.

For example, in 1970 commercial television in the United States grossed $3 billion from advertising. The cost of one minute of advertising time on television reaches $40,000. That is why television advertising shapes to a large extent the programme, not only by interrupting it, but often by so manipulating it that it distorts its content. In fact, advertising exercises a considerable control over television. At the same time reservations are being voiced against the tendentious character of some advertisements, which for example present in a stereotyped and traditional way the role of women.[3]

Large firms are exporting their products to many countries. This export, mostly composed of rather low-quality entertainment programmes, uses the channels of the former colonial system. It is therefore possible to speak of a *sui generis* 'imperialism of mass media' representing a tool of neocolonialism with respect to various countries.[4]

So-called 'educational' television is considered to counterbalance commercial television; however, television orientated towards information and education rather than towards entertainment disposes of incomparably smaller financial resources and therefore its scope is much more limited.

THE MECHANISM OF THE IMPACT OF TELEVISION ON THE ATTITUDES AND BEHAVIOUR OF CHILDREN AND YOUTH

The question whether the mass media, and especially television, affect clearly the attitudes and behaviour of children and youth, and if so, by what means, in other words the problem of the 'mechanism' of the impact, still requires further elucidation. Even assuming the reality of such impact, one would have to determine how to isolate it from other influences. That is why the diagnosis concerning that impact remains, at least for the time being, rather incomplete, unsure and ambivalent. It is incomplete, because research on the impact of television is carried out only in a few countries (it developed particularly in the United States). Unsure, because there are not enough experimental studies in which a genuine attempt has been made to isolate the impact of television from other factors.[5] Ambivalent, because the impact of television can in certain respects be considered as being definitely positive, while in other respects plainly negative; it is not easy to strike a balance between the two.

We may start our consideration of the impact of the cultural industry on the attitudes and behaviour of children and youth by assuming that this behaviour depends on the orientation towards values, in particular towards supreme values internalized in the process of socialization. The internalization of these values, or broadly speaking, the internalization of the contents transmitted by the mass media, depends most probably above all on three factors: (a) the possibility of recognizing values (to have access to these values in the objective sense and to perceive them in the subjective sense); (b) the emotional relation to the recognized values; (c) the degree of integration of the small group (family, peer-group) around the internalized values. The internalization of values depends, for example, in the case of reception of contents transmitted by television, also on the conditions which accompany such reception, on the type of the social organization of reception.

If we were to assume that in the process of shaping attitudes personal authority associated with existing positive emotional links (one can change only a person who is loved, etc.) plays a decisive role, one would have to conclude that the influence of television should not be overestimated. For the language of television is, above all, perceived as a language of information and not as a language designed to steer behaviour. On the other hand we know of the process of learning by imitation of behaviour observed on the cinema screen or on the television screen. This applies in particular to children. In this connection attention must be drawn to two problems. The first concerns the supposition that our attitudes and behaviour are influenced perhaps even more strongly by impacts that have no intended educational purposes than by factors deliberately set in motion. Should this supposition prove to be true, it would be of tremendous importance for the understanding of the force of impact, for example, of violence and sex in the cinema and on television and of the weak influence of intended educational programmes.

The second problem concerns the objectivity and veracity of the image of the world as projected by the mass media, and especially by television.

This image is, as a rule, one-sided, or simply false. Television has tremendous possibilities to manipulate facts freely and thus to falsify history.[6] It was Marshall McLuhan who coined the phrase: 'the medium is the message'; in other words, the way the message is being transmitted determines the contents which get through. American television offers its viewers a distorted and biased image of the world: it is more a man's than a woman's world, more a white man's world than a world of other races, a world of a specific professional structure than a world corresponding to its real structure, a world of rather traditional values, concerned to a minimum extent with the problems of the developing countries; finally a world in which the degree of violence and crime is higher than in the real world.[7]

The one-sidedness of the image of the world projected by the mass media is not something specific only to American television. In many other countries and on many levels a false image of the world is being presented on the television screen. It can be said without exaggeration that the fundamental crisis of the modern mass media is the crisis of truth.

Thus, the distortion of the process of internalization of values at the perception stage result from the fact that the information and content to be transmitted are being selected. Of course, they are also the result of the selection operated by the audience, but here we enter a very complex and specialized problem.

The distortions at the stage of the emotional shaping of the relation towards the received contents are connected with the objectionable or plainly low aesthetic level of the form and content of the transmitted values. It seems that only a high aesthetic level of the transmitted contents can ensure their internalization (the fascination with beauty). Equally, this internalization can be promoted by the peculiar concurrence of the symbolic language of the sender and the receiver, in particular the concurrence resulting from shared values. For obvious reasons such a situation is exceedingly difficult to create in the case of contents transmitted by television, cinema or radio.

Finally, the high degree of integration of the group of receivers (family, peer-group) no doubt facilitates the internalization of values, transforming these values in many cases into an essential element of the youth subculture (as regards integration of peer-groups).

To sum up, it is possible to maintain that the chances of internalization of values transmitted by mass media increase when these values are presented in a possibly objective and true manner, in a way corresponding to the criterion of beauty and in a language understandable to the audience; it is equally important that these values concur with the values of the reference group of the audience.

THE EFFECTS OF THE IMPACT OF TELEVISION ON THE ATTITUDES AND BEHAVIOUR OF CHILDREN AND YOUTH AND THEIR EVALUATION

The impact of the cultural industry (with particular reference to television) on the socio-cultural behaviour of youth was analysed in the course of a seminar organized by the Finnish National Unesco Commission in Espoo-Helsinki in December 1979.[8] Among others, two papers were presented; one by Dr Isaac Obeng-Quaido from the University of Ghana entitled 'The Impact of Cultural Industries in the Field of Audio-visual Media on the Socio-cultural Behaviour of Youth in Ghana' and the other by Dr Ritva Mitchell from the University of Helsinki entitled 'Youth Socialization and Culture Industries: Empirical Case Studies and their Interpretations from Developmental and Policy Perspectives'.

Dr Obeng-Quaido proposed to carry out 'longitudinal studies' which could provide the basis for the formulation of theses concerning the impact of mass media on the attitudes of youth.[9]

Summing up his paper he stated that: 'The case-study on Ghanaian youth consisted of two series of interviews: first the interviews with the producers of youth programmes and secondly with youth themselves in order to find out their opinions of these programmes.' The paper focused also on the reading habits of Ghanaian youth, as well as on their preferences in radio and television programmes, films and records. The paper showed clearly that young Ghanaian people prefer foreign cultural artefacts. For example, about 90 per cent of the fiction titles were of American or European origin. Books of Ghanaian or African origin were not favoured by these young people. Most of those in the sample listened to English-language youth programmes rather than ethnically indigenous youth programmes. It was assumed that the reason for the preference for English-language youth programmes was that they contain mostly Western music. The study claimed that 'it is in the area of musical taste and choice among the youth that the argument of "homogenizing effect" can be strongly made. There is a high degree of uniformity in the manner the Ghanaian youth appreciate Western music.' Since Ghana's national film production is small, most films shown are imported. Detective and adventure films are special favourites of Ghanaian youth. In general, records are, however, the most popular cultural products and most of them are of Western origin. The study recommended that ethnic youth clubs should be established as forums for monitoring youth reactions towards youth programmes. It also considered it important that the influence of Western music should be limited, for example by a quota stipulating that 60 per cent of broadcast music should be of Ghanaian or African origin and the rest of foreign origin.

The Finnish case-study was based on the theoretical concepts developed by Margaret Mead and her three patterns of socialization of youth: postfigurative, cofigurative and prefigurative socialization.[10] The study opens with four basic questions :

1. What is, and what in the future will be, the role of the cultural industries—especially in the field of audio-visual media—in shaping the socialization processes of children and adolescents?

2. How do the products of the cultural industries shape youth cultures and to what extent do they have a homogenizing and unifying, or a diversifying effect on these youth cultures?

3. What branches of the cultural industries and what major types of products are dominant in the shaping of youth culture and in the creation of subcultures?

4. What is the relative role of 'youth products' *vis-à-vis* the 'general audience products' of the culture industries and what makes youth products appealing to their audiences?

The study also differentiated between the mass media, which are mainly concerned with information, and the cultural industries, which are mainly focused on the transmission of creative artistic or popular culture items and ideas. Main concepts used in the report were socialization processes of childhood and adolescence, and socialization agents which transmit values and symbols.

The report also made a distinction between *creative socialization agents,* which provide the source of symbols and values, and the *transmitting and gate-keeping socialization agents,* which select, interpret and transfer these symbols and values. These concepts were used to analyse the data from two survey studies carried out among 10- and 14-year-old schoolchildren in the southern part of Finland. The researcher concluded her observations by the comment: 'It seems that the most pervasive impact of the products of culture industries on children and youth is on the level of general life-style.' She also stressed that the impact of cultural industries on children and youth should not be viewed merely from the perspective of individual social problems but that we should approach the issue with a more comprehensive analysis of the role of the culture industries as one among a wider range of socialization agents which interact with each other.

The Finnish case-study was carried out in 1977 on a sample of 242 10-year-old schoolchildren and in 1978 on a sample of 304 14-year-old schoolchildren. This provided the opportunity for comparisons, which must, however, be treated with caution because the population samples are not identical.

The key point for further study and discussion can be found on page 17 of the Finnish report where it is stated that:

This suggests that in a total socialization process the transmitting and gate-keeping agents are of primary importance, and the success of the original sources of new values and symbols in influencing the socialization process depends on the acceptance of their products by the major 'influentials' in the life of the children and the adolescents.[11]

Interesting and concurring with other findings is the statement that 'the modern Finnish youth culture is rather materialistic and money-consuming', and also that there are certain elements which point to an Americanization of culture. Important are also the remarks concerning two types of subculture: modern audio-visual culture and traditional home culture. Attention to this problem had been drawn some years ago by Joffre Dumazedier who drew a distinction between the subculture of the home and school and the subculture of leisure.

The controversy about the real effects of the impact of mass media, including television, on the attitudes and behaviour of youth has been going on for years. More than twenty years have passed since the publication of a book by B. Rosenberg and D. M. White, which offered two entirely different viewpoints on the matter under discussion: on the one hand an optimistic perspective with regard to the development of mass media, and on the other hand definite disapproval of them.

This controversy is still with us. It is argued that the mass media are to be credited for the increasing cultural integration of the world. Fifteen years ago McLuhan was defining the emergence of a new cultural structure as 'the global village'. Television was supposed to broaden the intellectual horizon of its audience, to take the place of the 'pub culture'.[12]

Television can take credit for the introduction of the authentic, for bringing real-life events closer to the audience. Thus, television and the other mass media perform important informative functions.

At the same time television teaches. It assists the school in performing its didactic tasks. Among other things, it teaches the alphabet to small children, it teaches how to use one's own language properly, it teaches foreign languages. This didactic function is particularly important in the developing countries.

Detailed studies carried out in the United States revealed also a positive influence of television on the shaping of the attitudes of children and youth: it has been established that television helps to develop in the child the need for sharing with others, that it enhances self-control, that it has also therapeutic effects in reducing fear and anxiety.[13] It can also be said—and this applies in particular to cable television—that to some extent it reduces the sense of loneliness and creates the possibility of establishing contacts with other people.

It must be recognized, however, that the drawbacks outweigh the list of the above-mentioned merits. In the first place, it has been pointed out that television projects an untrue or half-true image of the world. Television producers are accused of succumbing to the temptation of shallowness, of trying to accommodate the so-called average viewer, of degrading information, of 'packaging'. The Polish author Marcin Czerwinski uses the term 'information gibberish'.

However, the most important reproach is made in connection with television's shaping of aggressive attitudes in children and youth because of the amount of violence shown on the screen. R. M. Liebert, J. M. Neale and E. S. Davidson[14] analyse scores of case-studies carried out in this field and conclude that television, and at least American television, shows more crime than would be warranted by its place in real life, that in television violence constitutes a form of entertainment, and—which is particularly dangerous—that violence is presented as an effective way to achieve results.

Detailed studies discussed in this book describe the process of learning by children through observation; laboratory studies demonstrate that a single television show can affect the mind of the viewer even after a lapse of time and generate under favourable conditions aggressive attitudes; research carried out by a correlation method reveals the existence of a link between television viewing and delinquency. Experimental research (after elimination of the so-called third variable) reveals unequivocally a positive correlation between the reception of certain programmes (the cause) and aggressive behaviour (the effect).

Less studied, but no doubt of considerable importance, is the influence of television and other mass media on youth's attitudes towards sex and the excessive permissiveness which can be observed in this respect.

Another problem, of a broader nature, concerning not only children and youth but also grown-ups, is the role of television in shaping a passive, consumer orientated and—what is perhaps the most important thing—a 'free-wheeling' attitude towards life. In many countries television is viewed by producers primarily as a source of entertainment.[15] The basic features of television entertainment corresponding to man's essential needs, to his need to celebrate, to his yearning for rites, to his need to communicate, are reflected in the attempts to create the impression of a climate of celebration, the impression of community with what is happening on the screen. 'The escapist sense of entertainment lies in the fact that the desire for change of the described state is being channelled into a harmless and illusionistic direction which instead of fulfilling needs provides only illusions.'[16]

It seems that apart from what has been said above about the profound impact of television on the attitudes and behaviour of children and youth, especially as far as aggression is concerned, its influence is reflected above all in external behaviour, among other things, with respect to fashion, Children at play readily imitate the behaviour observed in favourite television shows (for example the behaviour of the heroes of some television serials).

It seems however that the impact, especially as regards youth, on the attitudes and behaviour connected with the orientation towards supreme values is all the stronger, all the more effective, the weaker the personality of the young viewer when his outlook and opinions are not definitely formed. It cannot be ruled out that the mass media bear to a certain extent the responsibility for that weakness, since they tend to isolate the viewer from more important problems (among other things by providing largely entertainment) thereby strengthening their grip over the audience. By causing that weakness they stimulate pathological phenomena, as witnessed by the results of the above-mentioned studies concerning the impact of television on aggressive behaviour.

The impact of cultural industry
and the tendencies towards change
in the attitudes and behaviour of youth

It is not easy to forecast the direction of the future impact of cultural industries, and especially those of the mass media, on the attitudes and behaviour of youth in the various regions of the world. This will depend not only on the maintenance of the present trends but also, and perhaps above all, on the action (if any) that will be undertaken within the framework of social policy by different countries in order to act against the prevailing negative phenomena.

Research carried out in the major developed capitalist countries such as the United States, in small developed countries like Finland, in some developing countries like Ghana, and also in several socialist countries, reveals (for the time being) some convergent or at least similar trends. This applies in the first place to the so-called homogenizing effect of television. Television is becoming a factor that is strengthening and broadening the youth subculture, one of the main features of that subculture being the craving for entertainment and, generally, consumer-orientated attitudes. The statement by Ritva Mitchell, author of the Finnish report, to the effect that 'the modern Finnish youth culture is rather materialistic and money-consuming', has, no doubt, a broader scope and applies not only to Finnish youth. Equally true, and of a broader scope, seem to be the statements by R. Mitchell as regards Finnish youth and by Dr Isaac Obeng-Quaido from Ghana referring to a certain 'Americanization' of the life-style of the young generation resulting from the preference shown to American television programmes. This phenomenon must be viewed in close connection with the massive expansion in the exportation of American television programmes.

It may also be surmised that further research would confirm the hypothesis concerning the increasing influence of television on the aggressive attitudes of children and youth and also on the attitudes of youth towards sex in countries other than the United States.

This is caused, among other things, by the above-mentioned commercialization of the cultural industry. Since by meeting the needs of a 'lower order' it is possible to make bigger profits, the natural trend in some countries is not only to adapt to the market requirements, but also to stimulate such needs by artificial means. Just as the production, traffic and contraband of alcohol and narcotics yields huge profits, the same is expected from the products provided by the mass media; their contents are responding less to educational needs and more to profit-making considerations.

On the other hand, in some countries these contents reflect, in the first place, specific ideological options which leave youth with no possibility of choice and create the false illusion that half truths can be substituted for the whole truth.

It is therefore necessary to see what measures can be taken in order to counteract these phenomena, what action can be taken by the countries themselves and what is the role Unesco can play.

POLICY RECOMMENDATIONS

The fundamental problem of social policy facing democratic societies which aim at developing supreme values in the process of educating children and youth is that of continuously solving the conflict between the threat of ethical relativism on the one hand and the danger of ideological indoctrination on the other.

The full liberalization of the contents transmitted by the cultural industries in the name of freedom and democracy, while maintaining the dominant position of various pressure groups whose action is motivated only by the search for profits, leads to the commercialization of the mass media and to the loss of man's supreme values, hence to a warping of the dispositions of children and youth, and results in ethical relativism, in the absence of permanent values, with the final effect of the spread of narcotic addiction, sexual permissiveness and suicide.

Full ideological indoctrination under the pretence of possessing a monopoly of truth, strict control of transmitted contents leads to the formation of attitudes of fanaticism and intolerance, provided these contents are accepted, or—and this may sound paradoxical—to attitudes of ethical relativism and a feeling of general frustration should these contents be rejected.

The only way, though the most difficult one, is that of the fullest honest and objective presentation of various supreme values, offering the possibility of their recognition by youth, of their emotional acceptance with the resulting voluntary choice and internalization of the accepted values.

I should like at this juncture to quote a few words which I wrote in the concluding part of my book entitled *Sociological Problems of Tourism*:

Unity of the world can only be accomplished through unity in diversity, through the integration of different cultures representing different values. Those values must, in the first place, be made familiar, and then exchanged. This means that our best values should be transmitted to other people and in return we should absorb their best ones. This is the only way to enrich mankind's cultural heritage.[17]

Radio and television must be, in the first place, the instruments of remote transmission of contents, instruments enabling man to overcome distance. These contents must be free of bias. They must represent the world and its most cherished values as they are, as the products of various ideologies and cultures, without becoming by themselves one of the sources of a specific ideology (including also the money-consuming ideology).

The achievement of such a goal is hampered, above all, by the existing dependence of cultural industries on the political authorities and on economic pressure groups. It is hampered also by the power exercised by these pressure groups, through the mass media, over the politicians[18] by the support they can lend or refuse to grant to the politicians, for example during election campaigns. The famous 'cigarette war' in the United States is a good case in point.[19] R. M. Liebert and his co-authors think that there is already an urgent need for 'immediate remedial action' as regards the influence of television on children and youth.

Financial resources must be concentrated in the hands of those who place the welfare of children and youth above all other considerations. Such a statement may sound somewhat utopian, however it may not be unrealistic to assume that in modern societies most people think and act in that way. The trouble is that in some societies control over the cultural industries and the mass media has been lost in the same way as in many countries control has been lost over governments.

The conclusions concerning policy recommendations for Unesco have been formulated in the Draft Report of the Helsinki Conference (December 1979). Here are some of them:

In view of the fact that cultural industries encourage consumerism . . . often dysfunctional to development—and in view of the lack of knowledge about whether cultural industries meet real needs or create these needs, Unesco should encourage Member States to engage in a serious critique of the sources, nature and influence of cultural industries.

Since little critical analysis of the output of cultural industries has been developed; Unesco should support formal and non-formal educational programmes directed towards promoting critical approaches.

Special emphasis should be given to policies which aim at broadening the range of socialization agents by bringing in new specialized agents for children and youth. So, special attention should be paid to *animateurs* working with children and youth.

RESEARCH IMPLICATIONS

Unesco, when programming international comparative studies on the impact of cultural industries on the attitudes and behaviour of children and youth, should aim at defining with the utmost precision their object and scope as well as their methodology, including the basic research tools (with the possibility of adapting them to the specific conditions prevailing in various countries). Only such a procedure will make it possible to arrive at a synthesis.

The fundamental questions that remain to be answered are the following:
What is the source of supreme values for youth?
Which values are transmitted by which ways?
How are they received?
What is the nature and mechanism of internalization of values?
What are the dynamics of change in this field?
Are we in fact witnessing a process of unification and if so around which values, or, on the contrary, is there a process of deepening diversification taking place?
If so, what are the types of youth subcultures which are emerging and what are the factors upon which they depend?

NOTES

1. K. T. Toeplitz, *Szkice edynburskie* [Edinburgh Essays], Warsaw, 1979.
2. Marcin Czerwinski, *Telewizja wobec kultury* [Television and Culture], Warsaw, 1973.
3. R. M. Liebert, J. M. Neale and E. S. Davidson, *The Early Window, Effects of Television on Children and Youth,* Elmsford, N. Y., 1976.

4. Toeplitz, op. cit.
5. Liebert et al., op. cit.
6. Toeplitz, op. cit.
7. Liebert et al., op. cit.
8. *Draft Report of the Expert Meeting on the Impact of Cultural Industries in the Field of Audio-visual Media on the Socio-cultural Behaviour of Youth and Women, Finland, Hanasaari, 11–14 December 1979* (mimeo).
9. Isaac Obeng-Quaido, *The Impact of Cultural Industries in the Field of Audiovisual Media on the Socio-cultural Behaviour of Youth in Ghana,* Espoo, Finland, 1979 (mimeo).
10. Ritva Mitchell, *Youth Socialization and Cultural Industries. Empirical Case Studies and their Interpretation from Development and Policy Perspectives,* Espoo, Finland, 1979 (mimeo).
11. *Draft Report . . .,* op. cit., p. 17.
12. Czerwinski, op. cit.
13. Liebert et al., op. cit.
14. Ibid.
15. Toeplitz, op. cit.
16. Ibid., p. 85.
17. Krzysztof Przeclawski, *Socjologiczne problemy turystyki* [Sociological Problems of Tourism], Warsaw, 1979.
18. Liebert et al., op. cit.
19. Ibid., pp. 136 et seq.

5   Women and the cultural industries

Margaret Gallagher

Institute of Educational Technology,
The Open University,
United Kingdom

CULTURE, CULTURAL INDUSTRIES AND THE PRODUCTION OF MEANINGS

Realization of the subordinate—and indeed largely unacknowledged—role which women play within the socio-economic system gives rise immediately to the question of how and why this role is broadly accepted by women themselves as inevitable and natural. The very placement of women within the personal rather than the public sphere is one answer. Gramsci in his *Prison Notebooks*[1] argued that for a subordinate group, working only through direct, personal experience and common sense does not allow the construction of a coherent oppositional world view. What is experienced may be in contradiction to available explanations, but it is very difficult to work out why or to understand how. So despite the *experience* of contradiction, what is often 'felt' is the naturalness of the way things are. The overarching role of culture—which can be defined as the socially and historically situated process of production of *meanings*—in this entire process of role and identity formation is fundamental.[2]

The cultural 'absences and exclusions' of women have begun to be noted by women themselves. Thus women can see that 'we have been defined negatively in relation to the culture into which we have been born: our experience has tended to be made invisible',[3] or can describe their 'inability to find ourselves in existing culture as we experience ourselves'.[4] Yet the step between the experience of contradiction and action to resolve the contradiction remains enormous in a world where—even for a majority of women—cultural meaning decrees that 'women mean love and the home, while men stand for work and the external world'.[5] The basic significance of the cultural exclusion or partial representation of women can be found in the relationship of cultural processes to the socio-economic system and in the economic determination of cultural practices and products. Consequently, cultural industries and their output can be seen as another link in the chain binding women in their particular relationship to socio-economic structures.

Raymond Williams, in a seminal study of modern communications in the United Kingdom,[6] writes of the 'long revolution' in culture, initiated by the extension of the education and communication systems, as a third current of change alongside the industrial revolution in the economy and the democratic revolution in the political sphere. These three processes together, he argues, define the texture and tempo of contemporary experience.

Consequently, it is necessary to study the complex interactions between the spheres of culture, policy and economy. In a later work,[7] Williams acknowledges the pivotal position of the economic structure and the determinations it exerts on cultural production. He suggests that the growing concentration of control in the hands of the large communications corporations is the key defining characteristic of the emerging situation, and that as a result the methods and attitudes of capitalist business have penetrated deeply into more and more areas and 'have established themselves near the centre of communication'.

However, the point is not simply that the communications media have an economic function (and Williams certainly does not suggest that it is), but that they play a fundamental ideological role which is articulated *through* their relationship to the economic structure. This is a point which is not always grasped. For instance, in Dallas Smythe's analysis[8] the media's primary function is to create stable audience blocs for sale to monopoly capitalist advertisers, thereby generating the propensities to consume which complete the circuit of production. A similar analysis is often applied to the media's treatment of women, in terms of their singling women out as the consumers *par excellence*.[9] Yet how do important media sectors with minimal dependence on advertising revenue—notably, paperback publishing, the cinema and the popular music industry—fit into this schema? The trap into which this type of theorizing falls is that by highlighting the role played by the media in the circulation of economic commodities, their independent role in the reproduction of ideologies is ignored. Consequently, there can be no exploration of the ways in which economic determinations shape the range and forms of media production and its resulting products.

It is these crucial links between the economic and ideological dimensions of media production which Peter Golding and Graham Murdock stress when they call for a comprehensive political economy of culture. Their argument is that the production of ideology cannot be separated from, or adequately understood except in relation to, the general economic dynamics of media production and the determinations they exert.[10] As they go on to suggest, these economic dynamics operate at a variety of levels and with varying degrees of intensity within different media sectors and different divisions within them. At the most general level the distribution of economic resources plays a decisive role in determining the range of available media: the absence of a mass circulation radical daily newspaper in the United Kingdom, for instance, is primarily due to the prohibitive costs of market entry and to the maldistribution of advertising revenue. Economic imperatives also help to determine the general form of available media. The lack of fit between the media systems of many developing countries and the social needs of their populations—the institutionalization of domestic, studio-based television in communally oriented outdoor cultures, for example—is due in large measure to the historical and economic dominance of the major multinational corporations. Similarly, dispersed rural populations are not particularly well served by urban-based daily newspapers. Within individual media organizations economic imperatives may play an important role in determining the allocation of production resources between divisions with varying ratios of costs to audience appeal, as between sports coverage and educational broadcasting, for instance.

Although Golding and Murdock make no mention of the fact, it is clear that each of the various levels of determination which they identify impinge, either singly or in combination, on the specific position of women as both subjects and objects in the media. Reasons ascribed to the absence of a radical newspaper, for example, apply just as well to the absence of a feminist one. If the needs of rural populations in developing countries are not well served by urban-based newspapers, the needs of rural women—the overwhelming majority of whom are illiterate—are particularly ignored. The differential ratio of costs to audience appeal as between sports coverage and educational broadcasting could equally obtain between sports coverage and programming directed at women. Clearly, then, the media do play a central ideological role in that their practices and products are both a source and a confirmation of the structural inequality of women in society.

SPECIFIC CHARACTERISTICS OF WOMEN'S RELATIONSHIP TO THE CULTURAL INDUSTRIES

Before discussing certain general aspects of the position of women in the media, in terms of both portrayal and participation, I should like to draw attention to some particular features which characterize women's relationship to the cultural industries and their products in quite a specific way. It should be clear that each of these features has its roots in both the economic and the ideological spheres, and furthermore that each has a distinct functional role to play in both of these areas.

In the first place, as Cornelia Butler Flora has pointed out, 'almost since the invention of the printing press, women's fiction has proved a lucrative venture. Middle-class women—women from the class that was literate and had the leisure and money to read—were avid audiences for the "romantic scribblers".'[11] Clearly, with increased access to education and the extension of female literacy, this particular market has expanded considerably in most industrialized countries. Moreover, the growth of the electronic, visual media has opened up completely new market groups among women (as well as men) and has led to a distribution of cultural products which is as diversified as the products themselves. However, an examination of some of the production processes involved even at the very earliest stages of the industrialization of cultural output indicates clearly those aspects of women's subordination in and through the culture industries that persist to the present day in a very wide variety of contexts.

In a study of the production and consumption of novels in the nineteenth century, Rachel Harrison has argued that this rested on a fourfold subordination of women.[12] First of all, there was the subordinate position of female novelists themselves. The writing of novels by women in the home was tolerated, rather than encouraged, so long as it did not disturb the routines of domestic life. Nevertheless, it was considered that writing should not be the business of a woman's life. In a direct allusion to one of Roland Barthes 'mythologies'[13] entitled 'Children and Novels', and arguing that children justify novel-writing, Michele Mattelart suggests that even now 'the woman who writes novels . . . must testify to her submission to the eternal female status quo in order not to become a symbol of rebellion'.[14] These contradictions are clearly internalized by women writers: so, for example, we find Lily Briscoe, Virginia Woolf's alter ego in *To the Lighthouse,* struggling to complete a painting against a mocking, insistent inner voice that whispers 'Women can't paint; women can't write.' Sallie Sears has argued that the strength of the contradictions has driven certain women writers, such as Sylvia Plath and Virginia Woolf herself, to despair and even suicide.[15] In another sense, women writers were subordinated through the discrimination that was practised against them in male-run publishing houses. Although the consumers were predominantly female, the attitudes of publishers dictated that authorship of novels should be male and led women to adopt pseudonyms—Currer Bell, George Eliot and George Sand among them. Content of the novels too was affected by predominating male values and assessments as to what was important. This led Virginia Woolf to argue that the whole structure of the nineteenth-century novel, when written by a woman, was 'made to alter its clear vision in deference to external authority' resulting in a high proportion of works which were centrally flawed.[16]

The second aspect of Harrison's fourfold characterization of the subordinates of women in the process of novel production refers to the position of women in the printing trade. Here technological changes had allowed the substitution of the unskilled labour of women (and of children) for skilled male labour. Karl Marx, in the first volume of *Capital,* noted that London print-shops had come to be known as 'slaughter-houses' and that the chief victims there, as well as in the sorting of rags for paper production and in the process of bookbinding, were 'chiefly women, girls and children'.[17] Thirdly, Harrison argues, a similar exploitation of women in domestic service (made possible by the greater volume of profit and wealth among businessmen, itself a result of the move from absolute to relative surplus value in nineteenth-century industrial economy) ensured that middle-class women had time to read—and sometimes write—the novels that were produced.

Finally, there is the aspect of the female consumer. Here, the particular form of subordination can be said to be primarily sexual, legitimated through the ideologies of romance, femininity, domesticity and motherhood which saturate the content of many of the novels produced at this time. It is important to realize that the ideology of love and marriage, with its corollary of virginity and monogamy, had, as well as a social function (that of ensuring dutiful daughters and chaste wives), a specifically economic role to play: indeed, its very roots lay in the emerging interests of new economic relationships. This is clearly expressed in the Finer Report:

Middle class families handled their accumulating industrial wealth within a system of partible inheritance which demanded a more severe morality imposing higher standards upon women than ever. An adulterous wife might be the means of planting a fraudulent claimant upon its property in the heart of the family; to avoid this ultimate catastrophe, middle class women were required to observe an inviolable role of chastity.[18]

The 'feminine illusion' to which, as various commentators have noted, this historical period gave birth[19] thus coincides both with radical shifts in the socio-economic system and with the emergence of an industrial mode of cultural production. Its illusory nature lies in the fact that it masks—or sets out to mask—the fundamental contradiction between the idealization and the structural subordination of women in society.

These problems in relation to women and cultural production, although they have been discussed in the context of a particular historical setting, are neither anachronistic nor culture-specific. Their modern corollaries should become apparent in the global review of issues affecting women in and through culture and the media which will follow. Prior to that discussion, however, I wish to touch briefly on one other factor that makes the relationship of women to cultural industries and their products a very distinct one. This is the way in which women as a group are *used* in cultural imagery for purposes both economic and ideological. Although this was raised to some extent above, the point is not simply that certain images of women which are mediated through the culture may affect the perceptions and behaviours of men and women in relation to each other. Beyond this, there is a sense in which the images of woman (which have been socially and culturally constructed) can be appealed to, or centrally placed in, the construction of much broader social images than those directly relating to women themselves.

For example, in her discussion of the construction and ideological function of the image of 'modernity', Michele Mattelart[20] highlights the prior image of 'woman' as the hub from which the media propagate their particular 'culture of modernity'. The image of womanhood, she argues, is basically—even mythical-ly—related to ideas of continuity, perpetuation and perdurability. 'Through the hidden power of its image, its unconscious insinuation, the female face . . . is the indication of a non-aggressive proposal, exuding security and lawfulness.' Yet, in an apparent paradox, the media continually associate—visually—women with the 'arsenal of symbols', fashions, new commodities, new designs, new life-styles which delineate the culture of modernity. What this means, for Mattelart, is that a *particular* image of modernity is being constructed, in which tradition acquires a new validation and perpetuation, in which alongside the appearance of movement and change there is a reassuring sense of order and permanence, and which is 'hiding the basic fact that the modern themes do no more than renew the old myths'.[21]

THE SOCIALIZATION PROCESS AND MEDIA IMAGES OF WOMEN

In theory, as one of a number of socializing agents, the media should carry no greater or lesser responsibility or power in the socialization process than any other cultural force. However, a number of factors particular to the structure and internal demands of media organizations have suggested to some theorists of sexual inequality that the mass media may play a particularly conservative role in socialization, reinforcing traditional values and beliefs. These factors include the sexual composition of the media workforce, which in almost every country is predominantly male—overwhelmingly so in the influential areas of management and production. Then there is the reliance of many mass media organizations on commercial backing and a consequent pressure to deal in known and accepted images and contents. Thirdly, mass media products—whether television or radio programmes, magazines, newspapers, records, films—are in general required to make an immediate and vivid impact and to be quickly and easily absorbed by their audiences: considerable reliance is therefore placed on the use of simplified, recognizable and standardized characterizations in media output. For these reasons, it has seemed possible to some commentators that the media present a social reality which, if not demonstrably false, feeds on the most conservative forces in society, ignoring new trends until they have become established and thus fulfilling a primarily reinforcing role, rather than a transforming one, in the culture. To take, for example, the 'standardized characterizations' or stereotypes through which much media output can be seen to depict both men and women: the concern of some media critics is that by repeatedly depicting women and men in stereotyped roles—and by tending to portray deviations from those roles in a negative way—the media may actually work against the potentially transforming effects of any experience of counter-stereotypes which women and men meet in ordinary social life. This would cast the media not simply in a neutral or even a conservative role, but as a reactionary force in the development of sexual equality.

It is not my intention to detail the basic images through which the world's media portray women. These are by now well known. The numerical under-representation of women, their depiction in terms of the familiar 'types' of wife and mother, sex object and glamour girl, the attribution to them of psychological characteristics denoting passivity, dependence, indecisiveness—all this is now well documented in both national and global accounts of images of women in the media.[22] Rather, I want to draw attention to some variations from the norm.

It is no accident that in those countries in which women have made quickest progress towards full social, economic and political participation (for example, the People's Republic of China, Cuba, the socialist countries of Eastern Europe) economic imperatives have underlain formulations of policies on women. The mass media have in general reflected government commitment to these policies. For example, media portrayals of women in China probably represent the most extreme example of how, in a historically brief time-span, the mass media can make a major contribution to a revolutionary reversal of women's self-image and of social definitions of women's roles. Clearly, however, the importance of government intervention in this process is paramount, the success of the media in promoting acceptance of change being directly related to the adequacy of political conceptualization of women's problems and their solution. For instance, Chinese women have expressed concern that by portraying heroines only in leadership roles—showing no hint of the competing demands which real women in such positions actually face—the media have ignored the specific difficulties inherited by women from their historical past or through their reproductive roles.[23]

As in China, most evidence points to the fact that the media of the socialist countries of Eastern Europe portray women in an overall positive way, stressing their contribution to economic and social development. Again as in China, however, the same dilemma for women—the conflicting demands of their economic and family roles—exists and is, according to some Polish and Soviet research, actually exacerbated by the media.[24]

Another variant which may be tentatively mentioned is that to be found in some parts of Africa. Although information is fragmentary and the evidence perilously thin, there is some indication that images of women in certain African countries may reflect and benefit from a relatively self-conscious use of the media in the general process of national development. For example, analysis of the Zambian daily press between 1971 and 1975 revealed positive and strong images of women as equal partners with men in development.[25] The appearance, in Ghana, Kenya and Senegal, of explicitly or implicitly feminist magazines in recent years is a further indication that alternative self-images are available for women. However, it must also be said that many negative features noted in media treatment of women elsewhere can also be detected in the younger media of Africa.

In sum, the total implication of these 'variations' is that it is notoriously difficult, even in those media controlled by governments with a strong commitment to social change, to uproot the deeply ingrained beliefs and assumptions that underlie dominant images of women in the media.

FUNCTIONAL ROLES AND THE MEDIA'S PORTRAYAL OF WOMEN

The mass media perform a number of quite different functions in society, providing news and entertainment as well as acting as vehicles for both education and advertising. It is a common assumption that within each of these separate functions the media's portrayal of women may be more or less damaging. By looking briefly at just two almost opposing media roles—advertising and education—we can see that the issue is by no means clear-cut.

Probably greatest concern has centred on images of women in advertising, whose reliance on women—particularly women's bodies—as sales bait is in almost universal evidence. The particularly degrading nature of many advertising images of women is well-documented, for example, in studies in Austria, Canada, Denmark, the Philippines and the United Kingdom.[26] Successful campaigns against particular advertisers or advertisements have been waged in a number of countries. However, these tend to be drops in the ocean of negative images projected in the name of commercial interests. Those interests control, or at least influence, not merely the advertisements themselves, but the context which surrounds them. Indeed, the purpose of much commercial media content— whether television, radio or print—is to attract an audience that will then be exposed to the advertising message. This, allied to the fact that advertising tends to deal in known, safe, traditional appeals, makes for an insidiously manipulative and conservative appeal to the audience.

On the other hand, to be successful, advertising must sell; it therefore needs to take account of the attitudes and behaviours of its target audience. There is no doubt that advertisements aimed at certain groups are taking account of changes in women's roles. In the United Kingdom, for instance, one series of successful advertisements for a popular daily newspaper plays on the words of a well-known saying with its slogan 'Behind every successful woman there is a *Daily Mail*'. Women in these advertisements are shown as business executives, lawyers and so on. In the United States, United Airlines, having found that, in 1978, 16 per cent of its business travellers were women, aims a quarter of its print advertising at them, while a third of the managers in its television advertisements are women.[27] Despite these and other instances,[28] and despite Canadian research which demonstrated that advertisements reflecting modern roles were rated as more effective by consumers and advertisers alike,[29] advertisers are unlikely to initiate change: they have a vested interest in the status quo.

Moreover, there are numerous instances of what has sometimes been called 'value prostitution' in advertising, cases in which a genuine value, which has nothing to do with a product, is used to sell it—for example, the appropriation of the value of independence for women in the 'You've Come a Long Way, Baby' series of the campaign to sell Virginia Slims cigarettes.[30] Stuart Ewen points out how, in a very similar way, the demand for equality for women in the 1920s in the United States was appropriated into the jargon of consumerism, in, for instance, the advertisements of the American Tobacco Company. These historical instances indicate the correctness of a definition of advertising as 'the rhetoric of modernity'.[31]

It is perhaps reasonable to assume that educational mass media may be more balanced in their portrayal of women, that educators may be more alert to sexual stereotyping and may seek to avoid bias in the projection of sex roles. However, as far as formal education is concerned, there is a growing literature from countries such as Bangladesh, France, India, Sweden, the United States and the Soviet Union,[32] to name only a few, attesting to sex-role stereotyping in children's textbooks. At the same time, some American research has demonstrated that aspects of sex-role stereotypes are present in 3-year-old children before they enter the formal educational system, indicating the crucial importance of pre-school informal education.[33] In this context, it is worth noting that the American television programme *Sesame Street,* in which female characters are outnumbered five to one by males, and in which males are stereotyped as dominant and aggressive, and females as traditional homemakers, was specifically *designed* so that pre-school children could 'model' behaviour.[34] Moreover, much research exists to show that *Sesame Street* has been successful in teaching children.[35]

Non-formal educational programmes for adults are not exempt from criticism. Although numerous television and radio programmes are directed towards the education of women, these tend to emphasize domestic skills and child-care to the exclusion of other, less traditional pursuits. This is not to deny that such things are important to women—particularly in many developing countries—but it is notable that in a country like the United Kingdom, television's 'further education' for women still consists mainly of series on cookery, dress-making, knitting and so on: programmes dealing with women's retraining and re-entry to the labour market hardly exist. Even programmes which deal with crucial topics such as health and contraception may contain sexist bias. In India, for example, a detailed analysis of two government family planning films found a heavy sexist and patriarchal bias in both.[36]

THE POSITION OF WOMEN WORKING WITHIN THE MEDIA

Concern with women's employment in the mass media industries springs from two basic preoccupations. The first is a simple interest in the development of job opportunities for women at all levels and in the removal of obstacles to their equal participation in every field of work. The second rests on an assumption that there is a link between media output and the producers of the output. The implication of this assumption is that by opening up the media to women workers on a larger scale, the images which have given cause for concern will gradually change for the better.

In many developing countries, the media form part of what is sometimes called the 'modern industrial' sector. In such countries, jobs in this sector are few, and as a general rule men predominate overwhelmingly. In the developed world, jobs in the media industries have themselves been subject to sex-types segregation. These factors, in addition to some media-specific variations on certain general problems—for example, occupational segregation in both vertical and horizontal terms, dual responsibilities of working women, inferior education and lack of training, weak unionization, aspects of protective legislation—underpin the overall position of women media workers.

The proportion of women employed in film, broadcasting or in the national press rarely exceeds 30 per cent in any country. Often the percentage is much lower. To give some examples from broadcasting: in the United States, 30 per cent of the work force at television-network headquarters and also at network-owned stations in 1977 was female;[37] in Italy, women accounted for 20 per cent of the jobs in RAI television in 1975;[38] in Canada, 25 per cent of the jobs in CBC were held by women in 1975.[39] It has been estimated that there were about 25 per cent of broadcasting jobs held by women in India in 1975. Women do slightly better in some Scandinavian countries: in Sweden women comprise 33 per cent and in Norway 38 per cent of all employees in the national broadcasting corporations (1976 figures). At the other end of the scale, only 6 per cent of those employed at NHK in Japan are women.[40]

When we see just where in the media women are employed it is clear that these global figures mask even greater disparities between men and women, brought about by a process of vertical and horizontal segregation. Thus, at the managerial level, women generally hold not more than 10 per cent of the jobs. At the creative/professional level too, access to top posts in very limited for women, although two broadcasting organizations with atypically high proportions of women producers are the Swedish and the Singaporean services, where women account for 30 and 38 per cent of all producers, respectively.[41] It is also true that women are found well away from the important areas of news, current affairs, economics and politics; in drama, sport and light entertainment, areas that are 'important' in terms of audience pull, they are again severely under-represented. In the United Kingdom in 1975, for example, the Association of Cinematograph, Television and Allied Technicians (ACTT) found its women members working primarily in the 'marginal areas of educational, arts and children's programming', a pattern which is common elsewhere.[42] At the technical level, there is a negligible number of women in any broadcasting or film organization anywhere. One exception is Finland, where 20 per cent of all technical staff in the Finnish Broadcasting Company were women in 1978.[43]

At the same time, the secretarial and clerical jobs are almost completely filled by women in most media organizations. In fact, when we talk of 'women in the media', we describe for the most part women working as production secretaries, script/continuity staff and clerk-typists. In the United Kingdom, 100 per cent of production secretaries/producers' assistants among ACTT members were female in 1975; in Taiwan, nearly 90 per cent of these staff across all three television networks in 1976 were women;[44] all continuity staff in the Finnish Broadcasting Company in 1978 were women. And so on. These facts become particularly important when seen in the context of earning levels and career development: not only are women's jobs lower paid than, for instance, the technical jobs dominated by men; they are also 'dead-end' jobs, with no obvious line of promotion.

In general, media women are relatively successful in less competitive areas—if that can be called real success. In many countries, television carries a particular glamour and prestige, along with high salaries, and competition for jobs is unusually strong. It is not surprising, then, that proportionately more women can be found in the upper echelons of the radio sector of the national broadcasting organizations of countries such as Canada, the United States, the United Kingdom and even Taiwan. In Egypt and France the national radio systems are actually headed by women. Local community media—an expanding sector of many developing media systems—are also unusually open to women, mainly because of their relatively low status within overall media structures.

THE RELATION BETWEEN MEDIA WOMEN AND MEDIA OUTPUT

It is difficult to find any hard evidence to support the proposition that the portrayal of women in the media differs when a woman is producing the images. This is partly a consequence of the way in which research in this area has typically been carried out. A heavy research focus on content analysis means that there have been virtually no attempts to establish links between the dominant images and the dominant values, beliefs or attitudes of media personnel. A few scattered studies have managed to establish that, for instance, the female editors of women's pages are on the whole oriented by the same traditional concerns and priorities as their male counterparts, and that women's judgements about newsworthiness resemble those of men.[45] Another study, examining the news perceptions of journalism students, found that women students had the same stereotyped picture of women as male students: although they themselves were interested in politics and not 'traditional' women's concerns, they thought that they were unusual and that 'ordinary' women would be more interested in mundane matters.[46]

It is also true that many instances can be found of individual women producers, journalists or decision-makers being associated with, or directly responsible for, anti-female material. For example, the most sexually explicit of a particular series of Venezuelan *fotonovelas* were almost all written by women.[47] This underlines the simplistic nature of some statements made about media output and male domination. The fact is that most women and most men share common cultural perspectives. The problem is not, therefore, simply to open up media employment to women, but at the same time to work towards changing women's self-perceptions, evolving and directing measures against a cultural value system which at present not only accords women lower status, but also frequently leaves them unaware of the fact.

A further problem in focusing on individual media workers, whether male or female, is that they often have very much less control over media output than is commonly assumed. Many research studies have documented, for example, the power of the American television networks in influencing both television-station practices and the programmes produced by independent production companies.[48] Journalists' output has been found to be conditioned by the reward system and political preferences of their employers.[49] Various studies of organizational control in the media have highlighted the difficulties experienced by individual communicators in attempting to innovate or deviate from organizational norms and ground rules.[50] In this context, it seems unlikely that women could or would have greater freedom than men within communication organizations.

At another level, problems arise from the complicated system of attitudes and practices that constitute media professionalism. It is difficult for media women to resist ideas and attitudes associated with success in their profession, even if such ideas demean them as women in the audience. Professional beliefs may undervalue women and women's interests—for instance, certain topics may be defined as uninteresting or unimportant—but professionally ambitious women are unlikely to go out on a limb and risk being identified with marginal or minority interests. The parameters of success are male-defined and women are not in a position to remake the rules.

Thus, for example, one study found that both male *and* female members of a talk show encouraged sexist comments from guests during the 'warm-up' preparations for the show.[51] At the same time, the subtlety with which professional norms and procedures operate make them difficult to isolate. A Canadian study of advertising found that many of the television advertisements that were considered totally acceptable in story-board or draft form seemed much less acceptable in their final version.[52] In other words, the bias arose in the course of detailed execution: in stereotyped acting, tone of voice, general 'style'. Briefly, it would seem that until a 'critical mass' of committed women is constituted within the media, the possibilities of working against cultural and professional values which demean or exclude women will be negligible.

THE IMPACT OF MEDIA PORTRAYALS OF WOMEN

Despite recent research which shatters many assumptions about the actual existence of, for example, psychological sex differences,[53] the old sex-role stereotypes persist and find their way into male and female self-perceptions and actions in a fundamental manner. Australian researchers, for instance, as part of an experiment in open planning for telecommunications, found that compared with four other groups surveyed, women's world-views reflected feelings of pessimism and powerlessness.[54] Given the ubiquity of the mass media, in many parts of the world at least, the question arises as to the role which they may play in the transmission of such ideas and beliefs. But although the *assumption* that media images of women have a negative effect on female self-perceptions and behaviours, as well as on general social life, underlies almost all analysis in this field, there is scant empirical evidence to bear out that assumption. The problem is basic to each media research, and revolves round the difficulty of establishing any direct causal relationship between media exposure and specific effects. Without wishing to engage in a discussion of these difficulties, I think it is worth bearing in mind that the question of what constitutes 'evidence' in the social sciences is itself deeply problematic. However, I take the liberty of leaving this conveniently to one side, while outlining what is 'known' about the effects of media portrayals of women.

A number of experimental studies, for example, in the United States, Canada and Australia,[55] have attempted to measure the impact of media imagery of women. Many findings have been replicated from one study to another.[56] Briefly, it has been fairly well established in this work that sex-stereotyped content leads children to describe women's roles in traditional ways; that content which contradicts sex-stereotyping leads to less traditional descriptions; that when watching television, boys and girls pay particular attention to children of their own sex performing sex-typed tasks; that the more television girls and boys watch, the more traditional are their attitudes and aspirations. It would appear from such studies that girls and boys—and by extension women and men—do tend to model themselves along lines suggested by media imagery. Some studies of advertising suggest that this may be particularly insidious and powerful in providing modelling behaviour. First, advertisements can present a complete—even if collapsed or telescoped—scenario or 'story', in which males and females accept their roles as natural. Sex-typing is usually implicit, rather than articulated. This implicitness may mean that while the explicit sales message is being discounted consciously, the subtle sex-typing can be absorbed unnoticed.[57]

Using another research approach, various surveys of women—in countries such as Brazil, Venezuela, the Netherlands and Japan[58]—suggest that women do identify with media situations, and indeed that they may apply to their own problems solutions offered by the media. For instance, in Venezuela it was found that 50 per cent of a sample of housewives believed that radio and television soap-opera derived from real life; 53 per cent believed that the solutions offered in these soap-operas could help them solve their own problems; 30 per cent said that their children tended to imitate the characters in these programmes. In Japan, 28 per cent of housewives surveyed said that they watched television soap-operas because of a feeling that they dealt with real-life problems and were a good education.

More recent research—particularly in Europe, but also in Latin America—has been attempting to analyse the ideological power of the media in building up and legitimating a central system of practices, meanings and values in society. Most analyses of this kind have concentrated on the detailed examination of media output, which has been found to reinforce existing power patterns.[59] Very recent studies, in an attempt to resolve the problems of inference attaching to this approach, have tried to link media output patterns with the perceptual patterns of audience members, finding for instance that women and girls tend to take for granted a 'natural' order in their lives.[60]

Although research of this last kind is still in its infancy, and is often approached at a high level of abstraction, it may prove more fruitful in explaining broad relationships between the media and social change than earlier studies, concentrating on individual or small group effects, have been able to do.

MEDIA PORTRAYALS AND THE SOCIAL REALITY OF WOMEN

Challenged with the negative aspects of media portrayals of women, a common response of media personnel is that the media simply show life as it is, however unpalatable this may be, and that they therefore reflect the reality of women's legal, political, economic and social subordination. Few systemative longitudinal studies of media exist to contradict this position; however, a recent piece of Swedish research concluded in its detailed analysis of magazine advertising over twenty-five years that advertising at least reflected conservative rather than liberal attitudes, and that it encouraged conformity in a culturally oppressive fashion.[61]

There is also plenty of evidence that the mass media under-represent women in terms of numbers, as a proportion of the work-force, in various age and class categories, in all parts of the world. That they misrepresent the majority of women in terms of characteristics, attitudes and behaviours is less easy to establish, since little research has so far been carried out into social perceptions and their congruence with media images. However, research findings in the Philippines, the United States and Canada report that women are enormously dissatisfied with their portrayal by the media.[62] In one American study, only 8 per cent of housewives thought the image of women projected by advertising was an accurate one.

Other research indicates that the media do respond to changes in the broader socio-economic fabric, and that the mainstream mass media are beginning to reflect or recognize greater diversity in images for women (although usually in the sense of accepting ideas that have become common currency rather than in terms of an active exploration of alternatives). For example, recent Japanese research[63] detects some slow response to changing social currents in the most recent media output, with some limited admission of the possibility of roles for women outside the strictly traditional sphere of home and family, in this most patriarchal of societies. Japan has even introduced a television news programme for women, directed by women themselves. Yet, as Anne Legaré points out in her study of the long-running Canadian programme, *Femme d'aujourd'hui*, the survival of such programmes is by no means assured. In the case of *Femme d'aujourd'hui*[64] it was won through the continual effort of its producer and its audience who defend it against successive management threats. A similar struggle has been fought by those involved in the Australian *Coming Out, Ready or Not Show,* a weekly programme produced since 1975 by a women's co-operative in the ABC, in the face of continual management pressure.

Outside the mainstream, there is evidence of the growth of an active body of feminist film-makers in certain countries, and an immense expansion of the feminist press in every world region. The range is enormous. For instance, *Viva* in Kenya, which started out in 1974 as a traditional women's magazine, has moved in a feminist direction through changes in editorial policy. Still commercially supported, *Viva* combines an appeal to middle-class Kenyan women's conventional tastes with a policy of publishing regular, comprehensive articles on issues such as prostitution, birth control, female circumcision, polygamy and sex education. The large-circulation feminist publications such as *Ms* in the United States (started in 1973, circulation about half a million) and *Emma* in Germany (started in 1977, circulation 300,000) have won readerships broad enough to be described as mass media, though their commercially palatable brand of feminism has been subject to criticism. Others, such as *Spare Rib* in the United Kingdom, Ghana's *Ideal Woman, Courage* in Germany, or Senegal's *Famille et développement* established in the early or mid-1970s, most with circulations around 20,000 (although *Courage* has a distribution of 65,000) are content to let rough edges show: ideas are more important than commercial slickness.

Run on a mainly voluntary basis, or foundation-supported, these magazines address themselves to serious problems and can influence not only their comparatively small audiences but can help shape policies affecting women. For instance, *Ideal Woman* is said to have been largely instrumental in the establishment of a government committee to review the laws on succession. Recently established and explicitly feminist journals, such as *Manushi* in India, or *Feminist* in Japan, appeal to similar markets. Most countries with well-developed media markets now support at least a few small feminist magazines and newspapers: the Federal Republic of Germany and the United Kingdom have at least twenty each; in the United States, there are hundreds. The proliferation and frequent success of this type of publication certainly suggests a growing audience interested in serious discussion about the reality of women's lives.

The growth in women-oriented programmes, pages and journals has been indeed substantial in many countries. Yet these ventures are often criticized for merely underlining women's marginality. It must be acknowledged, however, that in singling women out for special attention, media of this kind have had the effect of highlighting some of the specific problems that exist and that need to be solved. The very sensitivity of the women and media issues bears witness to their impact. That the problem of successfully integrating men's and women's interests in and through the media is at the moment being approached through concentration on women's needs seems to be an inevitable, though necessarily temporary, stage in the search for a new balance.

Meanwhile, the problems remain enormous. One of the most depressing developments in some countries is the extent to which certain media managements appear deliberately to exploit or co-opt for their own purposes the ideas and concerns of the women's movement. At a British seminar in 1979, for example, one producer spoke of her male colleagues' enthusiasm to become involved in the 'new growth industry' produced by women's programmes.[65] In the United States, a television writer, interviewed as part of an analysis of programmes planned for network transmission in 1978, commented that this was 'supposed to be a time for women's projects on TV', and that what the networks wanted were girls who were 'goodlooking, well-endowed and running towards the camera'.[66] Mass media have always been fashion and trend conscious: a problem for the future will be to ensure that women's concerns are neither dealt with as a passing fad, nor defused by media organizations' pressure to treat them as a token series of separate issues, designed to placate women working within the media as well as women in the audience.

NOTES

1. Antonio Gramsci, *Prison Notebooks: Selections,* London, Lawrence & Wishart, 1971.
2. Michele Barrett, Philip Corrigan, Annette Kuhn and Janet Wolff, 'Representation and Cultural Production', in M. Barrett et al. (eds.), *Ideology and Cultural Production,* London, Croom Helm, 1979.
3. Dalston Study Group, 'Was the Patriarchy Conference Patriarchal?', *Papers on Patriarchy,* Brighton, Women's Publishing Collective, 1976.
4. Sheila Rowbotham, *Woman's Consciousness, Man's World,* Harmondsworth, Penguin, 1973.
5. Sue Sharpe, 'The Role of the Nuclear Family in the Oppression of Women', *New Edinburgh Review,* Summer 1972.
6. Raymond Williams, *The Long Revolution,* Harmondsworth, Penguin, 1965.
7. Raymond Williams, *Communications,* Harmondsworth, Penguin, 1968.
8. Dallas Smythe, 'Communications: Blindspot of Western Marxism', *Canadian Journal of Political and Social Theory,* Vol. 1, No. 3, 1977.
9. See, for example: Alice Embree, 'Media Images. I: Madison Avenue Brainwashing—The Facts', in Robin Morgan (ed.), *Sisterhood is Powerful,* New York, Vintage Books, 1970; Ellen Cantarow et al., 'I Am Furious (Female)', in Michele Hoffnung Garskof (ed.), *Roles Women Play: Readings Toward Women's Liberation,* Belmont, Calif., Brooks/Cole, 1971; Carol Lopate, 'Daytime Television: You'll Never Want to Leave Home', *Feminist Studies,* Vol. 3, No. 3/4, 1976, pp. 69-82.
10. Peter Golding and Graham Murdock, 'Ideology and the Mass Media: The Question of Determination', in Barrett et al. (ed.), op. cit.
11. Cornelia Butler Flora, 'Women in Latin American Fotonovelas: From Cinderella to Mata Hari', *Women Studies International Quarterly,* Vol. 3, No. 1, 1980, pp. 95-104.
12. Rachel Harrison, '"Shirley": Relations of Reproduction and the Ideology of Romance', in Women's Studies Group, Centre for Contemporary Studies (ed.), *Women Take Issue,* London, Hutchinson, 1978.
13. Roland Barthes, *Mythologies,* London, Paladin, 1973.
14. Michele Mattelart, 'Reflections on Modernity: A Way of Reading Women's Magazines', *Two Worlds,* Vol. 1, No. 3, 1978/79, pp. 5-13.
15. Sallie Sears, *Psycho-sexual Imperatives: Their Role in Identity Formation,* New York, Human Sciences Press, 1979.

16. Virginia Woolf, *A Room of One's Own,* Harmondsworth, Penguin, 1975.
17. Karl Marx, *Capital,* Vol. I, London, Lawrence & Wishart, 1974.
18. *Piner Report,* London, Her Majesty's Stationery Office, 1974.
19. See, for example: Cynthia White, *Women's Magazines 1863-1968: A Sociological Study,* London, Michael Joseph, 1970; M. Cecil, *Heroines in Love 1750-1974,* London, Michael Joseph, 1974.
20. Mattelart, op. cit.
21. Ibid.
22. See, for example: Mieke Ceulemans and Guido Fauconnier, *Mass Media: The Image, Role and Social Conditions of Women,* Paris, Unesco, 1979 (Reports and Papers on Mass Communication, 84); Margaret Gallagher, *Images of Women in the Mass Media,* Paris, Unesco/International Commission for the Study of Communication Problems, 1980.
23. Elizabeth Croll, *Feminism and Socialism in China,* London, Routledge & Kegan Paul, 1978.
24. Magdalena Sokolowska, 'The Woman Image in the Awareness of Contemporary Polish Society', *Polish Sociological Bulletin,* Vol. 3, No. 35, 1976, pp. 41-50. V. S. Semenov, 'Obszory Braka i Ljukvi v Molodeznyh Zurnolov', *Molodez. Obrazovanie, Vospitanie, Professional' naja Dejatel'nost',* pp. 164-70, Leningrad, 1973. Mollie Rosenhan, 'Images of Male and Female in Soviet Children's Readers', in D. Atkinson et al. (eds.), *Women in Russia,* Stanford, Calif., Stanford University Press, 1977.
25. Ilsa Glazer Schuster, *New Women of Lusaka,* Palo Alto, Calif., Mayfield Publishing Co., 1979.
26. Task Force on Women and Advertising, *Women and Advertising: Today's Messages—Yesterday's Images?,* Toronto, Canadian Advertising Advisory Board, 1977. Trevor Millum, *Images of Women. Advertising in Women's Magazines,* London, Chatto & Windus, 1975. Arbeitsgruppe Frauenmaul, *Ich hab' Dir Keinen Rosengarten Versprochen: das Bild der Frau in vier österreichischen Tageszeitungen—eine Dokumentation,* Vienna, Frischfleisch & Lowenmaul, 1979. Preben Sepstrup, *En Undersagelse of mands og Kvindebilledet i den Danske Magasin og Dagspresseannoncering* (Report to the Danish Consumer Ombudsman), Copenhagen, 1978. National Commission on the Role of Filipino Women, *Image and Reality among Filipino Women: A Comparative Study of the Values Portrayed by the Female Lead Characters in Tagalog Films and the Values Held by Female College Students,* Manila, NCRFW, 1978 (mimeo).
27. Barbara Lovenheim, 'Admen Woo the Working Woman', *New York Times,* 18 June 1978.
28. Marlene Cuthbert, *The Impact of Audio-visual Media in the Socio-cultural Behaviour of Women in Jamaica,* Paris, Unesco, 1979 (mimeo).
29. Alice Courteney and Thomas Whipple, *Canadian Perspectives on Sex Stereotyping in Advertising,* Ottawa, Advisory Council on the Status of Women, 1978.
30. Gunnar Andren and Kjell Nowak, *Gender Structures in Swedish Magazine Advertising 1950-1975,* University of Stockholm, 1978 (mimeo).
31. Mattelart, op. cit.
32. Sultana Krippendorf, *Women's Education in Bangladesh: Needs and Issues,* Part II, Dacca, Foundation for Research on Educational Planning and Development, 1977. Susan Beraud, 'Sex Role Images in French Children's Books', *Journal of Marriage and the Family,* Vol. 37, 1975, pp. 194-207. Karen Berg, 'School Books and Roles of the Sexes', *Herta,* Vol. 5, 1969, pp. 45-53. Indian Federation of University Women's Association, *A Teacher-training Course on Sexism in the Classroom,* Geneva, UNICEF, 1977 (mimeo). A. Rickel and L. Grant, 'Sex Role Stereotypes in the Mass Media and Schools: Five Consistent Themes', *International Journal of Women's Studies,* Vol. 2, No. 2, 1979.
33. Vicki Flerx, Dorothy Fidler and Ronal Rogers, 'Sex Role Stereotypes: Developmental Aspects Early Intervention', *Child Development,* Vol. 47, No. 4, 1976, pp. 998-1007.
34. Nancy Signorelli and George Gerbner, *Women in Public Broadcasting: A Progress Report,* Philadelphia, University of Pennsylvania, 1978 (mimeo).

35. Gerald Lesser, *Children and Television: Lessons from Sesame Street*, New York, Random House, 1974.
36. Madhu Kishwar, 'Family Planning or Birth Control', *Manushi*, No. 1, January 1979, pp. 24-6.
37. United States Commission on Civil Rights, *Window Dressing on the Set: An Update*, Washington, D.C., U.S. Commission on Civil Rights, 1979.
38. Jerzy Toeplitz, *Women's Employment in Audio-visual Media Professions*, Paris, Unesco, 1978 (mimeo).
39. Canadian Broadcasting Corporation (CBC), *Women in the CBC. Report of the CBC Task Force on the Status of Women*, Ottawa, CBC, 1975.
40. Yoko Nuita, *The Impact of Audio-visual Media on Socio-cultural Behaviour of Women in Japan*, Paris, Unesco, 1979 (mimeo).
41. Sveriges Radio, *Saklighet, Opartishket... Jamstalldhet? Slutrapport fran Sveriges Radios Jamstalldhetsprojekt*, Stockholm, Sveriges Radio, 1978. Chong Wong Soon, 'Access to Education and Employment in Mass Communications in Singapore', in Timothy Lu and Leonard Chu (eds.), *Women and Media in Asia*, Hong Kong, Chinese University of Hong Kong, 1977.
42. Association of Cinematograph, Television and Allied Technicians (ACTT), *Patterns of Discrimination against Women in the Film and Television Industries*, London ACTT, 1975.
43. Joan Harms, *Yleisradion Selonteko Yk: N Kansainvalisen Raisten Vuosikyrmen Suomen Ohjelmaan*, Helsinki, Finnish Broadcasting Company, 1978 (mimeo).
44. Diane Ying, 'Access to Education and Employment in Mass Media for Women in the Republic of China', in Yu and Chu, op. cit.
45. Shayne Merritt and Harriet Gross, 'Women's Page/Life Style Editors: Does Sex make a Difference?', *Journalism Quarterly*, Vol. 55, 1978.
46. Jack Orwant and Muriel Cantor, 'How Sex Stereotyping Affects News Preferences', *Journalism Quarterly*, Vol. 54, 1977.
47. Flora, op. cit.
48. Les Brown, *Television: The Business Behind the Box*, New York, Basic Books, 1971.
49. Jeremy Tunstall, *Journalists at Work*, London, Constable, 1971.
50. Muriel Cantor, *The Hollywood TV Producer*, New York, Basic Books, 1971.
51. Gaye Tuchman, 'Women's Depiction by the Mass Media', *Signs*, Vol. 4, No. 3. 1979, pp. 528-42.
52. Task Force on Women and Advertising, op. cit.
53. Eleanor Maccoby and Carol Jacklin, *The Psychology of Sex Differences*, Stanford, Calif., Stanford University Press, 1974.
54. Lesley Albertson and Terrence Cutler, 'Delphi and the Image of the Future', *Futures*, October 1976, pp. 397-404.
55. Pamela Cheles-Miller, 'Reactions to Marital Roles in Commercials', *Journal of Advertising Research*, Vol. 15, No. 4, pp. 45-9. Courtney and Whipple, op. cit. Suzanne Pingree and Robert Hawkins, *American Programs on Australian Television: The Cultivation Effect in Australia*, Madison, University of Wisconsin, 1979 (mimeo).
56. Tuchman, op. cit.
57. Virginia Brown, *The Effect of TV Commercials on Women's Achievement Aspirations*, University of Delaware, 1979 (mimeo).
58. José Marques de Melo, 'Las telenovelas em São Paulo; estudio do publico receptor', *Comunicação social; teoria e pesquisa*, 2nd ed., Brazil, Vozes, 1971, pp. 247-54. Marta Colomina de Rivera, *El huesped alienante: un estudio sobre audiencia y efectos de las radio-telenovelas en Venezuela*, Maracaibo, Centro Audio-Visual, 1968. Marsha Berman et al., *De Waardering van vrouwen voor vrouwenfilms*, University of Amsterdam, 1977 (mimeo). Toshiko Miyazaki, *Housewives and Daytime Serials*, University of Leiden, 1978 (mimeo).
59. T. M. Quiroz and B. E. Larrain, *Imagen de la mujer que proyectan los medios de comunicación de masas en Costa Rica*, University of Costa Rica, 1978. Helen Butcher

et al., *Images of Women in the Media,* Centre for Contemporary Studies, University of Birmingham, 1974 (Occasional Paper, No. 32).

60. Angela McRobbie, 'Working Class Girls and the Culture of Femininity', in Women's Studies Group, Centre for Contemporary Cultural Studies (eds.), *Women Take Issue,* London, Hutchinson, 1978.
61. Andren and Nowak, op. cit.
62. National Commission on the Role of Filipino Women, op. cit.
63. Nuita, op. cit.
64. Anne Legaré, *L'impact des moyens de communication de masse dans le domaine de l'audiovisuel sur le comportement socioculturel des femmes: le cas de l'émission 'Femme d'aujourd'hui',* Paris, Unesco, 1979 (mimeo).
65. Penny Valentine, 'Women in TV—Feminists in Control?', *Time Out,* No. 473, May, 1979.
66. Ellen Farley and William Knoedelseder, 'Rub-a-Dub-Dub, Three Networks in a Tub; The Future is Now in TV's Titillation Sweepstakes', *Washington Post,* 19 February 1978.

Part Three

*Trends and prospects
in the culture industries:
concentration and
internationalization,
the changing role
of the artist*

There are two main trends characteristic of the recent development of the culture industries which seem likely to have important consequences in the long term. The first is the trend towards concentration—vertical and horizontal—and internationalization of the ownership of the means of production and distribution of cultural goods and services. The other is the changing—some say declining—role of artists in the production of cultural messages.

Where concentration and internationalization are concerned, a look at the development of the main branches of the audio-visual media shows that these are not two parallel trends, but one and the same trend, which is characteristic of the present stage of the increasing power of the cultural industries. Vertical and horizontal concentration makes it possible to reach the efficiency threshold, which is necessary for international coverage. International firms are always active where concentration is concerned, either by buying up small firms or investing in new countries, or by taking part in very extensive group reorganization. This leads to the establishment of a small number of very large groups with diversified interests (multimedia), whose expansion is limited solely by national anti-trust laws. However, even these laws can be evaded by means of indirect take-overs or by the system of subsidiaries. All in all, it is like a merger taking place on a world scale, first of producers of cultural goods and services (the big and affluent industrialized countries) and, second, of the consumers of those products (the smaller, less-prosperous developing countries). This is how the strategy of the multinational firms appears at any rate.

This trend is noticeable both at the production stage and at that of product distribution. Clearly, it presupposes the inducing of a trend towards standard consumer tastes on the principal markets so that the development and manufacture of the products can be rationalized. This means that just a few producers (the owners of the most powerful firms) are able to influence the style and appearance of the cultural products offered to consumers. What is more, the adoption of identical or different technical standards for broadcasting or playback equipment can make it possible to increase control over the market on the pretext of having made improvements in the public interest.

These trends can nevertheless be offset by policies for the safeguarding of cultural identity or by developing and supporting independent businesses at national level. However, it is important to realize that spontaneous small-scale efforts do not provide a credible answer here, any more than the 'alternative' circuits, which have only a limited impact. Then again, nationalizing the capital of transnational cinema, radio or television corporations, for instance, cannot suffice to stem the massive importation of foreign products and to reduce the dependence of national industries on these multinational firms.

Actually the one-way communication of messages cannot be reversed except through integrated global policies conducive to equilibrium between the international communication of messages and endogenous production. However, this implies that prior thought will have been given to the kind of internationalization predominating in each sector, the relation of national capital to international capital and the cultural impact of the transfer of technologies from the industrialized countries to the developing countries, for instance. Such transfers are beneficial only if the real needs and the limitations imposed by the environment, the culture and the employment situation in the receiving country are taken into account.

The same is true of the present role of artists faced with the very large-scale development of the cultural industries. First, it must be recognized that the economic imperatives of these industries profoundly change the living and working conditions of creative artists and performers generally. Any idea of continuous effort and the slow maturation of an idea is rejected as prejudicial to the exploitation of the market. Preserving a heritage and showing regard for historical remembrance, ideals essential to the maintenance and development of cultural identity, are disregarded by the cultural industries, especially when communicating to young people.

Some authors do dwell on the positive side to the development of the cultural industries, the audio-visual media in particular, in the sense of the provision of opportunities for employment and economic security for performers. However, one cannot be too dogmatic in asserting this. With the theatre, for instance, some increase in stage performances is to be found, but the situation is generally one of misunderstanding, inconsistent public support and economic insecurity, while the industrialized theatre of radio and television manufactures a faultless product, free from any mishap, which restricts the opportunity for experiment and for staging productions of another kind. Before stating an opinion, we must therefore accurately ascertain whether the cultural industries really represent a widening of the labour market and offer greater means of creative activity to performers who engage in 'traditional' forms of activity.

The predominance of the cultural industries also has important implications for the legal status of performers and the establishment of labour regulations. The regulations governing the participation of performers in the activities of the cultural industries, especially where entertainment is concerned, must be drawn up clearly. Indeed, although a few stars receive very large fees, for reasons not always unconnected with advertising techniques, performers in the main are underpaid, which is all the more serious because profits may be enormous.

Relations between authors, publishers or producers, at a time when a creative idea may be subjected to multimedia processing all over the world in a very short space of time, call for the drawing up of contracts and agreements on a realistic basis. Similarly, the extremely rapid development of equipment for making audio-visual, and especially audio, copies is raising a series of new and urgent problems relating to the protection of intellectual property. Some of the answers may be provided by national legislation and regulations. However, it is at the international level that measures must be taken or made tougher. In this connection, the recent adoption by the General Conference of Unesco of a Recommendation concerning the Status of the Artist represents an important step forward. Let us just mention here that it deals in turn with the problems involved in training in the arts, measures to be taken to consolidate the social status of artists, to protect their rights, to improve their living and working conditions and, lastly, to associate them more in the framing of new cultural policies. Finally, international conventions relating to the rights of artists would have to be re-examined in the light of the recent developments in the culture industries.

Where concentration and internationalization and their consequences in a small country are concerned, the study of the situation in Belgium, made by Armand Mattelart and Jean-Marie Piemme, brings out the dangers that this trend represents for the maintenance of cultural identity. The situation of performers confronted by the cultural industries was, in its turn, the subject of two highly contrasting studies in Montreal, one by a lawyer, Barbara D. Kibbs, concerning the United States, and one of a more comprehensive nature, by a sociologist, Ladislav Gawlik, concerning Czechoslovakia.

6   The internationalization of television in Belgium

Armand Mattelart and Jean-Marie Piemme

Summary report drawn up by Unesco on the basis of a survey carried out for the Belgian Ministry of French Culture (1978–80), the findings of which were published in *Télévision: enjeux sans frontière,* Presses Universitaires de Grenoble, 1980.

WHERE EUROPE'S TELEVISION CHANNELS MEET

Nineteen eighty-four is the year of George Orwell and also the year when multinational satellite-relayed television will come to Europe. Soon, national television organizations are going to have to face up to new challenges, some aspects of which are already apparent today.

Anyone who wants to study the conflict between a national state monopoly system and the present internationalization of a medium like television, will find a good example in the development of the situation in Belgium.

The establishment of a monopoly over sound broadcasting in Belgium dates back to 1930.[1] In that year, the authorities decided to create what was in effect a monopoly by granting all the frequencies available at the time to the Institut National de Radiodiffusion (INR). This decision was criticized for reasons of principle at the time. The monopoly was thought to be unconstitutional in that it ran counter to the freedom of expression that the Constitution guaranteed, and it was deemed culturally undesirable on the grounds that absence of competition might quickly cause the INR to become mediocre and unproductive. The minister responsible for broadcasting accepted these objections, 'while emphasizing that the INR was merely a technical umbrella organization made necessary by the existing state of science and the limited number of exclusive wave-lengths available'. He expressed the hope that 'echnical progress . . . would make it possible to give effect as soon as possible to that ideal, which certainly corresponded to constitutional principles more closely than the current project'.[2]

Provisional though it was, the state monopoly was to last. Between 1945 and 1959, two bills and four motions were tabled with the aim of adapting the broadcasting organization to the cultural pattern in Belgium, and challenging what amounted to a monopoly. The bill of 17 February 1948 aimed at providing for 'that sociological pluralism which enables all forms of thought to be freely expressed'. To this end, it was provided that 'the Belgian national broadcasting organization will make available to freely constituted associations of listeners a certain amount of time on the frequencies granted to it, while other frequencies with smaller coverage will be entirely devoted to these same associations of listeners operating at regional level'.[3]

The bill of 1948/49 went still further, granting very considerable powers to the minister regarding the allocation of frequencies to private persons. In fact, it provided that the minister could grant the use of a number of frequencies (particularly metric or ultra-short waves that were not needed by the state broadcasting service) to private broadcasting stations fulfilling the conditions laid down in a Royal Decree to be issued. The bill further said that associations of listeners (constituted as non-profitmaking bodies with cultural aims) consisting of at least two thousand members who had paid their licence fees, and constituted for the purpose of putting out radio broadcasts, would be able to obtain time on the air from the minister in accordance with procedures to be laid down by a Royal Decree issued after an opinion had been given by the Supreme Council on Broadcasting.

The bill prohibited advertising on national stations but authorized it on regional stations. These provisions were repeated in the main in a bill in 1953. However, none of these bills was discussed in public and the new statues of 1960 consolidated the actual state monopoly.[4]

Not until the 1970s did it begin to be seriously challenged.

From the outset the Belgian Television Organization had to face the problem of following the pattern set by other television corporations. It was even founded on the principle of following an alien model, since during the experimental period, roughly from 1953 to 1959, Belgian television was chiefly French and followed in the footsteps of French television. For several years, Belgian television relayed variety shows, television plays, games, sports coverage, and, for at least three years, news broadcasting from Paris. This latter point shows how little importance was attached to television as a means of information at the time. One can hardly imagine a sovereign country receiving its television news from a neighbouring country today. That was the situation in Belgium, however. It might be said that there were good reasons for this, such as unpreparedness, which made it necessary to call on specialists even if they were foreign, or again financial difficulties. However, these reasons are perfectly compatible with an underestimation of the importance of television news at the time. This was demonstrated in 1956 with the first serious political incident (the Suez crisis—is which Belgium did not back France's policy of intervention). The Belgian Television Organization then found a way to develop an embryonic news broadcast of its own.

Dependence on France dwindled as the Radio-Television Belge (RTB) developed its own programme policy. By 1966, only 15 per cent of programmes originated in France. This percentage is misleading, however, since it hides the fact that the proportion of French programmes varied considerably from one kind of broadcast to another. For example, in sectors which the RTB had made strong, such as investigative reporting, dependence on France was greatly reduced, but entertainment, particularly serials and series, was a different matter. Overall, 80 per cent of the programmes consisted of series and serials produced in France.[5]

Until about 1970, Belgium's dependence on France for fiction was apparent chiefly in its purchasing policy. Two other forms of dependence have since become apparent. Firstly, within the limits of its very small resources, Belgium has produced serials or television plays on the French pattern. One might mention serials with a regional setting where local accents are the rule, as also the setting of the action in a particular locality in Belgium. These serials are actually in the same vein as the new French ones. Mention might also be made of the serials adapted from popular nineteenth-century novels—there, too, the idea came from France—and the detective series. In one series filmed in Belgium, S. A. Steeman's hero, Inspector Wens, arrives just at the right moment to act as Inspector Bourrel's counterpart.

Secondly, dependence is also apparent today in the form of international co-production. Some internationalization of production has been seen for a few years now. This means that a foreign television organization is associated in the making of a particular series right from the production stage. For instance, in a given French series, Belgium produces its own episode set in Belgium with Belgian actors. On a broader scale, the television organizations of a number of countries, including Belgium, agree to make a series of films with a connecting link, a common theme or a general topic. Each participating country produces its own film. In this way, through exchanges and collaboration, an international stock of off-the-peg fiction programmes is built up from which not too much should be expected, either as regards the writing or as regards getting to grips with reality. Clearly, this kind of co-production can function only if it finds a level of maximum intelligibility. It must of necessity refrain from any departure from the prevailing code of narration. The content, too, must keep within accepted moral and political bounds—with the result that the experience of fiction and one's relationship with the world of the imagination are in danger of becoming an evening routine.

THE ARRIVAL OF CABLE TELEVISION

By sacrificing one sector so that another could live, the RTB acquired a kind of independence, but the development of cable television then profoundly altered the situation.[6] With thirteen channels available (some in foreign languages), Belgium occupies a unique place in Europe, being the only country offering such a wide range of programmes. With three German channels, two Netherlands channels, two Flemish-speaking Belgian channels, two French-speaking Belgian channels, three French channels, Radio-Télé Luxembourg (RTL), and three British channels, the situation is profoundly different from what it was scarcely ten years ago. The extent of this change cannot be measured solely in terms of technological innovation or the increase in the number of programmes available, however. This would leave out of account the fact that the development of cable television has given rise to profound socio-political conflict in the communication set-up.

This is no mere change or the unintentional consequences of the applications of a new technology. To think so would be to take too lightly the context in which cable television rapidly expanded, a content marked by attacks on the monopoly. More precisely, it would be to make light of the unrelenting presence of private interests at the heart of cable television. Add to that the fact that, apart from a few awkward features such as the broadcasting of advertising (which is not allowed on the air in Belgium, although viewers receive television advertising from their neighbours), this 'transgression' of the monopoly is perfectly legal and that its development is being organized in ways in which the authorities are very actively involved, and the reader will understand that study of cable television can throw a great deal of light on a wider problem, that of a communications policy in Belgium.

However, the leasons to be learned from the development of cable television there, the way in which it occurred, the action to which it led, or did not lead, the strategies or the lack of vision at work, have relevance beyond those geographical boundaries. What can be seen in Belgium today prefigures what will happen in certain other countries of Europe tomorrow. With the 1980s we are entering on an era of universal competition among the television channels. What cable distribution did in Belgium in the past, direct-broadcast satellites and cable television may do in other European countries in the future. The field of action of these satellites, which will be operational in less than three years, obviously does not coincide with national frontiers. This means that various places in some European countries may be offered unsolicited programmes (even though this may be foreseen), which may be conveyed by the cable distribution systems via relays to target localities that cannot be reached directly. As the direct broadcast satellites are likely to transmit commercial programmes, the state television organizations in Europe might be faced in 1980–90 with the situation that the Belgian national television organization has been up against since 1970. Some European countries—the Federal Republic of Germany, in particular[8]—have already taken steps to cope with this possibility. However, apart from the fact that no definitive answer has been found, one has to reckon with the existence in all of them of a large body of conservative opinion likely to prevent the government from concluding over-restrictive agreements with other governments. It will also be seen from the Belgian example how, even when legal guarantees exist, they cannot withstand the pressure brought to bear by industry.

Cable television is a way of distributing and receiving television pictures by wire. Although wireless transmission was considered a great step forward, it has been found that in some cases wire, or cable, is still necessary. As a rule it provides a better quality picture and may even be the only way of receiving television in areas where the lie of the land, or in some cases the urban environment, disturb or impede reception by aerial. The principle of cable television is fairly simple. A series of aerials pick up the transmission and the signals received are passed to a central station where they are processed before being fed into the cable network. This processing includes the amplification and rectification of the signals, frequency transposition, and the connection with the network proper and with amplifiers placed at regular intervals to boost the signals which tend to become weaker when transmitted by cable.

Belgium was the first country in Europe to take an active interest in cable television. Coditel, the first Belgian cable-television company, was set up in 1960, over twenty years ago. The reasons for starting this first network were of a technical nature. In Namur, a town lying in a valley, it was not possible to receive television broadcasts properly unless one had a quite expensive individual aerial, sometimes costing more than the television set itself. While technical reasons undoubtedly favoured the choice of Namur as the starting point for cable television, it would be wrong to think that these reasons were the only ones that lay behind its introduction. It must be borne in mind that Belgium's geographical situation makes it possible to receive broadcasts from outside the country. Such broadcasts, relayed by cable, offered potential customers a wide selection of programmes. Back in 1967, Coditel set up a radio-wave link between Namur, where France could be picked up with an aerial, and Liège, where this was not possible. At a later stage, the towns of Verviers and Visé were included. They, too, could receive French programmes and also those of RTL, which had in the meantime been added to the range made available by the cable-television company. Finally, a link-up was established with certain districts in Brussels, then certain municipalities in the Brussels area, previously equipped with cables by Coditel. This process and the pattern of its development clearly show that cable television from the outset was never intended solely to improve reception of programmes from the technical standpoint, but was introduced to help change the Belgian television scene.

Cable television received a new impetus around 1970 owing to the interest taken in it by various big companies producing or distributing electricity, the public authorities and the users. From that time on, cables were installed on a large scale, chiefly in thickly populated areas where cable television was potentially a profitable proposition. The number of programmes available and the number of subscribers increased very quickly. According to the Union Professionnelle de Télédistribution RTD, the number of subscribers was 23,989 in 1970, but topped 1.8 million in 1978. Annual figures are detailed in Table 1.

TABLE 1. Number of people possessing receivers and number of subscribers to cable television

| Year | TV N/B[1] | TV C[2] | Total TV | Cable TV | |
				RTT[3]	RTD
1970	2 099 893			?	23 989
1971	2 202 543			?	82 830
1972	2 237 865	50 702	2 288 567	185 792	213 350
1973	2 207 617	168 420	2 376 037	372 833	390 529
1974	2 106 456	357 743	2 464 201	785 216	654 434
1975	1 975 958	573 270	2 549 228	1 063 831	1 252 219
1976	1 818 808	827 042	2 645 850	1 388 236	1 501 273
1977	1 712 742	1 098 397	2 811 145	1 673 617	1 735 742
31–8–78	1 585 275	1 276 713	2 861 988	1 861 361	1 926 919[4]

1. Black and white.
2. Colour.
3. State-owned telegraph and telephone service.
4. As at 31 December 1978.
Source: Information communicated by the Régie des TT except for the figures in the last column, which come from the Union Professionnelle de Télédistribution RTD.

By 31 December 1978 forty-two cable television companies were affiliated to the Union Professionnelle de Télédistribution. Their legal status is that they are either purely intermunicipal, mixed intermunicipal, or private companies. It is estimated that the total number of subscribers to cable television is divided equally among these three categories.

The profitability of the network depends on the financial outlay for its installation, operation and maintenance set against the proceeds from individual installations and subscriptions. Clearly, cable television is likely to be profitable in thickly populated areas where there are the greatest number of potential subscribers. When financial interest is the only consideration, as is the case with private companies, urban centres are favoured for the installation of cable-television networks. When profitability is no longer an immediate imperative, as is the case with the purely intermunicipal companies, cable television is regarded as a public service to which everyone is entitled for the same price. The mixed intermunicipal companies combine these two approaches. They are associations in which a supervisory public authority joins forces with a private partner responsible for the actual management. They fix a ceiling for investment per household, and the municipality covers the additional expenses if it wants the whole of its area to have cables.

In contrast with the situation in other countries where cable television is quite widespread—the United States or Canada, for example—the Belgian cable-television companies have close links with the private electricity companies, whatever the legal status of the networks. This link between cable television and the electricity supply is easy to understand. It is not difficult for electricity companies to promote cable television since the existing electricity distribution network and the know-how acquired in this field make it possible to distribute television programmes without any serious technical problems and at the lowest cost. It is also a profitable business. In the first place, cable television is an activity which pays good dividends, but it can pay in a less immediate fashion. The development of the system cannot fail to increase domestic consumption of electricity. It has been suggested that Electrobel, by launching Coditel back in 1960, was trying in this way to reduce peak consumption in the evening. In addition, of the marketing ploys which electricity companies use against each other, cable television is one which enables them to get a firmer foothold in certain municipalities or regions, first, to distribute television programmes and then perhaps electricity.

The development of cable television in Belgium has been stimulated by private enterprise and is closely connected with it, directly or indirectly. It has therefore occurred in ways calculated more to respond to particular financial or electoral interests than to the demands of an overall communication policy. It is, after all, easy and effective to include in one's electoral platform firm support for the setting up of a cable-television network in one's municipality, town or region. The rather disordered way in which the networks have developed, state intervention being confined to the setting up of a national radio-wave relay system, the fact that advertising from relayed foreign channels was allowed in, despite the law prohibiting it on the RTFB (Radio-Télévision Française Belge, Belgian radio and television in the French language, are distinct from broadcasting in Flemish), ministerial laxity in the matter of control, and the conflicts between the cable television companies, the RTBF and the consumer associations, are all pointers to the fact that the only policy followed in respect of cable management was that of the *fait accompli*. The Ministry of Posts and Telecommunications confined itself to promoting a unified approach to cable television simply from the point of view of the technological infrastructure.

The effect of this *fait accompli* policy was to give specific and material answers to questions which had never been put or discussed in democratic debate—questions concerning the values connected with the development of certain communication models and the social choices those models implied. An irreversible situation has thus been created and now weighs in the balance existing between the liberal/private enterprise conception of communication and the conception of communication as a public service. The retransmission of advertising and the broadcasting of the RTL programme are good examples. If it kept to the letter of the law, the government could obstruct the distribution of both. However, it is quite clear that such a course has become politically unthinkable. No one, either on the right or on the left, would want to ban RTL. The *fait accompli* has, as is the way of such things, become a 'need' and a return to the previous situation seems impossible.

The process does not stop there, however, The *fait accompli* policy does not mean solely evading the law and developing alongside it what it expressly prohibited. It also serves—and this is perhaps where it is part of a strategy of broader scope—to challenge the validity of the law. The development of cable television is a *de facto* negation of the monopoly. The television programmes are quite lawfully distributed no doubt, but in the process, cable television changes qualitatively the conditions in which the monopoly is exercised. It makes general a competitiveness which already existed as a result of Belgium's geographical situation but which was not so widespread before the cable. The introduction of cable television on a massive scale has led to a dangerous decline in the RTB's audience, as can be seen from Table 2.

TABLE 2. Audience ratings for the French-speaking channels in Belgium (in percentages)

	Autumn 1974		Autumn 1975		Autumn 1976		Autumn 1977	
RTB	65		51		48		43 + 3	
TF1	11		16		16		18	
A2	10	22	17	38	14	38	14	40
FR3	1		5		8		8	
RTL	13		11		14		14	

Source : RTFB, *Rapport d'activités 1977.*

THE CONSEQUENCES OF CABLE TELEVISION

This table shows the inroads made by the French channels, inroads that today seem to have reached their maximum, and likewise by RTL. It should be noted, however, in the case of the RTB percentages, that the audience may drop below 40 per cent when investigations and feature programmes are screened and rise above 60 per cent when films are shown. As a result of cable television, the RTBF has to compete with channels with no great concern for culture or with channels possessing considerably greater resources. It is doubtless because of this competition that the number of films screened by the RTBF has increased—164 in 1974/75; 172 in 1975/76 and 218 in 1977.

The development of cable television is thus a threat to the RTBF audience, and this loss of audience is going to provide a reason for openly demanding the abolition of the monopoly. The consequence of a technological operation (the development of cable television) is to be used as a lever in the demand for another communication policy. However, the fact that private interests have a stake in cable television rules out the possibility that this challenging of the monopoly is motivated by anything but a desire to return to the conventionally liberal model of television, that is, a private and commercial model of communication. The way cable television was introduced into Belgium is a timely reminder that *laissez-faire* at the technological level never serves progressive interests. This is certainly not a new lesson, and it would suffice to turn to Italy, if need be, and consider the post-monopoly situation there to be convinced of that. The situation in Belgium is not on such a vast scale perhaps, but though it is not so obvious it is more complex.

In less than ten years, cable television has completely transformed the Belgian television scene. The reason for this transformation is to be found neither in a general government co-ordinated policy nor in some power peculiar to technology. Real though it may be, technological development has been determined by a number of economic and political factors that are part of a full-scale attempt to challenge the notion of monopoly and to defy the ban on commercials. This transformation was brought about with the active participation of elected representatives through the purely intermunicipal or mixed intermunicipal companies, more concerned with the short-term effects of cable television than with a consistent overall policy of television as a public service. Today that transformation is a fact and any communication policy has to reckon with the balance of forces resulting from the *laissez-faire* of the past ten years. This is clearly apparent in the negotiations which have been going on for several months on the need for new legislation. The cable distribution companies are displaying a strong determination to be more than just the neutral managers of a new technology. On the strength of the *fait accompli* they are making proposals or raising objections that show their commitment to a well-defined communication policy.

Looking now at the Belgian television scene from a more synchronic and structural standpoint, we can see that cable television is the hub of a complex system. It is here that the interplay of forces determining the whole set-up is most clearly apparent. Cable television is the focus, the object and the means of two kinds of conflict. First, it sets the supporters of commercial privately owned television against the advocates of communication as a public service. Second, it embraces two views of public service, divided on the question of the preservation of the RTB's monopoly. These two kinds of conflict do not develop independently, however. Through cable television they are closely linked together. To be more accurate, one could say that the first is seeking a solution with the backing of the second. Taking advantage of the challenge to the monopoly by way of community television,[8] the holders of the liberal/private enterprise view are trying to justify the ground already gained and to widen the breach by proposing to take over the planning and management of actual programmes. At the same time, the supporters of the public-service view are trying, through experiments indicative of a different idea of public service, to find a way of giving effect to a policy of new forms of communication while preventing the liberal view from profiting from the challenge to the monopoly implicit in that new policy.

NOTES

1. For more detailed information concerning the legal status of the Belgian radio and television organization and its evolution see M. Verheyden, *La radio-télévision face au pouvoir, l'expérience belge,* Louvain, Centre de Techniques de Diffusion, Université Catholique de Louvain, 1970.
2. Ibid., p. 23.
3. Ibid., p. 36.
4. Ibid., pp. 37–8.
5. RTBF, *Rapport d'activités, 1977,* p. 91.
6. See J. M. Piemme, 'La télédistribution', *Courrier hebdomadaire du CRISP,* No. 856, 20 April 1979.
7. H. Lhoest, La télévision en Belgique, interview in *Télémoustique,* 13 December 1979: 'And, in comparison with others, we don't defend ourselves. Take Germany, for instance, and its dispute with Luxembourg over the satellite.... RTL wanted to use the satellite, mostly to beam advertising to Germany. The first threat was a channel on the first French satellite with programmes post-synchronized or subtitled in German.... As the orbit of the French satellite covers a large part of Germany, that could quite well have been done. Meanwhile, however, there was the Franco-German agreement under which Schmidt obtained an assurance from Giscard that France would not accept any programmes on its satellite which might make things difficult for Germany. I saw the protocol of the agreement and the words used were *gêner l'Allemagne.* That was the first assurance. The French state said no to RTL, whereas the French state represents 29 per cent of the holdings in CTL through Havas.... RTL said, "We have the means of sending up our own satellite." This is true. They have financial and technological backing from Americans and others. The electronics multinationals are prepared to invest in the satellite, at a loss for a while, in order to sell all the televised trash to be shown throughout Europe. Then they said, "We'll launch our own satellite and aim at Germany, France, the Netherlands."... At that stage Schmidt took a different line. Now he wants a European convention prohibiting commercial transmitters directed chiefly towards a neighbouring country.
   T.M. : A new idea, a revolutionary idea, no?
   H.L. : Yes, but it's based on the Brussels Convention of 1977, which the Council of Europe took the initiative for. The object is to protect national sovereignty in the matter of radio and television. Luxembourg took it very badly. Mr Werner and Mr Thorn said in public that Germany was using methods which were very unpleasantly reminiscent of the past. As soon as you say that to Germans, their hair stands on end. . . . And nothing more was said by Chancellor Schmidt. However, the thing will be done in another way. A commission is meeting in Germany and it is going to examine all that in detail. What is more, the German television organization is putting up a good defence—six or seven programmes during the summer on the subject of the cable, which is becoming general in Germany, and on the problem of the satellite. Whereas for our part, we have done nothing.'

8. In February 1975 the French Minister of Culture set up a panel with a view to 'studying the development, the potential for economic and cultural exploration and the future organization of the new audio-visual media'. To begin with, its terms of reference were to study the 'active' uses of the cable in community television. Certain principles had been laid down by the minister—the experiments were not to ape the RTB: the distributors were not to have any role except the strictly technical one of transporter; the aims and purposes were defined as: local information, lifelong education, local community participation in the programme, the existence of a pluralistic group representative of the community to conduct the experiment. In March 1976 the minister decided, after considering the applications, to authorize a first series of experiments. Actually, it is not easy to form an opinion about the results. Most of the experiments have hardly been going two years. They are on the air for a relatively short time (at most a weekly programme of an hour or an hour and a half). Above all, the institutional arrangements for these programmes are and have been shaky. Yet these experiments were duly authorized by law in derogation of the law on the monopoly in force in Belgium. However, when it is realized that nine experiments are sharing between them the modest sum of 11 million Belgian francs, it will be understood that some caution is necessary in assessing the results. In some cases, the Ministry of Culture is not the only source of financing of the CTV, but with one exception it is the main source. So the CTV is constantly up against financial difficulties, which explains why they are often complaining they are treading a tightrope where production and management are concerned.

7 Creative and performing artists and the media in Czechoslovakia

Ladislav Gawlik

Director of the Institute of Cultural Research, Prague

In order to ensure the cultural development of society, the state, in co-operation with the organs of people's power and the social organizations, particularly the trade unions and youth organizations, has built up a wide material–technical basis making possible the creation, propagation, mediation and acquiring of cultural and artistic values. It should be mentioned, in this connection, that the first fundamental democratizing measures taken after the liberation of Czechoslovakia in 1945, concerned the broadest-based means of propagating artistic values, which were, at that time, the broadcasting, film,[1] printing and gramophone industries. Among them too, of course, was the theatre, which became a mass art in the true sense of the word. This is attested by the largest theatre network in the world, existing in Czechoslovakia since the second half of the 1970s. At present, there are sixty-two permanent theatres with eighty-eight stages for drama, opera, ballet, puppet plays and others; besides which, there are experimental studios and small theatres; there is one permanent stage for every 172,549 inhabitants, and for more than three decades, the number of theatre-goers has been about 9 million a year, without any noticeable decrease.

The measures taken in the years 1945–49 were aimed particularly at the nationalization of the film and gramophone industries (1945 and 1946), bringing broadcasting under state control (1948), abolishing private enterprise in the theatrical sphere (1948), integration of adult education into the powers of the people's organs (1945), the nationalization of the printing industry (1948), the promulgation of the law on publication and distribution of books, sheet music and other non-periodical publications (1949). A great number of important historical monuments came into the ownership and custodianship of the state.

These measures as a whole constituted the necessary prerequisite for an extensive democratization of culture and freed the creative intelligentsia from their former direct economic dependence on private ownership of the means of production in the sphere of culture, in particular, of the means of mass propagation and mediation of its products. Thus they abolished the main source of commercializing tendencies which, unless they are principally solved, represent, especially together with the so-called cultural industry, the mass propagation and production of cultural properties and works of art, a latent danger for futher cultural development of society, and for the creation and adoption of progressive and humanistic cultural values.

Characteristic of the contemporary development of Czechoslovak society in the period of construction of developed socialism in which the results of the scientific and technical revolution are particularly connected, to the new social relations, is a complex approach to the solution of political, socio-economic, cultural and ideological/educational problems. The development of culture and the arts, accompanied by the increasing cultural and educational function of the state, in which the organs of people's power of all grades participate together with social organizations and even the sphere of production itself, puts increasingly higher demands on the scientific and planned long-term control of cultural processes, which includes taking advantage of spontaneous cultural activities and of cultural creativity of the working people.

THE AUDIENCE OF THE ARTS AND THE MEDIA

The degree to which works in the different arts find a response among readers, spectators and listeners acts as an important precondition for the development of artistic creation, a criterion of the impressiveness of works of art and, at the same time, a certain indication of the cultural level of the inhabitants.

Statistical analyses of the number of visitors to theatres, concert halls, cinemas, art galleries and exhibitions, as well as research into reading, listening to artistic programmes on radio and television, show an incessant interest of the inhabitants in arts of a solid and distinct structure. Although cinema attendance was strongly influenced by the rapid spread of television at the end of the 1950s and the beginning of the 1960s, it can be said that after the first drop in the number of film audiences, this has stabilized again. Even with the present situation where every private home has a television set, film production can count on an increasing number of cinema-goers, especially among the young, and, moreover, on audiences with an increasing demand for films of artistic quality.[2]

With more than 15 million inhabitants in Czechoslovakia, the average annual number of visitors amounts to 9 million at theatre performances, about 2 million at concerts, over 18 million at museums, art galleries and exhibitions, and 86 million at film shows. Young people are the most active among visitors to artistic programmes, representing as much as 40 per cent in some branches of art.

Of course, statistical data are by no means the only indicators of the cultural level of the people, nor the most important ones. Therefore, scientific research concentrates particularly on the analysis of the real cultural needs, interests and activities of the people, trying to find ways in which these needs can not only be satisfied but also stimulated and further developed. Besides the sociological, psychological and aesthetic points of view, methods of scientific prognostication are also applied to a growing extent. These are of practical importance, for they help to make use of the results of scientific research in formulating long-term prospects for the cultural development of society.[3] New perspectives are opened up to scientific research itself as well in the effort to recognize the general laws of the present stage of development of culture and art.

SOCIAL AND ECONOMIC CONDITIONS OF PROFESSIONAL ARTISTS

The system of conditions for the development of artistic talents, built up systematically and according to a long-term plan, forms a basis for the selection of individuals with personal prerequisites and qualities that make them fit for creative artistic activity. The high social prestige of artists is accompanied by a corresponding material and social security.

Both creative and performing artists are members of a creative front, the core of which is formed by the artists' unions. Their members are the most outstanding creators of Czech and Slovak art.

The conditions of the artists' life and production are mainly ensured—in co-operation with the artists' unions—by the Cultural Funds, the mission of which is 'a purposeful support of progressive literary, scientific, and artistic activities of a high ideological and aesthetic level and social significance'.[4] They represent joint and executive organizations of the artists' unions and are responsible for their activities to the respective Ministry of Culture.[5] The funds and their sections are administered by committees appointed by a decree of the Minister of Culture. The economic funds are collected in the form of contributions from recipients of royalties or fees from artistic performances (2, 3 or 5 per cent, according to the total yearly income), plus subsidies from the Ministry of Culture derived from the profits made by the use of artistic and scientific works, and from payments by the users of these works (13 per cent). The funds are organized separately in each of the two Republics, one in Prague and the other in Bratislava. The authors' protective organizations and artistic agencies also take part in securing good social and economic conditions for the artists' activities (Fig. 1).

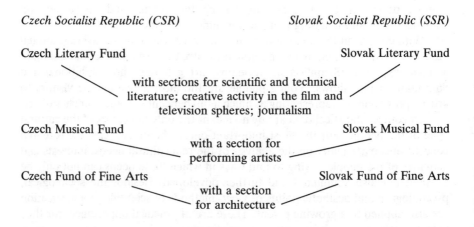

Czech Socialist Republic (CSR)   *Slovak Socialist Republic (SSR)*

Czech Literary Fund   Slovak Literary Fund

with sections for scientific and technical literature; creative activity in the film and television spheres; journalism

Czech Musical Fund   Slovak Musical Fund

with a section for performing artists

Czech Fund of Fine Arts   Slovak Fund of Fine Arts

with a section for architecture

FIG. 1. Cultural funds in Czechoslovakia.

From the economic point of view, the circumstance whether an artist has a full-time job or is free-lance is also reflected in his position. The number of free-lance and amateur artists who become professionals differ, of course, according to the different art branches.

For example, most writers and playwrights have occupations of different kinds as engineers, doctors, etc., or full-time jobs, often related to their creative activity, as editors, journalists, workers in adult-education institutions, etc.

ARTISTIC CREATION AND THE MASS MEDIA

The position and role of both art and artists in the contemporary world is undoubtedly influenced by the existence of the mass media which have developed since the 1950s into a relatively complete system embracing practically all ways and means of influencing people, in particular the audio-visual media. Besides their basic functions, they are capable of contributing in a marked way to a mass expansion of cultural and artistic values and, to some degree, to their preservation. If we speak about the relative completeness of the system of mass media, we can rightly speak also about the relative completeness of the system of art, or branches of art respectively. We are really concerned here with two independent systems whose contents overlap, and between which there exists a whole scale of functional bindings. They are developing, dynamic systems in both cases, and their relative completeness does not exclude a considerable extent of openness, even to each other. It can well be expected that due to developments in science and technology, new means of propagating works of art will arise, as is already indicated by the new types of records and magnetic tapes, video-cassettes, video-discs, the prospects of taking advantage of holography, etc. It is also to be expected that further development of the mass media will contribute to the crystallization of new artistic genres, or even to the emergence of new branches of art—as was the case with the film and with artistic photography.

The symbiosis of the two systems depends on a wider social context and can develop, on the one hand, in the direction of an equalization of the cultural level of people, a simplification of their spiritual needs and a growth of passivity in accepting cultural values as well as in the way of spending their leisure time; or, on the other, it can create a wide background for a many-sided and deeper communication between man and art, stronger and more differentiated value orientations, without any decrease in the creative participation of people in cultural and social life. What is important here is a purposeful cultural policy applied in relation to the mass media and, last but not least, an active participation of the artists themselves.

Art in Czechoslovakia occupies a significant place in the structure of the mass media. Artistic television programmes represent today over a third (37.9 per cent in 1978), music and literary-dramatic radio programmes more than half (55.4 per cent and 10.9 in the same year) of the air time. As far as television is concerned, this proportion is growing. For example, the percentage of artistic programmes in total broadcasting time is as follows: in 1965 it was 30.6; in 1970, 27.5; in 1975, 31.4; and in 1978, 37.9 per cent respectively.

Still more marked is the share of artistic programmes those imported from abroad, where it approaches 75 per cent of the air time.

Audience research shows that artistic programmes on television are among the most popular, and the most successful of them are watched by as much as 70 per cent of the population (practically every household has a television set).[6] However, comparative sociological research shows that the reading of books (by the population as a whole) and attendance at the cinema (by the young) maintain their popularity, which compares well with that of television. For example, in 1978 Czechoslovakia published 5.5 books per head of the population, 2.5 of them fiction.[7] Active citizens of Czechoslovakia (15–60 years) buy on average twenty-five numbers of cultural and artistic magazines on a year. About half of Czechoslovak households have small libraries of their own with a minimum of a hundred books.

A similar trend can be followed in the growing amount of gramophone records produced, serious music being markedly represented (over half the total number of recorded minutes; see Table 1).

TABLE 1. The development of gramophone records production group 1960–78

	1960	1965	1970	1975	1978
Gramophone records in recorded minutes	5 160	7 431	10 482	10 215	13 690
Musical recordings out of the total number	4 751	5 349	7 453	7 659	11 204
Percentage of serious music	60	65	58	60	53

Specific artistic genres have arisen and continue to do so within the framework of the mass media, such as television and radio plays, short comedies, and serials, which show a number of particular features.[8] During the short existence of television which can be expressed in a matter of decades, it has already filtered out the possibilities of the application of individual artistic types and genres and has replaced the former imports by programmes of its own creation. Moreover, there has been a marked turn of this creation to the solution of the problems of everyday life. The oscillation between the artistic and non-artistic, which is so typical of the mass media, influences to a considerable extent the character of artistic television and radio programmes; it is one of the natural sources of the genres arising here, through which it influences the whole structure of art, its themes and its subject-matter.

Czechoslovak television has been broadcasting a programme called *Bakaláři* (Bachelors) for more than eight years. It is based upon the narrative abilities of the viewers. The studios in Prague, Bratislava and some regional towns announce at regular intervals one theme or motive—usually a short sentence, proverb or saying—and invite the viewers throughout the whole country to 'narrate' a story on the given subject, which they have either experienced themselves or which has happened in their immediate neighbourhood. The three best ones are selected out of the hundreds of letters that come in,[9] and their dramatization is then entrusted to professional playwrights, directors and actors who try to combine the originality of the artistic treatment with the authenticity of the subject drawn from the sources of modern folk narratives.

The main focus of the artistic programmes of the mass media consists of original television, radio and other plays naturally including also possibilities of creative adaptations of both Czechoslovak and foreign works (serials based on novels by Balzac, Galsworthy, Tolstoy, Neff, etc.). Transmissions of plays from theatres or music from concert halls form a small part. In this case, they are mostly broadcasts from significant international festivals, festive performances or programmes given to support local cultural and artistic activities and traditions. The mass media also set up their own artistic ensembles and bodies, which participate not only in the programmes of a particular medium but also in other spheres of the cultural life of the country.[10]

Another circumstance worth mentioning is the growing importance and influence of their recreational function. For a considerable proportion of the population, the mass media serve as a source of relaxation and entertainment filling up their leisure time. If this tendency is left to develop spontaneously, it may have to a great degree a negative influence on the content level of the programmes. On the other hand, the solution does not consist in abolishing or reducing this recreational function, but in demanding criteria of a higher order in entertainment and undoubtedly also blending entertainment with the aesthetic function of the mass media.

Table 2 shows the structure of television programmes from the point of view of the presentation of entertaining and artistic performances.

TABLE 2. Structure of television programmes in Czechoslovakia in 1977

Type of programme	Broadcast time (%)
News, political commentaries, educational programmes, sport	47.1
Artistic and entertainment programmes	46.0
Connecting broadcasts (announcements, stills, switching over to other studios, etc.)	5.7
Advertising	1.2

There is a continuous dialogue between the artistic and the entertainment programmes on television as well as those on radio, for a number of artistic programmes have an entertainment function and, vice versa, the entertainment programmes endeavour to apply aesthetic criteria and improve their quality. The subjects of some entertainment programmes are drawn from the sphere of professional art (quizzes) or react to the spontaneous creativity of people (programmes of the *Zpívá celá rodina* (The Whole Family Sings) type, in which representatives of several generations of one family compete in singing.

Similar penetration of art can also be observed in the sphere of so-called educational programmes which represented 11.1 per cent of television broadcast time in 1978 and 14.3 per cent on the radio. Besides the extensive serial-programme, *Matematika převážně vážně* (Mathematics Mostly Seriously), there is another programme of a similar type, *Ceská filharmonie braje a hovoři* (The Czech Philharmonic Orchestra Plays and Talks) which guides the viewers, especially the young ones, in their understanding and aesthetic perception of serious music. Special programmes about art galleries, museums, historical monuments, nature reserves and others, have a similar educational, mainly aesthetic/educational, significance.[11] In the course of time, many programmes attract their own public, so that the original pedagogical aim seems to retreat into the background, and a new forum emerges where demanding artistic works can be shown. A programme of this type is the cycle of concerts of top orchestras and soloists which have been telecast under the title, *Hudba z respiria* (Music from the Respirium), in Prague for many years.

Television also verifies and introduces experimentally various types of programmes whose aim is to draw the viewer and listener into the creation of the programme. An example of this is *Televizní klub mladých* (Television Club of the Young), whose authors as well as participants are artists and members of the public representative of the younger generation; another example is *Návštěva v klubu* (Visit to a Club) popularizing local amateur artistic activity.

We have mentioned some concrete experiments by the mass media in Czechoslovakia, especially television, in applying art in the structure of programmes. These examples are a partial answer to the question whether there exists a tension between art (creativity and talent) and the standard productions characterizing the mass media. Not only theoretical considerations but also practice itself are proofs that this tension is no unsurmountable matter, and that an active, imaginative cultural policy can solve all the problems concerning the position and role of art in the mass media.

As the main economic causes of the commercializing tendencies which usually exert a negative influence on the position of art in the mass media do not exist, no antagonisms can arise, and the problem of the relation between artistic creativity, talent and series production is reduced, in principle, to the quality of television, radio and other artistic programmes. The demands put on quality come into the fore, in particular with regard to the mass influence of all modern audio-visual means. The aim of the mass propagation of cultural and artistic values is to create all the conditions required for the satisfaction and development of the cultural needs of the population, not leading to uniformity of cultural standards but to a rich variety of interests, value orientations and activities.

The mass media cannot fully answer the above question by themselves, not even in their fruitful connection with traditional cultural and artistic institutions, and fields. We know from experience that a person who is educated—not one-sidedly but with a broad general outlook—and is cultivated by aesthetic experiences, as well as by the direct impact of works of art, is also more resistent to the simplifying tendencies accompanying the operation of mass media, and applies more demanding criteria and a better discrimination in his choice of programmes. If this feedback works well, the public's standards can be influenced by the programme structure in a markedly positive way. Thus the achieved level of cultural democratization, i.e. the riches of the cultural values that have so far been made accessible to the public and which the people have adopted, is the basic prerequisite for the good and efficient operation of the mass media, particularly in cultural and artistic programming. The increasing democratization of culture is a dialectical process in which the wide range of cultural and artistic values that are being made accessible, should be necessarily accompanied by proper creative activities of the people for it is the people's conscious creativity that is the most important dynamic agent in a developed society.

NOTES

1. Even at that time, Czechoslovakia was one of the most developed European countries as far as the material and technical basis of the film industry, and the number of films produced, are concerned.
2. This interest is supported by organizing working people's film festivals all over the country. These have been taking place in all the larger towns since 1948, with the average attendance of more than a million visitors a year, and the so-called film spectators' clubs, where exacting spectators become familiar with the works of prominent film directors and producers from both Czechoslovakia and abroad, with film actors, schools and trends, as well as with the latest films from all over the world.
3. A study called 'A Prognosis of the Czech and Slovak Culture till the Year 2000' is being worked out at present in the Institute of Cultural Research in Prague and the Institute of Cultural Research in Bratislava.
4. Government Regulation of the Czech Socialist Republic of 5 December 1969.
5. Owing to the federal structure of the state, there is one Ministry of Culture in the Czech and one in the Slovak Socialist Republic.
6. At the end of 1978 there was one television set per 3.8 inhabitants.
7. Literature for children and adolescents, calculated for members of the age-group up to 19 years, amounts to four books per person per year.
8. There are also combinations of techniques used in the mass media and in the classical arts, as is attested, for example, by the Laterna Magica in Prague (founded in 1958) which combines theatre and film techniques with the use of poly-screen.
9. Five thousand letters arrived when the theme, 'My Unforgettable Experience with a Child' was announced in 1979 on the occasion of the International Year of the Child. On average about 2,000 letters with literary stories are received for every theme announced.
10. They are, for example, the Czechoslovak Radio Symphonic Orchestra, the Czechoslovak Radio Dance Orchestra, the Czechoslovak Radio Jazz Orchestra, Brno Radio Orchestra of Popular Instruments, the Czechoslovak Television Orchestra, the Czechoslovak Television Ballet, the Film Symphonic Orchestra, the Ostrava Radio Orchestra, and others.
11. Evaluation and popularization of film and television works on art are the aims of the ARSFILM Festival, which has been held annually at Kroměříž since 1964.

8   Creative workers, cultural industries and technology in the United States

Barbara D. Kibbe

TACT (The Arts, Culture and Technology),
School of Performing Arts,
University of Southern California,
Los Angeles

TENSIONS BETWEEN ART AND INDUSTRY

Clearly, not all art in the United States is the product of a well-defined 'cultural industry'. However, it is also clear that, in the twentieth century, the artist who functions outside or on the fringes of society, supported by a patron, is an outdated and romantic notion. In fact, those artists who hold themselves aloof from business are rare and becoming rarer. It is much more common to confront the artist who believes that, 'Business art is the step that comes after art.'[1] The role of the artist in society may not have changed philosophically, but, pragmatically, the artist finds fullfilment of that role a very different task in a highly industrialized, technological, service-oriented country from what it was 100 years ago. There are generally three choices available to the contemporary artist: The first is to seek economic self-sufficiency in employment outside the field of his art; or, secondly, to participate in the non-profit sector where financial gain is limited, activity is supported by charitable donations to the non-profit organization and where the subsidized activities of the artist are limited to those which satisfy the taxing authorities as educational or cultural activities for the public benefit;[2] or, thirdly, to seek employment in, or a market for, his or her creative work in the commercial sector of unsubsidized cultural industries such as broadcasting, publishing, music or film.

When artists choose the third of these alternatives, they thrust themselves headlong into industries often characterized by a high level of competition, little or no social security, chronically low financial compensation relative to other workers, and an incredibly high level of unemployment.[3]

What distinguishes these cultural industries from industries involving the manufacture and sale of fungible goods is that a tension exists by definition in cultural industries. Most industries are engaged in producing and marketing an item of trade such as clothing, motor-cars or food products which can be objectively valued. Art or cultural industries, on the other hand, face an interesting dilemma. When art objects or performances are offered for trade, the offering is not necessarily in direct response to an ascertainable market demand. Rather, the products of cultural industries are produced by artists, individually or collectively, who seek to give expression to a personal vision, aesthetic or message. The artist(s) may expect to communicate and may also expect to be compensated economically, but the main impetus for an artist is not always (nor should it be often) the satisfaction of a market demand. There is then an inherent—and arguably a permanent—tension present in all cultural industries; that is, the tension between a personalized world-view or aesthetic on the one hand, and, on the other, the economics of the industry which is based on the presumption of a market ready, willing and able to pay for the industry's product.[4]

For example, a ceramicist may be engaged in the production of clay sculptures which incidentally also serve a utilitarian purpose. There will come a time in the career of the ceramicist, if he is attempting to be economically self-sufficient through the sale of his wares, that a personal aesthetic may come into conflict with economic necessity. Stated simply, what is saleable may not be what artists consider their best work.

To take the example of the ceramicist one step further, the artist may find himself making 'production pots', repeating a popular saleable design. In such a case, the work of the artist is clearly affected by what may be easily marketed: the aesthetic is affected by the economic need.

The music business provides a more complex illustration of the same principle. But, unlike an independent potmaker, the composer or performing musician must first be initiated into the highly sophisticated business known as the recording industry.[5] The size and sophistication of the music business places the musical artist (composer and performer) in a position similar to that of the ceramicist in search of economic self-sufficiency. In either situation, the artist must be keenly aware of the demands of the business and must offer to the producers an art which contains the indications of marketability that record producers seek. However, once a producer is attracted to a musical artist, that artist, unless very careful when contracting with the producer, risks the probability that his contribution to the making of a recording will result in his receiving only a small fraction of the profits from the sale of sound recordings, leaving the bulk of those often substantial profits to the record producers.[6]

Each sound recording involves a composer, lyricist, one or more musicians and a producer or production company. The producer, in simplified terms, is the businessman who may provide the financial support necessary to make the recording, but who also transforms the musical composition into a sound recording. The producer assembles the technical persons necessary, oversees the recording process, and applies a variety of marketing skills in an attempt to secure a profit on his investment.[7]

Ironically, the technology of sound recordings, which was developed in an effort to preserve the beauty of live musical performances, has become such a significant industry in its own right that the role of live performance is used by performers first to attract the public's attention, and thereby the attention of a producer interested in facilitating the creation of a sound recording. Once a recording contract is signed, live performances often become simply a means of promoting or advertising the recording. An unfortunate effect of the current state of the music business is that performing artists find fewer occasions to perform publicly, reducing that source of income considerably. A further disadvantage for the musician lies in the fact that the current system of copyright laws in the United States provides no performer's right in sound recordings.[8] The obvious result of these facts is that the development of the sound-recording industry has not worked to the advantage of the musicians in all cases. Live performances are relegated to the position of advertisements for sound recordings and the sale of sound recordings brings no income to the musicians.

With respect to the composer's contribution to a sound recording, the United States copyright laws, through an unusual evolution, fall short in their protection.[9] That law, which secures to authors the exclusive right to distribute and reproduce their works, contains an exception with respect to sound recordings.[10]

Under the provision of the law called compulsory licence, anyone wishing to record the work of another may do so without the direct permission of the owner of the copyright of the musical composition. The law provides that the author of the work has the right to record it for the first time. After that, any other user simply notifies the author of his intent and pays the author a royalty of 2.75 cents for each record made and distributed.[11]

It has been argued that the compulsory licensing provision of the copyright law places an unreasonably low royalty on the use of another's musical composition, adding income for the producers of sound recordings and severely limiting the rights of the owners of copyrighted music. Clearly, in the case of the music business, it is the producer who is the most important individual (and the one likely to benefit most from sales of sound recordings).

None of the above should be in the least surprising. What it teaches us, in perhaps an oversimplified way, is useful in understanding the basic relationship between art and industry: a relationship fraught with tension, as the artist or creative worker struggles to participate in the cultural industry and yet retain his role as an artist, creator and visionary.

In my view, there are three basic questions to be answered on an industry-by-industry, case-by-case basis, by anyone considering the quality of that relationship and the quality of the products of the various industries, as well as the protection afforded to the workers in those industries:

First, in what way is the industry making the realization of the artist's vision possible, i.e. communicating a meaningful message to the participating public?

Secondly, in what way is the artist and his product the victim of exploitation by an industry? That is, to what extent does the consumer of the industry's product or service control the product and thereby the artist?

Thirdly, in what way has the role of facilitators (art dealers, producers, technicians) assisted the artist in attaining his goals and in what way have the facilitators alienated the artist from his product?

Simply stated, the ever-present tension between art and industry, or culture and trade, is that which must be present when a personal world-view or aesthetic runs headlong into objective economic considerations, which may be as simple as the requirements of an individual artist in search of a modicum of financial self-sufficiency, or as complex as the economic growth of a nationwide industry which deals in creative works.

My view is that a degree of such tension is desirable and militates against the nightmarish concept of cultural industries based entirely on economic factors.

TENSIONS INHERENT IN THE PROCESS OF COLLECTIVE CREATION

Thus far this study has focused primarily on the individual artist as a discrete and autonomous unit in American cultural industries. The ceramicist discussed above is ultimately responsible for the conception and excution of a final artistic product, such as a vase or sculpture. There are, however, thousands of American artists who do not command such autonomous control, but who function as joint contributors to a final artistic product. These artists are involved in a process that can best be termed 'collective creation'.

Collective creation may occur in virtually any artistic discipline; for example, two or more painters may jointly conceive and execute a mural. Likewise, a sound recording, as discussed briefly above, is often the product of collaborative efforts. While the dynamics of the creative process may change where more than one artist is involved, the social impact of collective creation in areas such as painting and sculpture is largely indistinguishable from that where only one artist is involved. For this reason, collective creation in areas such as those mentioned above will not be examined here.

Certain kinds of collective creation in the United States, however, do have an impact on society in a manner largely unlike that of individual creative efforts. These kinds of collective creation involve large numbers of collaborators and, not coincidentally, can be of a highly commercial nature, the most prominent examples being motion pictures and television. In an effort to understand something of the dynamics and impact of large-scale collective creation in the United States, the bulk of this section will be devoted to an examination of the established American motion-picture industry.

It will be noted that the tensions that reveal themselves in the process of creating films relate to the inevitable presence of conflicting visions among and between the creative workers who are called upon to co-operate in the project. I shall therefore pause to outline a brief biography of the film industry, which highlights these tensions and their symptoms and also indicates some of the provisional solutions that have from time to time assited in the growth of that industry. It may be useful to establish a historical perspective on film as an art-form possessed of semingly unlimited potential for conveying visual and aural messages. The discussion that follows also provides an appropriate introduction to a discussion of the influences of technology on art.

The 'crisis of film', as seen by the eminent art historian, Arnold Hauser, was to be found in the very fact that it was a technological, industrial art-form.

Considering its future while writing the final volume of his *Social History of Art* in the 1950s, Hauser stated:

The crisis of film, which seems to be developing into a chronic illness, is due above all to the fact that the film is not finding its writers, or, to put it more accurately, the writers are not finding their way to the film. Accustomed to doing as they like within their own four walls, they are now required to take into account producers, directors, script-writers, cameramen, art directors and technicians of all kinds, although they do not acknowledge the authority of this spirit of cooperation, or indeed the idea of artistic cooperation at all. Their feelings revolt against the idea of the production of works of art being surrendered to a collective, to a 'concern', and they feel that it is a disparagement of art that an extraneous dictate, or at best a majority, should have the last word in decisions of the motives which they are often unable to account for themselves.[12]

For Hauser and his contemporaries, film was a question of

two phenomena belonging to two different periods of time—the lonely, isolated writer dependent on his own resources and the problems of the film which can only be solved collectively. The cooperative film unit anticipates a social technique to which we are not yet equal, just as the newly invented camera anticipated an artistic technique of which no one at the time really knew the range and power.[13]

Happily or unhappily, the two decades since Hauser's portentious analysis has seen the development of this art-form to virtual pre-eminence.

The medium of film was the first among this century's new communication media to develop into an art-form.[14] It has been nearly a century since the expressive resources of the motion picture were first used by artists to put forward their personal and collective visions. Film in the United States can hardly be thought of as anything but a major and complex pooling of talents and resources in a collective and collaborative effort to produce and distribute an artistic product. In 1977, the American motion-picture industry grossed $2.4 billion. The tension between industry and art that has long characterized Hollywood film production has produced a complex of professional organizations, including numerous craft unions and guilds.[15] As the premier popular art-form of this century, motion pictures have become a key social institution and a showcase of American cultural values. What is the structure of this industry and how do artists function within it?

The American film industry can be divided into three distinct and vertically separated markets: production, distribution and exhibition. Production entails those things commonly viewed as being involved in 'making a film'. This includes casting, scripting, arranging technical support and financial backing, the actual shooting, as well as the hundreds of other tasks involved in creating the finished product. Distribution is quite distinct from production. It is the marketing and rental of the film to the cinema-owners who will then, in turn, exhibit the product to customers. In a somewhat simplified way, the production/distribution/exhibition triad is analogous to the manufacture/wholesale/retail relationship in other businesses.

The history of the motion-picture industry has been described as 'one of almost continuous innovations and a succession of combinations to control markets'.[16] From the early years of the industry, firms primarily involved in one market sought to extend their power into other sectors. After a number of years of constant consolidation and combination, a relatively few firms effectively controlled the production, the distribution as well as the exhibition of films.[17] The bargaining position of the smaller independent exhibitors was drastically reduced, and abusive practices developed on the part of the major firms.[18] In 1948, at the conclusion of a major anti-trust litigation; known as the Paramount case[19] the major firms were required to divest themselves of the exhibition aspects of their enterprises and to cease abusive practices. Despite the Paramount sanctions, the major studios continued to exert an overwhelming control over the American motion-picture industry well into the 1950s. That decade saw a sharp reduction in the production of American feature releases.[20] The new era of higher budgets, reduced schedules and a more selective market came about as the result of the loss of assured markets, increased numbers of foreign productions, and competition from television and other leisure activities. Reorganization within the film industry ensued, in which a radical shrinkage of the major studios took place.[21] An interesting example of how the structure of the industry has changed is provided by the case of United Artists. The founders of United Artists: Charlie Chaplin, Douglas Fairbanks, D. W. Griffith and Mary Pickford, set up the company in 1919 to distribute the films they produced. United Artists collapsed during the early 1950s but was revived by businessmen who reverted solely to distribution and investment; the firm ceased to produce its own films, but invested in those of others.

In the case of United Artists, the conglomerate, Transamerica Corporation, salvaged the corporation. The impact of conglomerates on feature-film production has had a mixed effect on the industry. On the one hand, conglomerates have the financial strength to assure a production programme on a continuing basis; on the other, fears of production by committee (as opposed to a more individual artistic control), banker control of content and minimization (the gradual reduction of interest in film activities in favour of more profitable aspects of conglomerates) are real concerns for the industry as a whole.[22]

The foregoing discussion points up the inherent tension that exists between the actual production of an artistic work (i.e., a film) and its sale and marketing. In a somewhat simplified way, this tension can be labelled as one between 'business' and 'art'. A second type of tension characterizes the film industry in the United States, one which derives from the nature of collective creation itself: the tension existing among the various artists actually responsible for making the film.

In Hollywood, specialized professional groups and discrete creative specialities have developed over the course of the industry's history. These groups have developed unique aesthetic, financial and career interests that often conflict with those of other groups involved in film production. There exist more than forty unions in Hollywood, twenty-four of which are affiliated with the International Alliance of Theatrical Stage Employees (IATSE).[23]

IATSE members work in craft and technical jobs such as film editors, hairdressers and sound technicians. Five guilds represent employees in the 'creative' unions: producers, directors, writers, actors and extras.[24] The unions and guilds have brought about better working conditions, craft guidelines and effective collective-bargaining procedures, but they have maintained strict rules regarding union membership making it difficult for non-union workers to be employed.[25]

The existence of many creative crafts in film-making results in relations of both co-operation and constraint between the various artists. An examination of several of the creative groups in film and their roles in the production process will serve to illustrate this point.

With the advent of sound films, Hollywood imported novelists and playwrights who were accustomed to function with relative autonomy under the protection of the Dramatists Guild, which prohibited unauthorized alterations to the work of their members.[26] In the studios of the 1930s to the end of the 1960s, these screenwriters were treated as factory employees whose output would be revamped to fit the studio's specifications.[27] However, it was the emergence of the so-called *auteur* theory in the 1960s, viewing the director as author of a film, regardless of whether he in fact wrote it, that has caused much unhappiness for screenwriters. Today the screenwriter is increasingly called upon to collaborate with the director. Often the screenwriter will contribute ideas to the editing process. One of the creative conflicts that can arise concerns an actor's conception of the writer's dialogue. The actor will often improvise on the script, with the director's acquiescence. In this case, the screenwriter may feel his or her dialogue is being compromised.

Actors are the interpretative artists in the film process and are seen alternatively as the puppets of the process and the centre of the cinematic universe. Since actors generally have their own unique career interests, there can be a conflict between how the actor conceives of his or her role and what the director envisions. The general unwritten rule is that the director's wishes are carried out.[28]

The art director or production designer is the creative worker who translates the director's conception of the film environment into visual terms. He works closely with the director, cinematographer and costumer designer in creating the total physical environment of the film. Despite the screenwriter's skill in writing or a director's skill in getting the actors to bring the lines to life, the environment in which the characters exist can largely determine the artistic success of a film. A good working relationship between the art director, director, cinematographer and set decorator is, therefore, essential.

The costume designer, the creator of clothes for the actors, can crystallize a director's visual conception of the characters. The costume designer must interact to a considerable degree with the art director. Predictably, the costume designer is often in conflict with the actors, who want to maintain or establish a particular visual image in the viewing public's eye. Likewise, interaction is necessary with other film artists: the designer's executed creations are not only worn by actors and handled by costumers, they are photographed by the cameraman against a set created by the art director.

The cinematographer directs the camera crew and works closely with the director to light the scene and direct the camera operator in the execution of the shot. The cinematographer has been called the painter of motion pictures, using lenses and lighting the way a painter uses a brush to achieve texture, emotion and weight. The photographic concept of a film is one of prime importance in this essentially visual medium. Since major delays in shooting are often occasioned by the details of lighting, there is always the potential for conflict between the producer and the cinematographer over aesthetic matters and the expense of scene lighting.

The preceding discussion has highlighted two kinds of tension inherent in the American motion-picture industry: that between business and art, and that among the various creative groups and individuals involved in the actual film-making process. The existence of these tensions is not unique to the film industry in the United States; what is unique is the development of highly complex modes of financial support and rules governing artistic interaction, that is, the ways of dealing with the tensions.

Whether the American motion-picture industry can be considered a success depends on what are viewed as the parameters of success. Viewed as a business, the magnitude of the film industry has certainly provided employment for numerous artists and technicians. As a producer of an art form, a determination of success becomes much more complex. In terms of total output, it has produced relatively few masterpieces. As one commentator has noted,

the triumph of Hollywood is the triumph of raising the general standard of films by concentrating on improving the quality of the average product. What is true of Hollywood efficiency is true of American efficiency in general: it aims to raise the general standard, the average, mostly by eroding the lower end of the scale, but also perhaps at the price of less encouragement to the higher end.[29]

The American film industry has of late exhibited signs of fiscal vitality. Sales to television have escalated, providing increasing sources of revenue. Some of the old studios, which have dealt only in distribution and investment over the past twenty years, have once again started to produce their own films.[30] In 1978, 133 million tickets were sold, and 204 major films were released (only 58 of these by major studios).

Despite this, however, the future of the motion-picture industry in the United States may continue to be tied to the larger phenomenon of technological development. In the 1950s, television was the technological development which threatened the industry; the film industry dealt effectively with this development and now sales to television are a major source of revenue. The 1980s present further technological innovations with which the industry will have to deal. Increasingly, films, like books and records, will be found in the home and under consumer control through the use of video equipment. Consumer control over films seen in the home promises new financial and legal changes, as well as drastic changes in the way we relate to film art.[31] As it has been called upon to do in the past, the American film industry collectively will have to develop ways of dealing with this problem.

TECHNOLOGY AND THE ARTS

As might be surmised from the preceding discussion of film, the combination of technology and art is a doubled-edged sword. At one and the same time, technology presents the artist with enormous potential for the accomplishment of aesthetic goals and a nightmarish danger of exploitation seemingly without end. No doubt, technological advancements are in each case new tools for artists. It has been postulated that:

In order to understand what is happening in contemporary art, one has to remind oneself that people are part of nature and that therefore the things that people make and discover are part of nature. Artists as well as scientists help us become aware of and relate to the very small and the very very large, for these newly discovered parts of nature are becoming more and more part of human experience.[32]

The partnership of art and technology has been tested in film and in music but yet more experimental possibilities are being explored. For example, the Los Angeles County Museum of Art developed a programme in Art and Technology which involved the co-operation of 76 artists and 225 corporation employees, as well as museum staff. The results of this experiment were works produced by artists who for perhaps the first time were able to use the advanced technology normally available only to industry, such as lasers, gas plasmas, advanced mirror-optic systems and the like.[33]

In the report on this experiment, the author states clearly two antithetical beliefs held by artists or scientists concerning the relationship of technology to the arts:

One of the fundamental dualisms inherent in the question of technology's uses in a humanist context has to do with the conflict between the belief that, in a word, technology *is* the metaphysics of this century, and therefore has to be accommodated from within, and the view that technology is somehow self-perpetuating, implacable and *essentially* inhuman, and that therefore humanist and artistic endeavor must function separated from it and even in opposition to it.[34]

The conclusion arrived at by the experimenters at the Los Angeles Museum is based on the premise that the artist exercises his or her prerogative to make use of technology or not; that the option is the artist's and that the result of an artist's option to use technology is, at its best, a way of humanizing technique and science.

Another project undertaken in the early 1970s[35] explores the voluntary interchange between art and technology through interviews with people active in each of those areas. The interviews present a fascinating display of attitudes and aptitudes concerning the collaboration of art and technology. In introducing his interviews, the editor shares his explanation for this undertaking.

If some hold that disaster is the stepchild of this macabre union [of science and art], an ever-growing segment of art-science protagonists has risen to challenge this premise. They argue . . . that the artist has always been a preeminent practitioner of technological innovation. Each art form has evolved, in this view, primarily through the advance of technical means.

In this conception of the functional value of technology for the artist, care has been taken to view technology as a vehicle but never a substitute for the creative act. *Technique and technology are neutral. Use of the most modern artefacts of science and technology [is] a logical extension of a long tradition.*[36]

One of the artists interviewed in *Science and Technology* is Alwin Nikolais, a choreographer who transforms the human body in his work by using costuming that is sculptural in design and which is playfully transformed by means of carefully used lighting effects. His music is a fascinating hybrid of electronic synthesized music and the more traditional type. Nikolais is not afraid of using technology in his art.

Nikolais' role as an innovator was recently reasserted when he wrote and choreographed the electronic ballet 'Limbo' . . . in collaboration with the producer . . . and a brilliant electronic engineer . . . Nikolais developed a videotape ballet that could only be realized in this medium.

The videotape ballet was realized with Chroma key switching. Chroma key switching enables the director to transform the screen into 2 or 3 totally independent visual fields. For example, a dancer's face and hands may appear as visible elements recorded from one studio camera. The dancer's body, however, can be visualized with input from a second camera. The 'background' can then be realized by switching to the input from a third camera. This flexibility enabled Nikolais to create a 'ballet without gravity' the ultimate realization of the choreographer's dream.[37]

In his own words, Nikolais describes his collaboration with technology thus:

One of the significant things about art is reaching for freedom. Technology is breaking another barrier. . . . Our whole sense of presence in the universe has been greatly shaken by new discoveries in science. . . . The artist has a feeling about this. Science and technology express our time but, more than that, they offer us new means to express it.[38]

The editor of the study notes:

Certainly the collaboration between art and technology has ancient roots. The artist has always worked with the tools of his time. . . . Art is, if noticed by the public, relevant to societal preoccupations. Today's artist is responding to the technical revolution that surrounds us.[39]

At the same time as some artists strive for relevance through uses of technology, a chronic problem exists with respect to access to that technology. Except for some experimentation, or involvement, in the well-developed film, music or publishing industries where innovation is somehow secondary to the available market, few artists are able to apply their vision through the uses of video, lasers and other advanced technology. The reason for this is, again, a simple one: artists do not command great economic resources.

I have no quarrel with those who hold that an artist, accepting the tools of technology, functions as a humanizer and that society benefits from that phenomenon. What I cannot agree with is that the artist always, or even most of the time, has the option of so doing. When seen through the lens of contemporary experiments, in art/science, the marriage seems to be a happy one, but it is not without its graver implications. A corollary to the use of new technologies by artists is the fact that the technology is often used against artists.

For example, since the invention of the printing press, there have been advancements in technology relating to reproduction of the printed word as well as visual imagery. The ownership and use of contemporary publishing techniques puts controls of the industry at a large distance from the writer. An experiment conducted recently by an American journalist illustrates the problem very graphically.[40] In an attempt to find out what happens when an unsolicited manuscript is submitted to a publishing firm, he chose an already published book: *Steps* by Jerzy Kosinski. *Steps* is a formidable piece of contemporary literature which received the National Book Award for fiction in 1979 and has sold over 400,000 copies. Clearly, *Steps* was worthy of publication from the point of view of aesthetic merit and was also an objective economic success in the publishing industry.

The experimenter retyped Kosinski's novel and submitted it, under his own name, to selected book publishers, three of which had in fact published works by Kosinski in the past. The results were unbelievable. All fourteen book publishers failed to recognize the work and all rejected the manuscript. A few suggested that the author obtain a literary agent (the commonplace intermediary between author and publisher). The advice was taken and twenty-six agents were contacted. Again, all refused the manuscript and one charged a twenty-five-dollar reading fee before he would offer an opinion.

Several important facts about the literary industry are well illustrated by this tragicomic sequence of events: (a) the literary industry in the United States is characterized by a high level of competition on the part of authors to get their works published; (b) there appears to be no committment on the part of major publishing firms to print the works of unknown authors; and (c) authors without professional literary agents are largely ineffectual in their attempts to deal directly with large publishing firms and literary agents are less impressed with skilful writing than with the reputation of the author, making it doubly difficult for an unknown writer to 'break into' the industry.

All this leads inevitably to the frustration of unknown, albeit talented, authors attempting to find a medium for communication of their art, to competition among colleagues to see books in print, and, ultimately, to the alienation of authors from the reading public and perhaps even from their art.

Visual artists, in light of the ease with which their imagery may be reproduced, are finding the protection of copyright laws less and less effectual. Clearly, the distance between the author or visual artist and the mechanism or technology used to reproduce and distribute the work is wide and getting wider.

New reproduction processes involving lasers, the large numbers of photo-copying devices, and the relatively small expense involved in reproducing an article or essay as compared with that of purchasing the original, all militate against the rights of authors and artists, often reducing their copyright ownership to an unenforceable ephemeral right.

We turn now to a discussion of the rights of artists and to a thoughful evaluation of the effectiveness of their protection in an age where culture is marketed on an industrial, international scale and technology is followed by its much slower step-brother, the law.

CURRENT COPYRIGHT LAWS IN THE UNITED STATES

Perhaps the most universal system of protection available to art and artists of all disciplines is the international system of copyright laws which guarantee that creators have the exclusive right to benefit economically from their creations. In the United States, copyright laws find their basis in the Constitution. Article I, Section 8 states that: 'The Congress shall have power . . . to promote the progress of science and useful arts, by securing for limited times to Authors and Inventors the exclusive right to their respective writings and discoveries.'

In 1978 the United States copyright law was completely revised in an effort to make a hopelessly out-of-date system of statutes and regulations relevant to the current state of art and technology. The revision work, though highly satisfactory in most areas, is already being outpaced by technological advances in copying machines and home video equipment.

CONTU

In an attempt to deal with the impact of developing technologies on copyrighted works, the Commission on New Technological Uses of Copyrighted Works (CONTU) was formed in 1975. The aims of the commission are twofold: first, to recognize the legitimate interests of copyright proprietors in controlling the uses to which their works are put, and secondly to improve public access to and availability of those works. Obviously, these two aims conflict at times; however, CONTU attempts to strike a balance between them so as to make copyright law effective through a national policy dealing with present and future advances in technology.[41]

The final report of CONTU contained a series of recommendations for the implementation of its aims. With respect to developments in the area of computers, CONTU recommended the extension of copyright protection to computer programs. The final report also called for a periodic review of the copyright law to ensure its adequacy in the light of technological change.

Some of the more significant recommendations concerned photocopying. CONTU recommended that the Copyright Office begin to plan and carry out a study of the overall impact of all photo-duplication practices on both proprietors' rights and the public's access to published information.

The Betamax case

In a recent case,[42] two producers of films and owners of copyrights brought a suit against a manufacturer of home video-recorders and a distributor, retailer and user of the product on the grounds of copyright infringement and unfair competition. The video equipment was sold exclusively for use in the home and no allegations were made that a commercial use was involved. The court held that non-commerical recording in the home, of material broadcast over the airwaves, does not constitute copyright infringement. The court further concluded that even if the activities involved in this case were found to come within the scope of the copyright law, such activity would fall under the law's 'fair use' exception and would, thus, not constitute an infringement.[43]

What is particularly instructive in this case, from the point of view of governmental attitude toward developing technologies in American cultural industries, is the reluctance of the court to delve behind the stated facts in the case: 'The ramifications of this new technology are greater than the boundaries of this lawsuit.' As a result, the court stated that it could not and should not undertake the role of 'a government commission or legislative body exploring and evaluating all the uses and consequences of the videotape recorder'.

This attitude reflects the general reluctance of the Federal Government to become involved in the regulation of developing technologies in American cultural industries. The position of the Federal Government seems to be to adopt a policy of *laissez-faire* with respect to technologies in their infancy. Only later, when the industry has matured and stabilized and more long-term problems emerge, will the government intervene.

CONCLUSIONS

The following points may be extracted from the foregoing discussion:

Art and industry are often in conflict with respect to the end-purpose of an activity but, at the same time, are frequently in agreement about the means to achieve those ends; hence, the possibility exists that healthy cultural industries which foster cultural development can, and do, exist in the United States.

Collective creation involves a democratic view of the participation of artists in collaboration, thereby producing an inherent conflict with regard to varying creative visions.

Technology itself is neutral *vis-à-vis* artists and art; the negative impact stems first from its inaccessibility to all artists, and secondly, from the fact that advanced techniques for reproduction of print, visual imagery and sound make exploitation of the work of others very simple.

The law lags behind technology in protecting the rights of artists and cultural workers.

In order to ensure and encourage cultural development through cultural industries and the contribution of artists to that development, I would therefore recommend the following:

That a survey be made of the active cultural industries in each nation, with special attention to the economic impact of those industries.

That the jobs or occupations within the various cultural industries be identified.

That the means of access to those industries be studied (i.e. formal education, apprenticeships or on-the-job training).

That the percentage of the profits earned by cultural industries which filters down to the workers be identified in each industry.

That the extent of unemployment in the various industries be studied comparatively.

That the percentage of a nation's work-force involved in cultural industries, as opposed to other occupations, be determined.

That a comparative study of the uses of tax-exemption as an indirect subsidy for arts and cultural activities be undertaken.

That Unesco sponsor experiments in the collaboration of art and technology in developing countries in a cautious way which meets the society's real needs using available resources and human potential.

That a survey of a country's population be undertaken in order to ascertain what segment or segments of that population are the consumers of the cultural industries' products and services, in order to facilitate broadening of the base of support for the arts and cultural industries.

That Unesco initiate further analysis of the potential means for the enforcement of existing protection for art and artists in the light of technological developments in the photo-reproduction and video areas.

NOTES

1. Andy Warhol, pop artist, from *The Philosophy of Andy Warhol: From A to B and Back Again.*
2. The non-profit organization acts as an important vehicle for cultural activities.
3. One good example of this is the film industry, which earned $2.4 billion in 1977. In spite of the level of economic activity, it is estimated that 85 per cent of the labour force is usually unemployed.
4. See M. Blaug (ed.), *Economics of the Arts.*
5. O. Shemel, *This Business of Music,* Los Angeles, Billboard Publications, 1971; *More About This Business,* Los Angeles, Billboard Publications, 1974.
6. This risk has induced many artists to form small independent record-producing companies in an effort to maximize the financial return to artists. At the same time, however, self-producing artists operate at great financial risk.
7. Retail sales of recorded music in the United States reached $1.7 billion in 1970; see Shemel, op.cit., p. XVII.
8. The United States Copyright Office is currently preparing recommendations to Congress regarding the impact of a performer's right on the industry and may amend the copyright laws to include such. See 'Performance Rights in the 1976 Copyright Act', *New York Law School Law Review,* Vol. XXII, No. 3, 1977.
9. Sound recordings were not in themselves subject to copyright protection because they were not seen as 'writings' in the meaning of the United States Constitution until 1971.
10. United States Copyright Law, Section 115.
11. For a brief discussion of the unusual growth of copyright protection for sound recordings, see 'Sound Recordings and the New Copyright Act', *New York Law School Law Review,* op. cit.

12. Arnold Hauser, *The Social History of Art,* Vol. IV, pp. 246-7.
13. Ibid.
14. See I. C. Jarvie, *Movies and Society,* 1970.
15. Examples are the Screen Actors Guild, the Producers Guild, the Screen Writers Guild, the Screen Extras Guild, plus groupings of virtually every other artistic and technical support group involved in the film-making process.
16. M. Conant, *Antitrust in the Motion Picture Industry: Economic and Legal Analysis,* 1960, p. 16.
17. Until 1948, the five major firms were Paramount, Loew's, RKO, Warner Brothers and Twentieth Century-Fox. The three minors were Columbia, Universal and United Artists. M. Conant, op. cit.
18. These abusive practices included 'blind selling' and 'block booking'. Blind selling means that a distributor licenses a feature before the exhibitor is afforded an opportunity to view it. Block-booking is the licensing of one film, or a group of films, on condition that the exhibitor will also accept another film or group of films.
19. *U.S.* v. *Paramount Inc. et. al.* 66F Supp. 323 (1946) modified 70F Supp. 53; remanded 85F Supp. 881; aff'd 339 US 947 (1950). See also Cassady, 'Impact of the Paramount Decision', *Southern California Law Review,* Vol. 31, p. 150, 1958. In 1948 the government won a victory confirmed by consent decrees accepted by defendants which: (a) mandated full complete divorcement of major producers-distributors from their exhibition outlets; (b) barred pooling of inter-corporate operations in controlled cinemas; (c) ended block booking of copyrighted films; (d) eliminated leasing of a film, sight-unseen; (e) found fixing of admission prices by distributors *per se* violative of antitrust law. Under new dispensation most licences are negotiated with individual cinemas.
20. Companies that once produced sixty films a year now produce twelve, and 'the unhappiness of union labor with the limited output of Hollywood is endemic. The industry entered an era of higher budgets, reduced schedules and a selective market.' M. Mayer, *The Film Industries,* 1978, p. 115.
21. Under the impact of television in the 1950s, audiences shrank and the larger studios became casualties. Many of those which survived have either sold their factories, or rent them out to television or independent producers.
22. Mayer, op. cit., pp. 117–21.
23. These unions include the costumers, film editors, illustrators, studio technicians, electricians, studio grips, publicists, script supervisors, screen cartoonists, set designers and model makers.
24. In 1977, there were approximately 35,000 members in the Screen Actors Guild, 4,600 in the Directors Guild, 4,000 in the Writers Guild of America (West), and 600 in the Producers Guild. These figures are deceptive in estimating the industry's work-force, since only a small percentage of guild members work at any given time. For example, the president of the Screen Actors Guild estimates that of that guild's 35,000 members, 85 per cent are usually unemployed. *Behind the Scenes,* September 1978, p. 5.
25. In an effort to facilitate entry into the various unions, internship programmes have been set up in Astoria, New York. Funded by the Department of Health, Education and Welfare, the City University of New York and Brooklyn College, these programmes have offered practical training to approximately forty film-school graduates each year. Graduates of the programmes are then admitted to the various locals according to their skills.
26. D. Chase, *Filmmaking: The Collaborative Art,* 1976, p. 39.
27. Ibid., p. 41.
28. Ibid., p. 79.
29. Jarvie, op. cit., note 1.
30. An example of this is Paramount Studios, which has had considerable success in producing its own films in the past two years.
31. For a description of possible copyright problems, see *Cleveland State Law Review,* Vol. 26, No. 3, p. 1.

32. Oppenheimer, Frant, 'Art and Science/Meancy Tools and Discipline', *The Exploratorium,* Vol. 3, No. 4, October/November 1979.
33. *A Report on the Art and Technology Program of the Los Angeles County Museum of Art 1967–71.*
34. Ibid., p. 43.
35. Stewart Kranz (ed.), *Science and Technology in the Arts,* New York, Van Nostrand Rheinhold, 1974.
36. Ibid., p. 19 (emphasis added).
37. Ibid., p. 36.
38. Ibid.
39. Ibid., p. 33.
40. *New West Magazine,* 12 February 1979.
41. See *The Journal of Management and Law of the Arts* (University of California at Los Angeles), Vol. 9, No. 1, 1979.
42. *Universal City Studios, Inc.* v. *Sony Corporation of America* (1979), as reported in *Patent, Trademark and Copyright Journal,* No. 448, p. D–1.
43. Section 107 of the United States Copyright law states that, 'the fair use of a copyrighted work, including such use by reproduction in copies or phono-records or by any other means specified for purposes such as criticism, comment, news reporting, teaching (including multiple copies for classroom use), scholarship, or research, is not an infringement of copyright. In determining whether the use made of a work in any particular case is a fair use, the factors to be considered shall include:
    (1) the purpose and character of the use, including whether such use is of a commercial nature or is for nonprofit educational purposes;
    (2) the nature of the copyrighted work;
    (3) the amount and substantiality of the portion used in relation to the copyrighted work as a whole; and
    (4) the effect of the use upon the potential market for or value of the copyrighted work.'

Part Four

The various strategies possible

What are the possible strategies, in national policy-making terms, that will provide responses commensurate with the challenge of the cultural industries? Clearly these will take entirely different forms depending on the socio-economic context and the political and administrative system of the country considered. The balance between action by the public authorities and the private sector (where such exists) is bound to vary according to the system in force, i.e. whether the economy is entirely free, mixed or wholly planned; similarly, the balance cannot be the same for countries whose language is spoken over a restricted area and for those where a large geographical area is involved. The case-studies prepared for the Montreal meeting show a very wide range of possible options. Japan is an example of a purely liberal strategy, where there is very wide scope for initiative by private enterprise. The case of the Canadian province of Quebec is interesting on two counts, since it represents at one and the same time an experiment in a mixed economy and an example of regional policy in a federal state. The study dealing with audio-visual media in Cuba provides an example of a cultural-industry strategy in a socialist country. The development of a particular industry, that of the book, is illustrated by two examples: that of a small industrialized country, Israel, and a developing country, the United Republic of Tanzania, where development planning follows the socialist model.

The experiments described provide lessons which may be relevant for the general study of the balance between political and private action with regard to the relations to be developed between cultural industries and other forms of cultural creation and organization, whether of public or private origin. Given the scope of the problem, no cultural development policy, if it is to be effective, can dispense with study of the facts or evade decisions that involve concrete issues.

Such study should relate basically, it would seem, to the different options open to the public authorities and private enterprise in respect of the creation and development of cultural industries, taking into consideration non-industrial forms of cultural activity. The aim is not to revert exclusively to craft production, nor to hand over to the public authorities the unprofitable leavings from industry, but to safeguard the cultural freedom of the people and their ability to participate, and to encourage the democratization of production and the development of endogenous industries, co-ordinating these with the overall cultural options of the society in question.

But how can we bring about the more effective integration of endogenous cultural values with the means of dissemination (in particular, the audio-visual media) which the public prefers, and which are economically profitable? How are we to devise a new kind of relationship between creative artists and the public, so that the latter will really be brought into contact with workers of the highest quality? And, in the developing countries, how can we create endogenous cultural industries which will not reproduce locally the shortcomings for which trans-national cultural industries are rightly criticized? The answer to all these major questions will determine to a great extent the practicability of national strategies designed to integrate cultural industries in overall cultural development policies.

We should not however confine ourselves to considerations of a general nature if our intention is to seek practical solutions. The following subjects deserve more specific study: legislative measures, regulations, measures relating to budgetary, fiscal and customs aspects, and direct or indirect action in respect of the production, dissemination or storage of industrially produced cultural objects. The public support accorded to cultural industries in comparison with other industrial sectors might also be studied. Thorough consideration should also be given to the limits to action by the public authorities in this field, such as the overall amount of budgetary resources, priority needs, the legal or constitutional division of responsibility at the various levels of authority (for example in federal countries) and the possible existence of international agreements applying in the territory of the country considered.

9 A purely liberal strategy: public and private intervention in cultural industries in Japan

Shigeo Minowa

Chief of Academic Services,
The United Nations University,
Tokyo

The concept of cultural industries is not so easy to define. It encompasses such typical mass-communication media as newspapers, radio and television and such sectors of the entertainment industry as motion pictures and gramophone records. Book and magazine publishing may be positioned somewhere in between. The Japanese Government's intervention in cultural industries is active and far-reaching in the mass-communication sector, but is so inconspicuous as to suggest virtual indifference in the entertainment-oriented sectors of motion pictures and records. Thus the Japanese Government has dual objectives when it intervenes in cultural industries. In the first place, it has a cultural nation-oriented aim of promoting cultural industries in general and, secondly, it seeks to achieve the urgent and vital purpose of ensuring unbiased news reporting by mass-communication media.

Governmental intervention is intended in some cases to protect and foster a given cultural industry as a whole, and in others to assist only a specific subsector of an industry. Exemption of publishing from business tax, for instance, belongs to the former, while the subsidy to scientific publications or the exemption of records of children's songs from commodity tax falls under the latter.

Furthermore, it seems possible to classify the purposes of government invention into those constantly continuing over long periods and temporary ones applicable only to specific situations.

The government can choose, out of the means available for achieving one or another of these purposes, what appears to be the most effective in a given situation. The following means of intervention so far used by the Japanese Government, consist of: (a) direct management (sometimes in the form of semi-governmental management); (b) licensing; (c) regulation of activities; (d) subsidization; (e) granting of privileges in taxation and assessment of public-service rates; (f) public spending to buy the products of cultural industries; (g) arrangement of legal environment (including legalization of resale price maintenance and institution of the copyright law); and (h) research and counselling.

The intensity of government intervention can be considered to decrease in the order of this listing. Besides those enumerated above, various quota systems provide powerful means in some countries. The effectiveness of each means in achieving its intended purpose will be analysed below in a comparative way.

DIRECT MANAGEMENT

The state can monopolize a cultural industry by either directly or semi-directly managing it to place it under its immediate control, or have it co-exist with private enterprises to achieve the same purpose while maintaining their mutual competitive stimuli. Examples of this technique include broadcasting in Japan and some other countries, and newspapers in socialist nations. However, such direct government intervention in news reporting by mass-communication media is not only apt to invite criticism from citizens suspecting it of having an adverse effect on the freedom of speech and impartiality, but also of being susceptible to bureaucratic inefficiency and apathy. Some effective mechanism to prevent such shortcomings has to be devised in a systematic and institutional way. In some cases, it may be desirable to start with direct government management until a given cultural industry sufficiently builds up its background and the general public accumulates adequate experience. A typical example of this process can be found in the history of Japan where the government in the early Meiji period undertook extensive translation and publication of Western scientific literature and fully handed these enterprises over to private publishers ten years later. Publication of bulletins by national universities and research institutes, and periodicals and other reference materials by public agencies, may be regarded as constituting a form of direct government management of publishing enterprises (amounting to 3,000 million yen a year). Elementary school textbooks are directly published by the governments of many developing countries.

LICENSING

This is a powerful means of control, next only to direct management. It is feasible and permissible only for broadcasting, which is dependent on finite radio waves, but generally incompatible with other cultural industries. While the government, the licensor, can have a very strong influence where licensing is feasible, the cultural industry will be unable to fulfil its responsibilities to mass news media adequately unless some outside control is exercised on the licensor. In contrast to the United States, where procedures to ensure impartiality, including the disclosure of reasons for licensing any broadcaster, are well established, Japan lacks such a mechanism, the absence of which invites strong dissatisfaction and suspicion from citizens.

REGULATION OF ACTIVITIES

As we saw above, various means have been taken by the government to regulate the activities of the broadcasting industry. What makes this regulation possible is the licensing system, and why it is necessary (for the government) is because broadcasting can be so influential that any bias in information disseminated might endanger sound development of the nation (in the government's opinion).

The same can be said of newspapers and other publications, but there is little possibility, if there is much need, for government intervention because they are less influential than broadcasting and not subject to effective means of regulation such as the licensing system.

The regulation of the content of broadcasting is obviously a double-edged sword. For instance, Japanese television programmes are said to have recently deteriorated in quality because, it is alleged, government intervention with respect to content and pressures from the profit-seeking management of broadcasting companies have discouraged production staffs and driven them into apathy. Certainly, commercial broadcasters' 'logic of capital' which drives them to seek ever higher audience ratings, and through them greater profits, and their self-regulation in order to avoid government intervention, have overwhelmed the opposing forces of programming autonomy abiding by the 'logic of journalism' or the 'logic of culture'. It has to be kept in mind that government regulation of the activities of any cultural industry will always entail this danger.

SUBSIDIZATION

Subsidization is a means of intervention to which the government can deliberately and selectively resort in trying to achieve a specific purpose. If the difficulty that exists and is to be overcome is a purely financial one, subsidization can of course be an effective means. A case in point is the publication of scientific books, which involves no problems either in production technology or marketing system but simply does not pay off. Intervention in the form of subsidization enables the government to discontinue it when the situation which necessitated it has disappeared (more readily than any other form of intervention requiring the amendment or abolition of a law). However, in an organization-minded and pseudo-egalitarian society like that of Japan, subsidization tends to become diffusive in an all-around manner, and each individual subsidy often fails to achieve its intended purpose with reasonable effectiveness. Thus it is difficult to make a break-through by concentrative subsidization. In this context, publication of scientific books may be an area where subsidization can be applied with relative success. In the Federal Republic of Germany, subsidies for scientific publication are not outright grants but have to be partially repaid to the government for each individual project if and when it proves successful and recovers a certain proportion of the invested funds. Such a flexible system can make subsidization of cultural industries more active and penetrating, because cultural projects usually entail considerable uncertainty.

GRANTING OF PRIVILEGES IN TAXATION AND ASSESSMENT
OF PUBLIC-SERVICE RATES

Taxation and assessment of public-service rates are of vital importance to cultural industries. As postage and rail-freight rates are cost items directly passed on to the readers of books, magazines or newspapers, any reduction in them can directly alleviate the financial burdens on the ultimate readers, whose access to such publications would be correspondingly facilitated. In Japan, however, the progress of inflation and, above all, a sharp rise in labour costs in recent years have substantially pushed up postage rates and are thereby severely affecting cultural industries.

Although tax exemption (for instance, commodity tax) and discounting of public-service rates are to be welcomed in principle, one of the difficulties in protecting cultural industries is that selective granting of these privileges is virtually impossible and eventually the good and the bad enjoy equal protection. In the case of books and magazines, for example, vulgar weeklies and comic books are given undeserving assistance, resulting in correspondingly reduced aid to publications that truly deserve and need it. In cultural industries where pluralism of values is a major premise, however, selection based on value judgement is essentially difficult and moreover dangerous, and therefore this indiscriminate granting of privilege perhaps should be accepted as a necessary evil. Similarly, the exemption from income tax, like business tax, can never benefit any enterprise operating at a deficit, in spite of, or rather because of, the culturally valuable character of its business, but it does render additional assistance to those not necessarily engaged in culturally valuable activities but earning substantial profits.

PUBLIC SPENDING TO BUY THE PRODUCTS
OF CULTURAL INDUSTRIES

Government purchases are sometimes effected either in place of or in combination with subsidies to encourage individual projects. They should rather be regarded as disguised subsidies, and are no different from genuine subsidies in their effect, except that they are calculated differently. Apart from these instances, however, the government may fully sponsor a radio or television programme or have a private publisher issue a magazine for its publicity. These are disguised direct presentations by the government. In still other instances, the government may buy existing publications or films for some purpose other than publicity, but the economic effect of these purchases is negligible.

Generally speaking, the government buys the products of cultural industries more often in its own interest than to assist their producers, but its purchases can play a stimulative role.

ARRANGEMENT OF THE LEGAL ENVIRONMENT

It is an important task of the government to see that freedom of speech and the press, and the exercise thereof, be legally guaranteed, to ensure adequate protection of authors' rights over the fruits of their intellectual labour and to exercise legal regulation, as required, to facilitate maintenance of as efficient a distribution system as practicable for the proliferation of the products of each cultural industry in a manner suited to their characteristics. Lacking any one of these environmental arrangements, cultural industries cannot give full rein to their potential. Countries, however, cannot accomplish these tasks in a uniform way because of their differences in political, economic and social circumstances. For instance, socialist countries cannot avoid taking a different stand on the freedom of speech, and there is some conflict of interest regarding copyright as between developing and advanced industrial nations. In Japan, for example, there is as yet little legal control over unauthorized copying with photocopying machines or tape recorders. The lack of legal regulation of photocopying is attributable to insufficient pressures from the publishing industry. Although the government referred the matter to an advisory council in which authors, publishers, libraries and copyright experts were represented, its work made no substantial progress because the publishing industry, which would be the greatest victim of un- authorized copying, remained lukewarm. As no democratic government can propose legislation in disregard of public opinion, there is the danger of regulation lagging behind the prevalence of what has to be regulated. In fact, the absence of legal control over unauthorized copying is undermining the very basis on which the concept of copyright stands.

RESEARCH AND COUNSELLING

The government, as the administrative organ of the state, is in a position to guide and supervise industries. The first step in fulfilling its guiding and supervising responsibilites is to find out how things stand, and hence the need for research by the government. Research findings are analysed and studied by experts and scholars in and out of the government bureaucracy, and translated into desirable policies through discussions by advisory bodies. If these policies are found truly desirable and feasible, counselling and recommendations will be given to industries on this basis.

As far as cultural industries are concerned, the Japanese Government has done relatively little to intervene, partly because of the aversion of Japanese cultural industries to government intervention. Because of their unfortunate experience before and during the Second World War, every cultural industry in Japan has maintained a rigid position in refusing intervention by the government and has remained independent of state finance. Probably no other sector of Japanese industry is so independent of state finance as its cultural sector. Japan's cultural industries have thus been able to keep their immunity from government intervention and are determined to do so in the future as well. Here lies the reason why government intervention, even by such unobtrusive means as research and counselling, is not necessarily well accepted by the cultural industries. The rationalization of physical distribution, for instance, which is undertaken in many sectors under the guidance of the Ministry of International Trade and Industry, is suspected by many publishers as being likely to benefit only big businesses, and accordingly has failed to make much progress in this industry. There is no doubt, however, that research and counselling are practical and effective means of government intervention.

AID TO CULTURAL INDUSTRIES IN THE FRAMEWORK OF CULTURAL AND ECONOMIC DEVELOPMENT POLICIES

The concept of culture is not necessarily uniform worldwide. Accordingly, the different governments cover more or less different scopes with their respective cultural policies. Whereas such fine arts as theatre, music and dance, are commonly included in the realm of culture in most countries, not a few nations also regard newspapers, broadcasting and other areas of mass communication as constituents of culture. An increasing number of national governments are making conservation of cultural assets a priority item in their cultural policies, and in some countries such policies cover their museums, archives, libraries and consequently literature together with publishing. In probably the broadest interpretation of the term, culture further includes sports, tourism, cinema, conservation of natural environment, cooking, weaving and folklore. In extreme instances, even education is considered a part of culture.

Because the concept of culture can cover so broad a spectrum of human activities, governments seem unable to establish a unitary cultural policy encompassing all the areas and spelling out only general principles. Thus they may have to formulate a separate policy or strategy for each individual area of culture.

In Japan, numerous ministries and government agencies have competence in these different areas of culture, instead of an agency or a ministry of cultural affairs being responsible for all of them. The central government body in charge of cultural affairs obviously is the Ministry of Education, with its affiliate body the Cultural Agency, but responsibilities are shared among its many bureaux and divisions, thus making consistent cultural administration difficult.

The presence in Japan of the Cultural Agency, relatively independent of the Ministry of Education, is attributed to the view that, unlike education and science which are basically forward looking, cultural administration primarily concerns preservation of the past and as such differs in task from the ministry proper. Although this view of culture is highly questionable, the agency in reality, reflecting the view which underlay its establishment, is responsible for administration involving the Japanese language, fine arts, copyright, religion and conservation of cultural assets.

The Cultural Agency thus has nothing to do with mass communications, and its intervention in cultural affairs lacks the viewpoint of promoting 'industries'. For instance, the agency grants subsidies to superior motion pictures, but these economic contributions, totalling $400,000 a year, can have no effect in alleviating the critical situation in which the Japanese cinema industry now finds itself. They may help conserve the brilliant tradition of film production in Japan in the way traditional arts and natural monuments are conserved, but they can by no means facilitate the production of motion pictures—which now constitutes an industry and can exist in no other from—as works of culture or sources of amusement. In other words, the Cultural Agency can only intervene in the film industry in a marginal way. It may be out of place to count on the Cultural Agency, primarily founded for conservation of intangible cultural assets including traditional arts, to foster or protect an industry, but motion-picture production as well as the publishing of books or records is a sector of culture that exists in an industrial form, and its true protection and fostering requires government intervention in industrial dimensions. Assistance to cultural industries in such dimensions could also be effective and significant as cultural policy tools, but unfortunately no such cultural policies have ever existed in the history of Japan.

Perhaps it may be more to the point to say that aid to cultural industries has more likely than not to be considered in the framework of economic development policy. As the newspaper, broadcasting and book-publishing industries employ thousands of people each and account for a substantial proportion of the national income, they in themselves constitute major economic forces. Of course, in this respect as well, cultural industries have often been ignored. It is true that these industries, too, have tended to alienate themselves from political power, but the worlds of publishers and broadcasters have had least to do with the national budget, and here lies one of their peculiarities. They have been least adaptable to government intervention.

Notable in this context has been the role of television. In the process of the rapid proliferation of television sets in Japan, there were a number of events which served as spring-boards, such as the wedding of the Crown Prince and the Olympic Games in Tokyo. Sociologists now refer to them as pseudo-events in the sense that they were deliberately planned events. Through the impetus they give to the dissemination of television sets, these events generally stimulate the economic activites of society, including not only the broadcasting and electrical industries but also all other related sectors. This stimulative effect is well recognized by economic circles in Japan, and consequently by the bureaucracy as well as political leaders, so that pseudo-events are devised solely for economic purposes. Thus, rather than enabling cultural industries to facilitate the implementation of economic policies directly, economic and cultural-industry policies are worked out in an integrated way.

Today television has taken over from newspapers and magazines the role of the most powerful tool for stimulating the development of the mass market. Stimulating mass consumption through television results in increased sales by business corporations, which are thereby able to create additional employment opportunities and personal incomes, and this in turn serves to expand the demand. Television is now positioned at a strategic point of this cycle of economic development, though newspapers and magazines continue to play similar roles.

COMPARISON OF PUBLIC AID TO CULTURAL INDUSTRIES
AND THAT GIVEN TO OTHER SECTORS

Out of the $114 billion budget of the Japanese Government for the fiscal year 1977, subsidies accounted for $38.4 billion or 33.6 per cent. In the implementation of present-day economic policies which govern what is dubbed as a controlled society, subsidies play an important role, and the whole national economy is affected to a considerable extent by subsidization policies. Many industries now depend heavily on the fiscal policy of the government for their prosperity. However, cultural industries are least influenced by subsidization, presumably because:

First, people engaged in cultural industries, which indispensably require freedom of speech for their very survival, have a strong spirit of independence and reject outside interference. They think that in order to maintain their independence from the government it would be dangerous to rely on its economic assistance. At least they have no intention of actively seeking government aid. This trend is particularly conspicuous among publishers of books and periodicals.

Secondly, from the viewpoint of the government, cultural industries generally pose no urgent need for assistance. Since the government is constantly called on to meet more urgent needs such as those for national security, a steady food supply and economic development, aiding cultural industries has ranked low on its priority list. This basic stand of the government has not changed even today when Japan is being called on to shift the basis of its national identity to culture and to promote cultural industries in a broader sense of the term.

Thirdly, public aid to cultural industries also involves technical difficulties. Promotion of these industries is not just a matter of quantity but always entails qualitative judgement, which poses an extremely difficult problem to administrators. Granting interest-differential subsidies to help finance shipbuilding does involve complex control of the qualities of the ships so built, but these qualities can somehow be objectively evaluated. In contrast, supposing similar interest subsidies were to be applied to publishers' inventories of scientific publications, objective assessment of their qualities would be practically impossible.

CONSTRAINTS ON GOVERNMENT INTERVENTION

Government intervention in cultural industries is obviously subject to various constraints. Thus the government intervenes in cultural industries against the counterbalancing forces of these constraints but not in a vacuum. The constraints may be considered in the following three aspects.

Public acceptance

Public criticism of the financial aspect of government intervention in cultural industries has been generally weak in Japan. The government has been criticized for not being generous enough in subsidization, but not for being inappropriate, unreasonable or unfair in its granting of subsidies, because its economic contributions to cultural industries have been quite modest and have never exerted any appreciable psychological impact on the general public. Thus there is no room for the public to feel that an unduly large proportion of state expenditure is appropriated for subsidizing cultural industries at the sacrifice of more urgent needs (because the total of such subsidies is so small).

However, government intervention in non-fiscal aspects usually meets strong resistance from the general public and from industry. Citizens are highly sensitive to, for instance, the action of the government to license radio or television broadcasters or to control the activities of already licensed broadcasters. Efforts are required on the part of the government to win more willing public acceptance of its action by holding public hearings on the choice of licensees or setting up a screening committee in which citizens' views can be well reflected, to cite but a few conceivable examples.

On the other hand, where there is a major conflict of interest between different sectors of the public (publishers versus libraries and so on), as in the case of unauthorized copying of books or records, the government will have a hard time trying to win the gratest possible support from the greatest possible segment of the country.

Financial resources and order of priority

Government assistance to cultural industries outlined above, including both active subsidies and exemption from, or alleviation of, financial burdens, are estimated to account for 0.1 to 0.2 per cent of the total annual expenditure of the state.

Public spending in cultural undertakings other than those by cultural industries, even including the whole expenditure of the Cultural Agency, total only 0.1 per cent of Japan's $137.2 billion yearly budget. As already pointed out, culture has been particularly neglected by the administrators of Japan, which undeservingly reidentified itself as a cultural nation after its defeat in the Second World War. It is therefore theoretically possible to expand substantially the financial resources available for subsidization of culture by only slightly modifying the budgeting policy of the state; but in reality the government, suffering from enormous deficits, would sacrifice first of all the realm of culture, which is a marginal area where effective pressure groups are absent. For instance, a general consumption tax, whose introduction is now suggested, would cancel the discount of the admission tax on cinema audiences, which currently has an effect virtually equal to outright exemption, and the motion-picture industry accordingly is strongly opposing its imposition.

International agreements

Some international agreements inevitably limit government intervention in cultural industries. For example, the international allocation of radio channels physically restricts broadcasting licences that can be issued to radio or television stations in any given country. Fortunately Japan enjoys the vested rights of an advanced nation in this respect, but many developing countries are unequally restricted, unavoidably resulting in greater constraints on their domestic broadcasting administration. Liberalization of capital transactions typically affects the gramophone-record industry. The language barrier in Japan protects its publishing industry from being severely affected by competition from abroad, which often impedes the development of the local publishing industry in developing countries. A notable example of the protection of local publishers was the Japanese provision for a ten-year reservation of translation rights.

PURPOSES AND METHODS OF PHILANTHROPY

The large number of philanthropic foundations and funds that existed in pre-war Japan were reduced to naught by the inflation which followed the Second World War. Although the nation was too much preoccupied with economic reconstruction for such foundations to find any opportunity for revival during the first two decades of post-war Japan, moves for their reinstatement have finally begun over the last ten years or so. As industrial corporations which achieved tremendous growths came to be criticized by the general public for the environmental pollution and destruction they caused, they have increasingly set up philanthropic foundations with an eye to improving their own public image or that of the industry to which they belong and to channeling the back-flow of their profits to society at large. However, philanthropy in Japan is still on the whole underdeveloped, and its overall financial resources are far smaller than those in other major advanced countries. This situation stems from the centralization philosophy of the national government, which prefers to absorb as much of personal and corporate incomes as possible and redistribute it through the state fiscal system to what the government regards as deserving undertakings.

Although activities by these foundations cover a wide range of fields including science, education, culture and conservation of the natural environment, each individual foundation usually limits itself to a narrowly defined scope or a few strategic themes with a view to preventing the diffusion of funds and instead achieving a concentrative effect. A typical example of this policy is the concentration of the Toyota Foundation on traffic safety as one of the pillars of its activities.

These foundations mostly operate through the granting of subsidies but are rarely engaged in active projects of their own. Although there are many foundations which do undertake research activities or specific projects of their own, the present review will be restricted to philanthropic foundations.

These philanthropic organizations are managed by experts in the operation of foundations, but they are limited by the lack of tradition in Japan, and accordingly the accumulation of their own experience and transfers of similar experience from other advanced nations are hoped for.

Although these foundations can exert effective influences on one specific field or another through their activities, their overall impact on Japanese cultural industries seems to be still very small. One of the notable examples of their activities is the 'Know Your Neighbours' project of the Toyota Foundation, under which translation into Japanese of literary or scientific works from other Asian countries is subsidized to facilitate publication (in Japanese) of works so far virtually unknown in Japan.

10 A model devised for a mixed economy: the Société Québécoise de Développement des Industries Culturelles

Guy Morin

Managing Director

THE SITUATION IN QUEBEC

In Quebec the thought devoted to culture and to the means of ensuring its development and full flowering has led the government to take action, having regard to the present precarious situation of the cultural industries, whether radio, television, the press, publishing, gramophone records, the performing arts or handicrafts, all of which draw on substantial financial and human resources. Given their repercussions for the cultural life of society, the state cannot abandon them simply to all and sundry. The government has moreover already observed that these sectors of activity occupy a marginal position in the interests of Quebec, with the result that these industries are unable to fulfil their role adequately in supporting and disseminating the products of cultural creation.

It has therefore been necessary for the legislative authorities to take action, in order to provide specially favourable conditions for both the production and the dissemination of Quebec's cultural works, while continuing to guarantee access by the people of Quebec to foreign cultural production as before.

Taking into account the stance adopted by the government on this matter, and also the fact that the inquiry into the various functions of cultural industries has already resulted in a number of papers, and that speakers will be adding further material, we have considered it preferable to devote this text to the Société de Développement des Industries Culturelles, which had been created by the government very recently in order to provide these industries with a place and role that will match the aspirations and needs of Quebecers.

Obviously there is no seeking after complete self-sufficiency (which would in any case be most undesirable), nor is there any question of passively accepting dependence on external cultural contributions (which, to a certain extent, encourage creativity). Rather than retreat into futile and apathetic isolation, it was considered preferable to rely on the initiative and determination of the people of Quebec.

Briefly, what is at stake is to acquire a mastery of the major instruments of cultural expression and to establish, in so far as is possible, 'ground rules' that will be suited on the one hand to the North American context and, on the other, to French-speaking Quebec.

The government's attitude has been dictated by considerations of two kinds: those that are actually inherent in the situation of firms in the cultural industry sector, and those which result from Quebec's geopolitical situations.

The fact is that weaknesses specific to Quebec's cultural industries prevent firms from developing, thus making them vulnerable to concerted attacks by foreign companies. With the exception of the book sector, most of the firms engaged in cultural production have been established only recently, and are small in scale and poorly structured from the administrative and financial point of view. It is precisely the internal integration of the various functions that constitutes the strength of foreign companies, and organizations of this kind in Quebec are few and far between. In addition, Quebec interests are under-represented in the distribution networks for records, films and, to a lesser but still considerable degree, books and periodicals.

Thus when things take the slightest turn for the worse, Quebec firms find themselves in situations that are sometimes fraught with danger, and inevitably exploited by foreign investors, as is only to be expected given the market economy system.

Quebec covers a very large geographical area, but its primary market is nevertheless restricted to its 6 million French-speaking inhabitants. If in addition we take into account the neighbouring 'catchment area' of 250 million inhabitants, with a different language and different values, we can gauge the scope of the challenge in Quebec, particularly since the other culture and language, copiously transmitted by both electronic and printed media, exercise a great attraction in Quebec, thus proving McLuhan's dictum that the media and the message are practically indistinguishable. Further, the history of Quebec links it culturally to French culture, which also inevitably exerts its influence through its own cultural industries. In addition to these historical, geographical and demographic features, there are several other problems arising from the behaviour and advantageous situation of the immense cultural industry of the foreign neighbour.

Thus in the field not only of the cinema, but also of gramophone records and books, foreign investment is to be found everywhere, above all in the distribution sector, which proves to be outstandingly profitable, precisely for the reason that Quebec frequently provides a natural extension of the foreign firms' domestic market.

Having regard on the one hand to the restricted size of their market of 6 million consumers, the difficulties encountered by firms hampered financially and administratively in penetrating foreign markets, the fears that local interests in Quebec's cultural industries were being undermined, and the widespread weaknesses of Quebec firms; and, on the other, to the fact that foreign firms were already established and had taken firm root on its soil, Quebec took steps to create the Société Québécoise de Développement des Industries Culturelles in the autumn of 1978.

The situation described above called for early action by the Quebec Government, which in creating this body wished to associate itself with the private sector in order to preserve Quebec culture from being developed through foreign networks which were likely, sooner or later, to replace Quebec's cultural production by foreign products transmitting entirely different values and experiences.

Realization of this situation of virtual underdevelopment inevitably led to consideration of the complementary functions to which the government should direct its efforts.

In the first place, there were a number of firms capable of playing a more extensive role: these were well structured, but frequently too small to raise the resources required for their expansion, since traditional financial bodies were reluctant to take risks for the kind of products that depend on the creative artist's talents. In addition, there was the need to reconquer markets controlled by other interests; in other words, a change was necessary, not in the 'ground rules', but actually in the ownership of the firms that frequently dominated the markets. This aim, which required much greater capital, called for a structure on the lines of a 'tourist development agency'.

In the light of these considerations, two courses of action were open to the government: (a) to establish two state enterprises, one responsible for promoting a more traditional kind of development and dealing mainly with existing firms or with the setting up of new ones having the same aims, and the other a 'development agency' dealing mainly with cultural industry as a whole; or (b) to set up a single enterprise, which would perform both functions.

The government chose to set up a single enterprise. This solution avoided a proliferation of government institutions, and above all enabled the government to demonstrate its resolve to work with the firms in Quebec which have efficiently fulfilled their role in their own sphere, which are capable of expansion beyond that sphere, in association with a partner having the necessary financial resources, and which are the obvious choice for taking these economic sectors of cultural activity in hand.

As the corner-stone of a policy for expanding cultural industries, this body was intended to help to reduce the number of government agencies involved, channel financial resource, avoid costly duplication, simplify the relations between 'cultural entrepreneurs' and the government, and make them more efficient. By entrusting the implementation of its policy for providing finance and investment for cultural industries to a single supervisory body of a quasi-public nature, the government avoided imposing too heavy an administrative burden on cultural industries, and associated itself in the simplest possible way with the expectations of those representing the cultural sector.

The fact was that, over a number of years, this sector had repeatedly called on the government, either the present one or its predecessors, to submit legislation to the National Assembly for the establishment of a financial body that would provide support for the development of cultural industries. It was however necessary to hold comprehensive consultations at all levels concerned before deciding on the choice of a satisfactory formula.

As soon as it was established, the Société Québécoise proceeded to develop the tools for its work, in particular by adopting its own regulations and financial policy. In addition, a number of measures have already been defined with a view to meeting the wishes of the cultural sectors.

ACTION PLAN

The plan for development and action drawn up by the Société Québécoise sets forth both the approach it has adopted to the problem in terms of the context in which Quebec's cultural industries operate, and the programmes of support for development and the promotional action it will have to carry out, either by means of a partnership arrangement or as a supervisory body.

This action programme has been prepared in close co-operation with the heads of firms in the various sectors, and reflects their expectations. It is not a statement of government policy, but a document actually produced by the firms concerned. Before drafting the bill constituting the society, the government brought together the leaders of the various industrial sectors, who put forward their recommendations, taking account naturally of the difficulties they encountered in their work and the kind of association with the government which they wished to see introduced by means of the Société Québécoise.

Following the constitution of this quasi-public body, representatives of the different private firms were consulted again by the society before it established its programme of specific activities to be carried out. Lastly, it was necessary for the programme to be approved by the government before the start of work; it is vital, in fact, for the government to bring the forms of assistance it provides to the cultural sector into line with one another, whether these are subventions through its ministries or financing by the Société Québécoise itself.

STRATEGY

Thus legislation, regulations and financial policy have now resulted in a plan, but in order to carry it out as successfully as possible and further its aims to the maximum, the society intends to emphasize that part of its strategy concerned with methods of finance, whatever their nature. On the basis of both the deficiencies felt by the cultural sector and the methods used by multinational corporations established in the territory of Quebec, the society has identified a number of common features, specific to these foreign firms, which can be summed up in the main as their administrative pattern on the one hand, and on the other, operations that have a multiplier effect. The following features will accordingly be an integral part of its strategy:

Support for the amalgamation and consolidation of small firms that prove they have an appreciable 'profitability' potential, either culturally or financially speaking.

An effort to find ways of integrating firms that are capable of bringing together all the functions of a sector under the same roof, and of maximizing the use of their financial and human resources.

The drawing up for firms of promotion and advertising programmes adapted to
    marketing techniques.
Encouragement of exports by means of an agency that will act as a channel for
    cultural firms' products.
The search for concepts that will promote new products.

ACTION

As an example of the work which the Société Québécoise will perform in
connection with the two functions described above, we may mention the following
activities.

As a development agent, it will deal with all applications from firms wishing
to increase their capacity. It is not difficult to see what this role involves, and the
society's methods of action have already been outlined.

The second aspect of its functions, that of a 'cultural development agency',
is of much greater importance, since here the society plans to come to grips with
the major problems encountered by the people of Quebec, in order to help them
both to acquire control of the ownership of the means of production and
distribution of cultural goods and to fulfil a role commensurate with their capacity
in the key sectors for the future. The society's philosophy is thus to give priority
to action that is likely to have the maximum possible impact on the sphere
concerned, and the most substantial effects in stimulating the growth of the
economy. In this respect, the society may even, when necessary, fulfil a co-
ordinating role. In the book sector, for example, the society might foster the
establishment of better basic services so as to enable publishers or booksellers to
meet specific needs satisfactorily from the operational point of view. As regards
gramophone records, it is prepared to study the desirability of support for the
grouping of independent dealers. Its programme also envisages the creation of an
integrated production, distribution and sales centre. As regards handicrafts,
Quebec is in a somewhat special situation, since supply falls short of demand.
Accordingly, any applicant wishing to increase his turnover will have his
application approved by the Société Québécoise, provided naturally that he
complies with its administrative and financial requirements. Lastly, as regards the
video-recording field and audio-visual media in general, which have been barely
mentioned so far, it should be noted that the Société Québécoise is paying special
attention to this rapidly expanding key sector. Using the means already available
to it and with assistance from the ministries concerned, it will arrange for the
necessary research to be carried out in order to ensure that Quebec will not find
itself in a few year's time in a situation in these fields similar to that now experienced, for example, by the book and record industries.

This is not an exhaustive list of the society's activities: these examples are
intended merely to show the practical forms that its action will take, in constant
co-operation with cultural enterprise in the private sector.

11   The book industry in a small industrial country: Israel

Ari Avnerre

Member of the Israel Book Council,
Israel National Commission for Unesco

Whether original or translated, with well over a thousand titles per million inhabitants, Israel is among the most prolific book producers in the world. An American trade journal recently quoted much lower figures for Western Europe (558 per million) the USSR (310 per million) and North America (310 per million) computed from Unesco statistics.[1] More detailed comparisons attempted elsewhere[2] find only a few Western European countries exceeding Israel in this respect (according to one calculation, Denmark and Switzerland; according to another, the Netherlands and Sweden). Over the decade ending 1976/77, the number of titles grew 1.65 times and reached 3,760 a year. The number of first editions and re-editions grew at the same time 1.46 times and reached 1,926 a year. With minor fluctuations, too small to warrant interpretation, the picture is one of steady growth.[3] The average number of copies per title also rose from 2,700 in 1969/70 and 1970/71[4] to 3,500 in 1975/76 and 1976/77.[5] No later statistics are available for the entire industry, but interviews by the author with individual leading publishers and with officials of the Publishers Association—as well as some newspaper reports—suggest that the pace has not slackened.

Almost 60 per cent of all books published in 1976/77 were first editions or re-editions. Comparison with the previous year shows a 16 per cent rise in the number of titles of this type and 5 per cent in the number of reprints.[6] The percentage of reprints is especially high in school textbooks (61.7 per cent) and much lower in literature (31.8 per cent). Of all titles published, literature represents the largest single class (20.5 per cent), and the same is true if first editions and re-editions only are taken into account (23.7 per cent). In terms of the number of copies printed, pride of place goes to school textbooks (24.2 per cent), with 4,900 copies per average title (for literature the average is 3,100; for children's literature—4,500.[7]

The latest statistics available for periodicals are for 1978.[8] And while the polyglot antecedents of the population hardly show in the language of book publication (in 1976/77, 86.7 per cent of all first-edition and re-edition titles were in Hebrew),[9] with imports adequately satisfying the needs of foreign-language readers, periodicals offer a different picture. About half the daily newspapers published in Israel are in languages other than Hebrew: in 1978, 13 out of 27. This by no means represents readership (see below) but that is another story. Of the 679 non-daily periodicals 433 (or 63.8 per cent) are in Hebrew and 246 (32.2 per cent) in other languages. English, with 78 non-daily periodicals, is the most heavily represented single foreign language. This is not a function of massive immigration from English-speaking countries (in fact such immigration has always been numerically small) but is due to a different reason altogether: 583 periodicals are professional, and because of close ties with the Western world there seems to be a predilection for the language often presumed to have attained the status of an unofficial lingua franca in that world. Though 96 of Israel's non-daily periodicals are classified as dealing in 'actualia', few of them are socially significant. As for frequency of publication, 13.6 per cent of all periodicals appear more than once a month; 30.7 per cent five to twelve times a year; 27.3 per cent twice to four times a year; 13.5 per cent are annual, and the rest irregular. Comparing these 1978 figures with the situation two years previously, one finds stability in the number of dailies and, more or less, in the number of weeklies and fortnightlies, and an increase in all other types (except irregular publications, the number of which was almost halved). Among the 583 specialized (professional) periodicals, the most heavily represented subjects are economics (10.3 per cent), the social sciences (8.9 per cent), the humanities (8.7 per cent), law, the army and public administration (7.4 per cent) and Judaism and other religions (7.2 per cent).[10]

Unfortunately, precise figures on the number of copies printed by each periodical (especially by dailies) are jealously guarded secrets in Israel, but an estimate made about a decade ago puts the number of copies of dailies per thousand inhabitants at 208 (similar to the ratio in Canada),[11] though this figure seems too low to most experts.

As mentioned before, both evening dailies *Maariv* and *Yedioth Aharonoth* enjoy a wide circulation. Together they have a circulation close to 400,000, probably more or less evenly divided between the two, with each quoting readership surveys (not, one must add, audited circulation data) to prove it is ahead of its competitor. The most widely circulated morning paper, *Haaretz,* is estimated to be printing under 50,000 copies. The next in line, *Davar,* about 20,000 less than that, and there is some red ink on its balance sheet. The other papers (nine in Hebrew, four in Arabic and nine in other languages) fare worse, though some of them may do better financially than others because of less pretentious operations, or for other reasons (six non-Hebrew dailies are published by one syndicate, controlled by the Labour Party). Circulation of all papers is higher at week-ends, with their supplement magazines largely taking the place of weeklies.

The daily press has joined forces with the Israel Broadcasting Authority to maintain an associated national press agency, Itim (acronym of the Hebrew words meaning United Israel Press). This agency also jointly distributes copy from most major foreign news-agencies, in the original languages or in Hebrew translation, or both, as required. Three-quarters of its budget is covered, rather inequitably, by members' fees, with the Israel Broadcasting Authority paying more than two-fifths, and the widely circulated evening papers each paying less than twice the sum levied from *Davar,* etc. The rest of the budget is financed by distribution fees for disseminating non-commercial press releases of the government press office and other public bodies (distinctly so marked on the copy emerging from the agency's tickers), as well as stock-exchange information and the like. It is a measure of the partisan political traditions of the Israeli press, that papers do not want the agency to cover some party-political sensitive areas, such as parliamentary debates: each paper wants to see such events through its own eyes.[12]

Vehement political criticism and hard-hitting investigative reporting have made the Israeli press feared, sometimes viewed with respect and sometimes with exasperated rage, by the country's politicians. Libel laws involve complex litigation, and are therefore not widely used in attempts to overcome hostile criticism. There is however a very active Press Council (its first president was a retired chief justice) adjudicating complaints and, where it sees fit, offering remedy by publication (obligatory for offending members) of its findings. Because of a permanent warlike situation, intermittently breaking out into hostilities, there is censorship on national-security information, but a joint committee including the Daily Newspapers' Editors Committee representative adjudicates disputes and ensures that such censorship is not used for political ends.[13]

Israel's publishing industry serves a wide reading public. 1979 statistics[14] show 52.8 per cent of adults (aged 14 and over) in the Jewish population to be reading at least one book a month, with 45.3 of them reading three books or more a month, and with a fifth of the readership reading five books or more. Comparing these figures with data from two previous years (1969 and 1975/76) shows current rates to be slightly higher than a decade ago (50.7 per cent) with an intervening decline a few years ago (45.1 per cent for 1975/76), possibly because of the initial impact of television (introduced in 1969). Significantly, the most avid readers (five or more books a month) were not affected by the temporary decline, and their numbers have been growing steadily (7.1 per cent of the adult population in 1969, 8.1 per cent in 1975/76 and 10.5 per cent in 1979).

In the early 1970s, Elibu Katz and Michael Gurevitch[15] attempted a comparison of reading rates in Israel and Western Europe. Their figures for Israel are slightly lower than the above-mentioned findings of the Central Bureau of Statistics (42 per cent of the adult population reading 'more than eight books a year' versus the Bureau's 45.1 per cent reading 'at least one book a month' in 1975/76); but since Katz and Gurevitch only surveyed 18-year-olds and above, as against 14-year-olds and above in the bureau's sample, the figures may not be comparable. With compulsory education, the 7 per cent illiterates in the Jewish population of Israel are mostly to be found in the higher age-groups; in addition, reading rates among the 9–13 age-groups have been found to be very high (almost 90 per cent 'at least one book a month' readers;[16] see below), and thus the 14–18 age-groups probably also have a higher reading rate than older people, and their inclusion in the bureau's sample may tend to increase the total number of regular readers. In any case, Katz and Gurevitch conclude that while Israel has a higher readership percentage (reading 'at least one book a year') than any Western European country (77 per cent of the adult population, as against 69 per cent in Switzerland, the second highest rate), and the same holds true for the percentage of the population reading regularly more than eight books a year (42 per cent for Israel as against 39 per cent for the United Kingdom and Denmark, the second highest figure), the percentage of regular readers (more than eight books a year) among the general readership (more than one a year) is lower than in some Western European countries (the United Kingdom, 61 per cent; France, 59 per cent; Denmark, 58 per cent; Israel, 55 per cent; the rest have lower rates). They also note especially high reading rates among Israelis of low and medium education, and assume that this is due to traditional Jewish values emphasizing the paramount importance of learning.

As for contents of reading, respondents reading at least one book a month in 1979 reported having read,[17] in descending order: novels and plays (68.8 per cent); detective literature, thrillers and science-fiction (28 per cent); journalistic literature and biographies (16.3 per cent); general non-fiction (15.5 per cent); religious literature (7.6 per cent); poetry (3.9 per cent); and other categories (2 per cent combined). Using different methods and classifications, in the early 1970s, Katz and Gurevitch[18] arrived at a slightly different order, putting detective stories below journalistic literature. They also make the useful observation that many readers of professional and religious literature may not have classified this activity as reading but rather as study. This may also explain the difference between the percentage of religious books published[19] (15.7 per cent of all titles in 1976/77, 16.3 per cent of first-edition and re-edition titles, 13.1 per cent of all copies) and read (7.6 per cent for 1974). Interestingly, Katz and Gurevitch also note, that while reading of most kinds increases with education, the peak for reading religious literature is found among those with partial higher education; unsurprisingly 'sex and suspense' (a category—different from 'detective literature'—absent in the Central Bureau of Statistics surveys) reading is higher among less-educated people. In addition they find that women tend to read much more fiction, plays and poetry while men have the edge in professional literature, general non-fiction and religious literature.

It is a measure of cultural integration, that 77.3 per cent of all readers in 1979[20] read Hebrew books (62.1 per cent Hebrew only, and 15.2 per cent both Hebrew and other languages). Using a different criterion ('the language of the last book read'), and excluding younger age groups (14–18) from their survey, Katz and Gurevitch[21] found 69 per cent of readers to have had last read a Hebrew book. They also found English to be the most widely read foreign language (7 per cent—'last book read', and 25 per cent of readers reporting reading books in English in general). Though relatively large numbers reported reading books in languages other than Hebrew (besides English, 14 per cent each for French, German, Russian and other Slavonic languages; 13 per cent Yiddish; 8 per cent Romanian; 4 per cent each for Spanish and Italian; this was before immigration from the USSR reached its peak), the authors conclude: 'It seems that—as opposed to the image of pluralistic multilinguality current in Israel's society—the trend is toward linguistic homogeneity in reading.'

The authors also examined the significance of the differences between Jews of European/American and Afro-Asian origin as a factor in reading, concluding that:

The findings . . . show, that there are indeed no considerable differences in the amount of reading between readers of different origin. . . . Possibly such differences [as do exist, favouring those of European origin] between respondents of different ethnic origins may be ascribed to differences in parents' level of education. *Second generation [Israelis] with . . . more than 11 years of schooling, of all ethnic groups, read more than the immigrant generation of the same origin.*[22]

This has an additional significance, since at the time, before large-scale immigration from the USSR tipped the scales, 'Afro-Asian origin' was largely synonymous with recent immigration.

To turn from books to newspapers, 83 per cent of the Jewish population in 1979[23] read newspapers at least once a week. The overwhelming majority (69.8 per cent of the population or 84.1 per cent of newspaper readers) read an evening (Hebrew) newspaper, fewer (27.2 per cent and 32.8 per cent respectively) a Hebrew morning paper; still fewer (15.9 per cent and 18.2 per cent respectively) a non-Hebrew morning paper. A vast majority of the readers of any given type of paper read it regularly, i.e. more than four times a week (68.4 per cent for evening papers. 67.7 per cent for morning papers in Hebrew and 60.4 per cent for morning papers in other languages). This should offer a picture of 55–60 per cent of the adult population reading their paper every day.

In the early 1970s Katz Gurevitch[24] arrived at a much higher figure (77 per cent), incompatible with either the latest or previous figures given by the Bureau of Statistics,[25] since they show readership to have risen since 1969, not the other way round. If, here again, the discrepancy is to be ascribed to the exclusion of 14–18-year-olds from the Katz and Gurevitch survey, one must arrive at the conclusion that younger people tend to read more books and fewer newspapers. And if a recent study conducted among students in California[26] is right in concluding that 'age 18 may be the milestone after which the likelihood of begining a newspaper reading habit is greatly reduced,[27] an ominous caveat should here be audible to the press. Especially so, since the California survey also shows the habit to be 'hereditary'.[28] Things, however, may not be so bad after all, since the teenagers of the early 1970s are adults by now, and as readership has risen, not fallen, they must have acquired the newspaper-reading habit in subsequent years.

Comparison over the years tends to show,[29] that the overall rise in total newspaper readership in the last decade betrays a picture of decline under the initial impact of television, followed by a recovery: 79.6 per cent in 1969, 78 per cent in 1975/76 and 83 per cent in 1979. Broken down by type of newspaper, the evening papers seem not to have been affected all that much and endured a deceleration of rise where other papers experienced a real decline: 60 per cent read them (at least once a week) in 1969, 62.3 per cent in 1975/76, and 69.8 per cent in 1979, while the figures for Hebrew morning papers are 31.6, 25.3 and 27.2 per cent respectively, and for newspapers in other languages 22.7, 17 and 15.9 per cent respectively. The steady decline in reading non-Hebrew papers may also add proof to the above-mentioned trend toward 'linguistic homogeneity' in reading.

Apart from the already-mentioned trend away from party-political affiliation of the press, two other characteristics of the tastes of readers should be noted here, both in negative terms. While at least eight party-politically affiliated Hebrew newspapers have ceased publication over the last forty years or so,[30] infant mortality among local ('home town') newspapers has been total. The only non-national newspapers now in existence are throw-away advertising sheets. The entire daily press in Hebrew is now based in Tel Aviv, though some papers feature regional supplements. The reasons for this phenomenon may be the heavy concentration of the population in and around the Tel Aviv megalopolitan area as well as the fact that a large proportion of the population is composed of relatively recent arrivals, with the small size of both country and population as a contributing factor. Another feature is the non-existence of a true tabloid, as known elsewhere (one attempt was made, but proved abortive).[31] Both evening papers, though in many ways 'lighter' than the morning papers, are closer to what is known as 'quality' papers in the West, and one of them—the lighter of the two to boot—sports the most highbrow literary supplement in the business.

Non-daily periodicals are less widely read in Israel than elsewhere. In 1979[32] 42.7 per cent of the adult population read at least one periodical published in Israel in a month (excluding professional periodicals and weekly supplements to daily newspapers) while 15.3 per cent read such periodicals published abroad. Scarcity of 'general interest' periodicals, the function similar to that of periodicals performed by week-end supplements to the dailies, the relative popularity of foreign periodicals, as well as the short week-end in a country at work six days a week have all been advanced as explanations of this fact.[33]

One final remark on reading habits concerns the impact of the introduction of television (in 1969). As we have seen from the figures concerning the reading of books and newspapers alike, there was an initial slackening followed by recovery and upsurge once the novelty of the visual medium wore off (interestingly, without a corresponding decline in television audiences). The already extensively quoted study by Katz and Gurevitch is of especial interest here, since the field-work was conducted almost at the time of initial impact. Even then the authors reported[34] the decline in radio listening and some social activities to be much more pronounced than the decline in time spent reading books or newspapers. Even so, the effect was slightest at both ends of the educational spectrum, and the sale and readership of books serialized on television actually shot up. Attempting to arrive at a computation of substitutability of means of communication, the authors conclude[35] that, from the point of view of gratifying specific needs, books are lowest in substitutability by the electronic mass media, and newspapers tend to be more substitutable by radio than by television. Later on, in 1979, Professor Katz concluded[36] that newspapers still had the edge as 'the main source of political information' while books are not superseded by television 'in the minds of the audience' in terms of its functions for 'learning, for self improvement, even for aesthetic experience'. He tentatively suggests a possible decline in the reading of fiction, but statistical data do not seem to support such an hypothesis. Television did inflict a severe, and perhaps irreversible, blow on the cinema,[37] the theatre was somewhat affected, but probably not live light entertainment.

To serve the needs of the expanding readership, a large number of publishers operate in Israel. 'Too many', according to the managing director of one large firm.[38] At first sight the number does look staggering, both for the size of the country and the numbers of books published: The Central Bureau of Statistics lists 250 publishers for 1976/77,[39] slightly fewer than in preceding years (278 for 1974/75 and 261 for 1975/76: the membership list of the Publishers Association[40] for August 1979 lists 78; a trade directory[41] lists 150 (after mentioning a lower figure in its own introduction). But all these figures are deceptive: 160 'publishers'[42] (64 per cent are listed in the '0–9 books a year' class, and were jointly responsible for 5.5 per cent of the titles published (3 per cent of the reprints and 7.4 per cent first edition and re-editions); at the other end of the spectrum, seven (!) publishers (2.8 per cent) jointly put on the market almost a quarter (22.8 per cent) of all titles published, having printed more than 100 titles each in that year; using a slightly more generous criterion—publication of more than fifty titles a year—we find twenty-one publishers (8.4 per cent) responsible for 54.9 per cent of all titles. In all, ninety publishers (36 per cent) were active enough to have more than ten titles published in 1976/77, putting out between them almost all the books in the market (94.5 per cent). Incomplete data for subsequent years show the tendency of concentration to be unabated.[43]

Apart from relatively high concentration, another prominent feature of the publishing industry in Israel is widespread public ownership of publishing houses. To a certain extent this is in accord with the general structure of the country's mixed economy, where the General Federation of Labour (Histadruth) also controls, directly or indirectly, a large part of manufacturing. But there are also other reasons for it. Historically, the Zionist movement and all its major components, such as political parties, have made it their business to shoulder the burden of the cultural renascence of the Jewish people, and went into publishing in order to accomplish it. Thus the Histadruth publishing house is probably the largest firm (by number of titles) in the country.[44] Kibbutz movements maintain two flourishing publishing houses,[45] each having become, in its turn, the *cunabula gentis* of the modern literature of the day, especially poetry. The World Zionist Organization maintains several publishing houses, one of them highly prestigious as a publisher of classics and encyclopedias,[46] and another very prominent in religious publishing.[47] Improbably, the Publishers' Association itself,[48] besides dealing with such mundane matters as getting paper at a discount for members and organizing book fairs, competes with its own members, as it were, in maintaining two publishing houses to turn out textbooks and publicly subsidized books.[49] To this one must add the multifarious publishing activities of the government itself, by no means confined to production of official documents. In particular, the Ministry of Defence publishes numerous books in various fields, in fact anything that may be of service, not merely in improving soldiers' professional qualifications but generally educating or even entertaining them (including a paperback series of reprinted classics and old favourites). Universities, learned societies, the Academy of Sciences, the Academy of the Hebrew Language, the Writers' Association, etc., are all active in the field of publishing and some of their lists are very impressive and rich.[50] A prominent publishing house holding rights to many modern Hebrew classics (including Bialik, who was a director),[51] though ostensibly private, operates as a self-styled non-profit national trust.[52]

All this does not mean that commercial publishing proper either does not exist or is unimportant. On the contrary, the largest privately owned publishing house, operating as several interlocked companies,[53] is also the largest publishing house in terms of cash turnover (probably second largest in the number of titles)[54] and is, among other things, publisher of the *Hebrew Encyclopaedia* as well as a host of reference works, and also specializes in books for children. A fairly recent venture (1973) jointly embarked upon by three publishers has been a spectacular success,[55] publishing many foreign modern classics in translation. Two veteran publishing houses hailing from pre-war Berlin are still going strong,[56] one of them—with a sister enterprise in New York—controlling rights for both Franz Kafka and S. Y. Agnon.[57] A firm started under government auspices[58] to publish science translations (see above) was eventually transferred to a private company, published the *Encyclopaedia Judaica* and branched out into divers fields, from university textbooks to children's literature. A businessman-turned-publisher published numerous titles of light reading, including many translated best-sellers.[59]

Another feature of publishing in Israel is the active part played by newspapers, with their built-in distribution facilities, in the publication of books, including—apart from 'natural' items, such as journalistic-political literature— almost anything, from cookery books to novels, albums and reference works. Newspapers either have their own publishing firms,[60] or are in partnership with others,[61] or publish and distribute books by arrangement with publishing houses, sometimes ordering a special edition for their readers.

Thus an author whose books have been established as commercial successes is unlikely to have much trouble finding a publisher; the prevalence of publicly owned non-profit firms, as well as prestige considerations of the wealthier private ones, more or less assure as much to an author, or work, of proven merit. But no more than 'more or less': even publicly owned publishers' purses are never deep enough to publish at a heavy loss. Moreover, young authors, whose books have neither proven market value nor proven merit, face a hard uphill climb. For some kinds of book, subsidies may be available: there is a special fund, in the Ministry of Education and Culture, for financing translations of classics; many authors have been helped by the Tel Aviv Foundation for the Arts; the Writers Union subsidizes some books; various public institutions may finance research in their fields of activity; the literature branch of the Culture and Arts Council has embarked on certain projects (such as financing books for children written by well-known authors of general fiction), and this list is very far from exhausted. The most heinous form of subsidy is, however 'subsidy by the author'. In plain language this means that many publishers, even highly respectable ones, in many cases simply act for the author as contractors for publishing services, incurring no risk, and usually not mentioning the fact in the book itself. Publishers with a high reputation to maintain are particular as to what they put their name to, even at the author's expense; others are not. Serious writers and graphomaniacs, poets and poetasters alike, have been known to go into heavy debt to see their works in print.

It was this state of affairs that prompted the Israel Book Council, formed under the auspices of the Culture and Arts Council, to embark on an ambitious scheme, emulous of Norway: to use funds provided by the Ministry of Education and Culture, in order to buy a fair number of copies of every original work of fiction by a living author, thus bringing the publisher within sight of a break-even volume of sales, without recourse to financing by the author (and with the publisher specially required to undertake not to accept such financing). The result has, unfortunately, been somewhat reminiscent of the provincial penniless teacher in Jewish folklore, who could not understand why the rich so much appreciated something called an omelette, after he had prevailed upon his wife to make one for him—with neither eggs nor butter, nor even a frying pan. The money available for this project was not even within hailing distance of its ambitious goal. Out of 525 titles listed for 1976/77, under 'first editions and re-editions' classified as 'literature'[62] the council bought less than 5 per cent—twenty-five titles, including ten prose works and fifteen poetry,[63] with a mean number of 608 copies each (instead of the envisaged 1,000 copies), thus failing to make a significant contribution to approaching the break-even point in sales, even for the titles actually bought; in 1977/78, twenty-nine items were bought (mean number of copies, 712); in 1978/79, fifty-two (608); in 1979/80, sixty-seven (528). Future prospects are not certain because of severe budget restrictions undertaken by the government as an anti-inflationary measure. Even so, public libraries, the recipients of the books thus bought, complained that they were being saddled with some items for which they had no demand. The selection of books for purchase has been entrusted to a panel of expert readers, often using divergent yardsticks for their recommendations and causing much bad blood in the process. At best, selection by merit (as opposed to some technical criteria, such as 'living author', 'publisher who is a member of the trade association', etc.) involves value-judgement by somebody who is neither the author nor the publisher, and smacks of *dirigisme*.

The 'break-even' number of sales is often claimed by publishers to be 3,000 copies,[64] with 3,500 copies being the average number per title.[65] With a fairly high number of best-sellers pushing this average up, this would mean that most books are published at a loss. There are however several explanations why publishers are able to keep their heads above water: part of the story concerns the already-mentioned subsidies; also, by publishing such sure-fire sellers as school textbooks and works of reference, a publisher may be able to afford some losses on prestige-titles; finally, some publishers do admit in private that the true break-even point may be much lower.

In any case, a title reaching the 5,000-copy mark is considered a success, and 20.4 per cent of all titles[66] (15.2 per cent of first editions and re-editions) go that high, with pride of place belonging to children's books (35.1 per cent of all titles). Some 5.4 per cent of all titles (3.4 per cent of first editions and re-editions) are published at more than 10,000 copies each (by population size, this is the equivalent of a 600,000-copy edition in the United States). Nor is this a record. Besides a popular cookery book, which sold 150,000 copies, there are instances of novels, both original and translated (such as *Cien Años de Soledad* by Gabriel

García Márquez), selling at 50,000–70,000 copies each (the equivalent of 3–4 million in the United States).[67] A fiction series has 25,000–30,000 subscribers, in addition to single sales. Notable successes have followed serialization on television: John Galsworthy's *Forsyte Saga*, Leo Tolstoy's *War and Peace* and Robert Graves's *I, Claudius* are all cases in point (this last offers a tragi-comic case history: the sequel, though part of the televised series, sold only half the number of copies, because the title was different: *Claudius the God*).[68] Interestingly enough, even well-loved poets achieve wide circulation, in the 10,000 class, though the average first edition of modern poetry only runs as high as 1,500 to 2,000 copies, often subsidized.[69]

In this situation authors can hardly make a living by their pen or typewriter, unless a publisher chooses to play Maecenas[70] and not content himself with the standard fee of '15 per cent of the take minus the cost of two bindings (less for paperbacks)'. Translators are payed by volume of work, and though fees may not be unfair, this source of income lacks the steadiness to make it in most cases more than a part-time occupation. In this kind of market, it comes as a matter of little surprise that literary agents play a negligible rôle in the internal market. A 1979 trade directory[71] characteristically lists no more than three, all of them in fact specializing in Israeli authors' foreign rights and the rights of foreign authors and publishers in Israel (copyright is secured by Berne Convention and the Universal Copyright Convention standards, extending now to seventy years after the author's death). Something of a consolation to authors is the large number of literary prizes offered by various funds and organizations; many of them are general in nature and some are specialized. The most prestigious of them are the annual Israel Prizes (for achievement in various fields, including literature) and the veteran of them all, the Bialik Prize (one for *belles-lettres* and one for Judaic scholarship). Special mention should be made of the Prime Minister's Creativity Prize (founded by the late L. Eshkol), given to authors not for past achievement but as a means of enabling them to forgo employment for a year (this is a condition) and be free to write or do research. A number of prizes exist for achievements in journalism. Though the extreme proliferation of literary prizes may be a boon to authors, their very number, with in-bred literary coteries sometimes alternately serving as judges and recipients, provoked a famous poet (the late A. Shlonski) to talk of 'prizetitution'.

The practical value of prizes has of course undergone serious depletion in times of three-digit inflation, a factor which plays havoc with publishers' calculations. A veteran publisher[72] reckons that with financing costs running as high as 36 per cent for four months, prices have to be fixed at six times the cost for fiction (less for textbooks) in order to leave publishers with a very modest profit of 2.5 per cent, though a lower ratio could be feasible by establishing a proper mechanism that pegged prices to the cost of living. Some publishers feel this to be an exaggeration, and maintain that such a prohibitive pricing policy may hurt sales, in a market already weakened by recession. One publisher[73] maintains that in the past, appreciation of stock value in slow-moving items used to compensate publishers for inflation, but the keeping of large stocks has been rendered uneconomical in the face of high financing costs, and as a result there is a decline in publication of such items as art albums and reference works, which require long-term investment.

Still, whatever the contingencies of the economy, Israel is not only a nation of readers but a nation of book-owners. With 57 per cent of all households mustering a private collection of more than fifty books (with 4 per cent having no books and 5 per cent more than 500),[74] it has been the personal experience of many of us never to have come across a home without a library of some sort. Ninety-three per cent of homes have a Bible, 82 per cent a prayer-book and 49 per cent the Talmud (some of them incomplete). When Katz and Gurevitch[75] inquired into the source from which the 'last book read' was obtained, at least 44 per cent of respondents referred to buying the book (36 per cent bought it themselves and another 8 per cent received it as a gift; to this one may add the 2 per cent from 'other sources', such as 'had it at home'). Others borrowed the book from friends (35 per cent) or a library (19 per cent). Apparently the tendency to obtain books from public libraries has been on the increase: the Bureau of Statistics[76] lists library registration rising from 16.6 per cent of the total Jewish adult population in 1969 to 21.9 per cent in 1975/76 and to 25.5 per cent in 1979, with a steady four-fifths of those registered regularly borrowing more than one book a month. Superimposing these figures on the earlier-mentioned readership figures, would mean that about two-fifths (37.3 per cent) of the 'more than one book a month' readers are 'more than one book a month' library borrowers.

To serve the buyers, more than a 1,000 retail outlets are available all over the country, though only a minority, mainly in the largest centres of population, sell books exclusively.[77] Most booksellers award regular customers with discounts, and though some publishers[78] feel rigid-list pricing should be introduced to discourage such practices, others consider it counterproductive,[79] especially since numerous books are sold in bulk, at a discount, via staff-committees in places of work. This method of sales also serves as an effective promotion technique, since the size of editions is usually not large enough to finance a fully fledged orthodox promotion campaign. One leading publisher[80] reckons a 30,000-copy edition to be the minimum for such a campaign to be justified. With no more than 5.4 per cent of all titles printed in editions of more than 10,000 copies,[81] this is a rarity. Thus publishers tend to concentrate on catalogue-like advertisements in newspapers and to focus on specific audiences, such as the readers of the literary supplements of the dailies. Display advertisements in the press and radio advertising are rare (television advertising does not exist in Israel; brief daily reviews of books on the midnight news on television are known to have a marked though short-term positive effect on sales.[82] An annual event contributes much to sales promotion: it is the national Bookweek. Experimentally started some twenty years ago, Bookweek has become a nationwide celebration. For one summer (no rain hazard) week open-air book markets are established everywhere. The central ones are in the big cities, and more than a score in smaller towns, with mobile market vans reaching even places too small to have a year-round regular retail outlet for books. The Israel Book Publishers Association, the Union of Writers, the Ministry of Education and Culture, and municipal authorities all join in organizing Bookweek. Publishers and booksellers maintain stands, with authors at hand to autograph copies. Books are sold at a discount, up to 35 per cent (except textbooks etc.). In 1979 the cash-flow during Bookweek was estimated at $2.5 million,[83] and though some booksellers complain that the multitudes thronging into the open-air markets are, at least in part, siphoned off from their regular clientele, the trade as a whole benefits, and even authors are content with diminished earnings per copy (because of the discounts), willingly trading in cash for the added popularity.

Bookweek is often referred to as Hebrew Book Week. Small wonder: 90.2 per cent of all first editions and re-editions published in 1976/77 were in Hebrew (including 3.4 per cent bilingual publications and 0.7 per cent dictionaries, mostly in Hebrew with another language).[84] Of the books published in other languages, some 70 per cent are in English. The numerous readers of foreign languages (see above) thus almost exclusively depend on imports (about 6.5 million dollars' worth in 1978,[85] about a third from the United States, less than a quarter from the United Kingdom, 13 per cent from France and 6 per cent from the Federal Republic of Germany). Non-Hebrew books published in Israel are thus to a large extent meant for export. Publications in English for 1976/77 give pride of place to the humanities (26.1 per cent) followed by religion (15 per cent) science and mathematics (9.8 per cent) and art (9.8 per cent).[86] This is a clearly export-oriented picture, a conclusion that becomes even more pronounced when compared with the (much scantier) internally oriented publication operations in Yiddish: practically all books published are *belles-lettres*.[87] A typical immigrant-oriented picture emerges from a select list of publications in Russian;[88] while the list is incomplete, it is fairly extensive, enumerating some sixty titles for the last decade. The total is too small to be statistically significant, but the distribution by subjects presents a picture of great variety: an abridged version of the *Encyclopaedia Judaica,* original writings by Israelis in Russian, translations of classical Hebrew works and even of popular English detective stories.

Export trade in books, periodicals, printing and publishing services in 1978 reached a total of more than $14 million (58.2 per cent books, 12.4 per cent newspapers and periodicals);[89] 40.8 per cent of all exports go to the United States, 7.1 per cent to the United Kingdom, 7.3 per cent to the Federal Republic of Germany. One publishing and printing conglomerate alone[90] exported last year half a million dollars' worth of books, and 750,000 dollars' worth of publishing services. This particular house, as well as one or two more, have their own outlets abroad. It was recently reported[91] that thirty publishers are combining to organize a joint United States-based company for export. The Israel Book and Printing Centre, operating as part of the Israel Export Institute, makes it its regular task to facilitate exports.

To project the picture of reading and publishing in Israel into the future, there is no better way than turning to the children. Since the last widely available general description of the subject was published some two years ago,[92] a pioneering survey of 9- to 13-year-olds has been carried out by the Bureau of Statistics.[93] Though it may come as no surprise that practically all children (87 per cent read one book a month or more) did some book-reading in 1979 (schools do induce certain reading habits and, as mentioned before, illiteracy is concentrated in the higher age-groups), the large number of avid readers (43 per cent read a book a week or more) is heartening indeed. Girls tend to read more than boys (91 per cent read more than a book a month, 51 per cent more than a book a week),[94] with boys more heavily represented in other social activities.[95] Children are also steady library-users (61 per cent used the ubiquitous school libraries, 55 per cent public libraries, 33 per cent both; total: 75 per cent as against 25.5 per cent of adults).[96]

This phenomenon has not developed in a vacuum: the beginnings of modern Hebrew literature for children almost coincide with the beginnings of modern Hebrew literature in general (late eighteenth century) and few of the classic authors have not written for children.[97] As early as 1875 a Warsaw publishing house specialized in children's literature. Between 1896 and 1899 one publishing house produced 300 titles for children.[98] All this, one must be reminded, happened before the young readers had a Hebrew-speaking environment. The first children's book in Hebrew to appear in the land of Israel was published in 1887—by E. Ben-Yehuda of course—and it was he who published the first periodical for children in 1893.[99] At present, there are thirty-nine periodicals for children in Israel,[100] and nearly half (46 per cent) the 9- to 13-year-olds read them.[101]

As for books, in 1976/77, 546 children's books, practically all in Hebrew, constituted 14.5 per cent of all titles published and 20.9 per cent of all copies printed. Of first editions and re-editions (213 titles) about a fifth were translations (20.3 per cent). Children's books, though running a larger average number of copies than other kinds of books (4,500 per title, as against the 3,500 general average, 3,100 for adult fiction) tend to be smaller in size: 55 per cent of all first editions and re-editions were under 99 pages (as against 27.6 per cent for 'literature', including poetry).[102]

In spite of the widespread use of libraries by children and the school library being a fixture in practically every school,[103] a leading publisher of children's books[104] complained that, as opposed to other countries, libraries are not a decisive factor in distribution. The gift market is highly important, and it demands beautifully produced books in hard covers. Their quality has greatly improved over the years (texts, graphics and illustrations are as handsome as can be found anywhere); what is still sorely lacking is reasonably priced and produced paperbacks for children.

With the young generation's reading behaviour, in the face of the recent impact of the visual electronic media (there is a television set in practically every home, and children view it assiduously), one may feel assured, that the 'special relationship' between our people and our books is bound to continue. Turn-of-the-century forebodings[105] that being the People of the Book actually means enslavement to the Book and therefore contradicts the evolvement of a living literature and of an active interrelationship between a people and its literature have been belied by subsequent cultural history. The readers are there, active, growing in numbers, expecting books and periodicals to yield knowledge, a sense of belonging, aesthetic pleasure and entertainment. It is up to the publishing industry not to let them down, and it is up to the polity to help it to satisfy their needs and to provide authors with the means to reach the public and to go on writing.

In terms of broad national objectives, publishing is inseparable from the general trends of the cultural renascence of the Jewish people. Some of these are pursued by the industry—like the West Wind—by its very presence, namely, developing the revived language, forging it into an adequate vehicle of communication held in common, integrating a nation of immigrants into a society already united by its basic cultural roots and values but in need of broadening and enriching this cohesion, and linking cultural life, via translations, to the winds of change and mainstays of continuity in the modern world. Other objectives need special attention if the industry is to attain them. The main public concern should be with two things; in the field of native literature: to ensure a publishing outlet for authors, especially young ones, irrespective of immediate marketing prospects, and to make possible the re-issue of old literary treasures lying dormant in rare old editions and manuscripts; in the field of translated literature: to ensure that the main body of world culture is available to the increasing proportion of monoglot Hebrew readers (including students) without undue deference to ephemeral vogue or demand.

The relatively large publicly owned sector in the industry could go a long way towards ensuring both. The question obviously presents itself, whether such publishing houses—while to some extent liberated from the tyranny of the market place—would not be open to the no less insidious influences of power-holders in the public bodies behind them, seeking what might ensure their political power. Past experience does not justify such apprehensions. By virtue of the already-mentioned special place occupied by culture in the Jewish revival, it should come as no surprise that it was one of the founding fathers of socialist Zionism, Berl Katznelson, who also founded the Histadruth publishing house. Declining to start with a formal manifesto, he chose to elucidate some guiding principles after some two score of books had already been allowed to speak for themselves.[106] He likened the work of a publisher in the service of the public to that of a judge:

When the public appoints a judge, it does not stipulate that he should do what the public wants, but rather that he should do justice. . . . And it is a good judge who remains loyal to justice, even when he knows it may displease the majority or the powers that be. This is what the injunction 'ye shall not be afraid of the face of man' [meaning 'fear no one]'[107] is all about. . . . Society may depose the judge . . . but may not demand that he should be in default of his duty.[108]

Almost universally, the people in charge of publicly owned publishing houses have kept faith with this creed. Public bodies owning publishing houses should however let them do justice by long-term objectives, through making them still less dependent on the short-term contingencies of the market.

As for the government, it should channel its aid in such a way that it involves a minimum of value-judgements: what a reputable publisher (public or private) considers worth publishing should by the same token be worth supporting, subject to purely technical criteria (such as 'an original work by a living author' or 'translation of a book considered an established classic in a foreign literature', etc.). Something, of course, should be done about inflation, though not primarily for reasons connected with publishers' calculations.

A word should be said here about foreign influences in publishing, a subject specifically mentioned in the agenda of this meeting. At present, none exist in Israel in any significant form. One worldwide organization did attempt to establish an Israeli outlet, but it did not survive, and even if it had stayed in the market, it was difficult to see what specific influence this could have: the local industry is strong enough to stand a little more competition. Such joint publishing ventures as do occur, mainly take the form of Israeli houses selling publishing services to a larger market, growing stronger in the process, and becoming more efficient in performing their domestic functions. Commercial competition from abroad— foreign-language book imports—does shrink the market for the local product, but curtailing this kind of competition by administrative or fiscal means is culturally undesirable and politically not feasible. In any case, the growing tendency of the public to do most of its reading in Hebrew minimizes the impact of imports on the book market.

There is no doubt about the integrative effect of the printed word, whether books or periodicals, in Israel. One need not go further than the already-mentioned study by Katz and Gurevitch,[109] who investigated the list of objectives pursued by book-readers and found that apart from individual values, uses and gratifications—obviously highest on the list—a large percentage of respondents mentioned such objectives as 'getting closer to Jewish tradition' (38 per cent of all readers), feeling pride in having a state of our own (37 per cent; here newspapers top the list with 68 per cent). Specific case-studies of reading of literature dealing with two momentous recent national events (the Holocaust, the 1967 war) revealed 67 per cent of readers to have read such books, with the result of creating 'a common national experience' and fulfilling 'much like exposure to a fixed set of contents in traditional society, an integrative function of strengthening national identity'.

NOTES

1. *Publishers Weekly* (New York), Vol. 215, No. 12, 19 March 1979, p. 34.
2. Elihu Katz and Michael Gurevitch, *The Culture of Leisure in Israel*, p. 243, Tel Aviv, 1973 (referring to Robert Escarpit, *The Book Revolution*, London, 1966).
3. Israel Central Bureau of Statistics, *Statistical Abstract* (ICBS 30 (6)), p. 27, Table 1; Katz and Gurevitch, op. cit., p. 245 (based on earlier ICBS publications).
4. Katz and Gurevitch, op. cit.
5. ICBS 30 (6), op. cit., pp. 27–9.
6. Ibid., pp. 25 and 27, Table 1.
7. Ibid., pp. 28, 29 and 31, Tables 2, 3 and 5.
8. Israel Central Bureau of Statistics, *Statistical Abstract* (ICBS 30), 1980, p. 709, Table XXVI/10.
9. ICBS 30 (6), op. cit., p. 34, Table 10.
10. ICBS 30, op. cit.
11. *Encyclopaedia Britannica* (1974 ed.) *Macropaedia*, Vol. 15, pp. 237, with note on sources.

12. Interview with Itim management by the author, 28 February 1980.
13. A. Dor-Un, *Journalism,* pp. 205 (censorship agreement text), 209 (Press Council regulations), Tel Aviv, 1976– (in Hebrew).
14. Israel Central Bureau of Statistics, Ministry of Education and Culture, Israel Broadcasting Authority, *Reading Habits and Leisure Activities of the Jewish Population 1979,* p. 23, Table 2, Jerusalem, 1979 (Education and Culture Statistics, 101). This is a reprint from *Supplement to the Monthly Bulletin of Statistics,* No. 5, 1979 (subsequently quoted as ICBS 101).
15. Katz and Gurevitch, op. cit., pp. 226–7.
16. ICBS 101, op. cit., p. 106, Table 4.
17. Ibid., p. 103, Table 2.
18. Katz and Gurevitch, op. cit., pp. 250–4.
19. ICBS 30 (6), op. cit., pp. 28–9, 31.
20. ICBS 101, op. cit., p. 103, Table 2.
21. Katz and Gurevitch, op. cit., pp. 247–9 (emphasis added).
22. Ibid., p. 231.
23. ICBS 101, op. cit., p. 102, Table 1.
24. Katz and Gurevitch, op. cit., pp. 146–7.
25. ICBS 101, op. cit., p. 102, Table 1.
26. Gerald C. Stone and Roger V. Wetherington Jr, 'Confirming the Newspaper Reading Habit', *Journalism Quarterly,* Autumn 1979, pp. 554 et seq.
27. Ibid., p. 559.
28. Ibid., p. 558.
29. ICBS 101, op. cit., p. 102, Table 1.
30. The morning newspapers, *Hamashkif, Heruth, Haboker, Hayom, Zmanim, Hakol* and *Lamerhav,* and the evenings, *Hadshoth Haerev* and *Hador; Hayom* was a merger of *Heruth* and *Haboker,* which did not survive; *Lamerhav* has been incorporated in *Davar.* The two defunct evening papers were abortive attempts to compete with the two independents in the field. Another defunct evening paper, *Mivrak,* was quasi-affiliated.
31. By the publishers of the weekly, *Haolam Haze,* which combines erotica, muck-raking and multidirectional radicalism.
32. ICBS 101, op. cit., p. 102, Table 1.
33. Katz and Gurevitch, op. cit., pp. 148–51.
34. Ibid., pp. 194–5, 199–200.
35. Ibid. p. 294.
36. Elihu Katz, 'Modern Media and Publishing', *Proceedings of the International Publishing and Printing Committee of the Jerusalem Economic Conference, Jerusalem, 23 April 1979,* pp. 59–60, Jerusalem, 1979.
37. ICBS 101, op. cit., p. 104, Table 3.
38. Interview with Yoav Barash of Massada by the author, 28 February 1980.
39. ICBS 30 (6), op. cit., p. 36, Tables 12 and 13.
40. Obtained from its secretary.
41. *Directory 1979,* pp. 6–40.
42. ICBS 30 (6), op. cit., p. 36, Tables 12 and 13.
43. *Directory 1979,* op. cit.
44. Am Oved, founded in 1940, published about 100 new titles and 120 reprints in 1978.
45. Hakibbutz Hameuhad (founded in 1939) and Sifrivat Paolim (founded in 1942).
46. Mossad Bialik (founded in 1935).
47. Mossad Harav Kook (founded in 1937).
48. The Israel Book Publishers' Association, founded forty years ago. Source of the information here is its official leaflet published in April 1979.
49. These are Yahdav and Ma'aloth.
50. For example, the Jerusalem University (Magnes) Press, publishes scores of scholarly works every year.

51. Dvir, a non-linear descendant of a nineteenth-century pioneering publishing house in Russia.
52. Interview with its former director-general.
53. The Massada-Peli group.
54. It published 150 books in 1978.
55. Zmora, Bitan and Modan.
56. Schocken Books and Rubin Mass.
57. Schocken.
58. Keter.
59. Mizrahi.
60. For example *Ma'ariv* and *Davar.*
61. *Yedioth Aharonoth* partly owns *Edanim,* for example.
62. ICBS 30 (6), op. cit., p. 28, Table 2.
63. Interim report by the Centre for Public Libraries, 1980, made available to the author.
64. *Publishers Weekly,* op. cit., p. 58.
65. ICBS 30 (6), op. cit., p. 30, Table 4.
66. Ibid.
67. *Publishers Weekly,* op. cit., pp. 35–40.
68. Barash interview (see note 38).
69. Ibid.
70. S. Y. Agnon and S. Tschernichovski were both supported by Schocken Books, and N. Altermann by the *Davar* newspaper. In some case authors are paid for certain editorial duties as a semi-sinecure.
71. *Trade Directory 1979,* op. cit., pp. 66–7.
72. M. Bernstein, in Publishers' Association circulars for 11 and 17 February 1980.
73. Anonymously quoted in *Ha'aretz,* 25 February 1980.
74. Y. Barash, in ibid., and in interview (see note 38).
75. Katz and Gurevitch, op. cit., p. 242.
76. ICBS 101, op. cit., p. 103, Table 2.
77. Katz and Gurevitch, op. cit., p. 237.
78. *Publishers Weekly,* op. cit., p. 35.
79. For example, M. Bernstein, during meetings of the Book Council attended by the author.
80. Barash interview (see note 38).
81. ICBS 30 (6), op. cit. p. 30, Table 4.
82. Barash interview (see note 38).
83. *Israel Book World,* No. 36/37, October 1979, p. 6.
84. ICBS 30 (6), op. cit., p. 32, Table 7.
85. Israel Export Institute leaflet, July 1979.
86. ICBS 30 (6), op. cit., p. 34, Table 10.
87. Ibid., p. 33, Tables 8 and 9.
88. *Israel Book World,* op. cit., pp. 44 et seq.
89. ICBS 30 (6), op. cit., p. 34, Table 10.
90. Massada, as reported in Barash interview (see note 38).
91. *Ha'aretz,* 26 February 1980.
92. Alex Zehavi, *Printed for Children,* pp. 215 et seq., London/Munich/Paris, K.G. Saur, 1978.
93. ICBS 101, op. cit., pp. 105–7.
94. Ibid., p. 106, Table 4.
95. Ibid., p. 107, Table 5.
96. Ibid., pp. 103 and 106.
97. Zehavi, op. cit., bibliography.
98. *Encyclopaedia Judaica,* Vol. 5, pp. 432–3, Jerusalem, 1973.
99. Ibid., pp. 435 and 441.
100. ICBS 30, op. cit., p. 30, Table XXVI/10.
101. ICBS 101, op. cit., p. 106, Table 4.

102. ICBS 30 (6), op. cit., pp. 28–31, 33–5.
103. Zehavi, op. cit.
104. Barash interview (see note 38).
105. For example, A. Ginzberg, 'Ahad-Ha'am [At the Crossroads]', *Works of A. Ginzberg,* pp. 51–3, Tel Aviv, 1947 (article written in 1894; in Hebrew).
106. Article by B. Katznelson, *Works of Berl Katznelson,* Vol. XII, pp. 29 et seq., Tel Aviv, 1949/50 (article written in 1943; in Hebrew).
107. Deuteronomy, 1:17.
108. Katznelson, op. cit., p. 30.
109. Katz and Gurevitch, op. cit., pp. 256, 260, 282–5.

12   The book industry in the United Republic of Tanzania

E. E. Kaungamno
Director,
Tanganyika Library Service

In order to understand the book industry in the United Republic of Tanzania it is advisable to study, as a prelude, the book industry in Kenya, which is the hub of the industry in East and Central Africa. Many of the publishing firms in Kenya had or still have their branches in Tanzania. The publishing situation in Kenya has been well documented by John Ndegwa.[1]

THE EAST AFRICAN LITERATURE BUREAU

In 1945 Elspeth Huxley was appointed by the East African Governors' Conference to examine the problem of the provision of reading material for literate Africans in East Africa (Kenya, Tanganyika, Uganda and Zanzibar) and to submit proposals for consideration. Mrs Huxley's report recommended the formation of an East African Literature Bureau with the following functions: (a) to publish books for Africans, both for general reading and educational purposes, in English and African languages; (b) to edit and publish popular magazines; (c) to encourage actively and assist African authorship; (d) to assist in the development of book distribution; and (e) to establish and administer a lending-library service for Africain readers.

The Huxley report was accepted, and in 1947 Charles Richards was appointed adviser to the East African governments on literature for Africans. He advised, among other things, that in the first instance publishing should be in Kiswahili and Luganda and then extended to other vernacular languages.

In 1947 the East African High Commission was established as an interterritorial organ to deal with special services. Richards's proposals were accepted by the British and East African governments, and as a result the East African Literature Bureau was formed in 1948, as a Department of the East African High Commission. The East African Literature Bureau Headquarters was in Kenya and had branches at Kampala in Uganda and at Dar es Salaam for Tanganyika and Zanzibar. Soon after it was established, the Bureau produced a variety of books in different subjects and by the end of 1949 had published forty-six titles in English and eleven in East African languages. Since the need for books was great, the Bureau encouraged commercial publishers to produce books for East Africa.

In order to encourage African authorship, literature committees were formed for different languages, and these stimulated interest in literature writing. Authorship competitions were arranged for African writers, and the best entries were published by the Bureau or a commercial publisher. A series of very useful leaflets was also published by the Bureau to guide potential authors. By June 1956 the Bureau had published over 350 titles, making a total of 1.7 million volumes, while 50 titles (about 330,000 volumes) had been reprinted. The Bureau had indeed been a successful venture.

In 1963 Richards recommended that as more and more publishers were then active in East Africa, the Bureau should concentrate on adult-literacy primers and readers as well as other follow-up reading material for new literates. The Bureau was also advised to concentrate on producing books in East African languages particularly where the market was not big enough to attract commercial publishers.

In addition to publishing books, the Bureau was responsible for producing magazines and journals. Many of the scholarly journals of the East African universities have been produced by the Bureau. With the increase in the volume of business, it was decided that the Bureau should establish a printing press in 1968. With such printing facilities, it was possible for the Bureau to publish all its books as well as fulfil all the requirements of the East African Community of which the Bureau was a department.

The East African Literature Bureau was also responsible for running library services. With its headquarters in Nairobi, Kenya, the Bureau organized small library centres all over East Africa and ran postal library services until 1964. Following recommendations by Sidney W. Hockey, libraries organizer for East Africa, the East African Literature Bureau became the nucleus of national library services in Kenya, Uganda and Tanzania. More details about libraries later.

COMMERCIAL PUBLISHERS

As indicated before, in his final report as Director of the East African Literature Bureau in 1963, Richards recommended that the Bureau should concentrate on publishing materials for adult literacy projects and leave the rest of publishing to commercial publishers. The Bureau encouraged commercial publishers, passing the more viable publications to them and, when necessary, guaranteed sales by buying the books. However, although it is true that British publishers like Longmans Green, Macmillan and the Oxford University Press were publishing for the East African market, hardly any of them actually published in Kenya, Uganda, Tanganyika and Zanzibar before 1963. Most of their publications were in fact issued in London and then sent over to East Africa.

Among the early British publishers who established their offices in East Africa were Longmans in 1950 and Oxford University Press in 1954. Later on, other British publishers also established local bases. They set up warehouses, engaged local authors to write textbooks, and sent local representatives to visit schools, universities, teacher-training colleges and ministries of education to introduce new books conforming with new syllabuses. The existence of those foreign publishers has generated a vigorous debate.

There have been some criticisms of the position held by British publishers in East Africa. It has been alleged that the publishing industry in East Africa is still almost entirely dominated by the British firms, which are primarily interested in making money. It is further argued that their local financial strength and their considerable profits have largely been built up by their share of the market of educational books, particularly school-books, on which the profit is large, assured and sustaining. There has been, therefore, a big cry for the development of a strong and genuine local publishing industry where both policy and editorial control are firmly in the hands of East Africans.

A special mention of the East African Publishing House is necessary. In 1964, the East African Institute of Social and Cultural Affairs considered the possibility of starting a local publishing concern that would cater more satisfactorily to the aspirations and requirements of the local people and mirror the African heritage more actively. The outcome was the establishment of the East African Publishing House in 1965. However, for lack of adequate capital to finance the venture, the Institute approached André Deutsch, who agreed to have a partnership in the publishing business. The East African Publishing House therefore became a joint concern between these two bodies until 1966, when André Deutsch was bought out and the East African Cultural Trust, formed for this purpose, took over the complete management of the East African Publishing House. Right from the beginning, the East African Publishing House went out looking for authors, taking many more risks than any other publishers were willing to take. It started publishing readers for primary schools, and later on for secondary schools. As time went on, the firm published university-level books and other scholarly material. The East African Publishing House also publishes in local languages, mainly in Kiswahili. The firm is, on the whole, making a great contribution to the book industry.

Tanzania, being one of the East African countries where foreign publishing firms have branches, has had its share of problems.

THE TANZANIA PUBLISHING HOUSE

Tanzania Publishing House was established in 1966 as a partnership venture between the National Development Corporation (60 per cent shareholding) and Macmillan (40 per cent shareholding). From 1966 to 1972, the firm encountered various problems. Robert Hutchison, the former and last expatriate General Manager of Tanzania Publishing House (TPH) has been very critical of Macmillan's policy.[2] He points out that during the 'first five years TPH was dominated and largely controlled by Macmillan and was very little more than a vehicle, albeit at times a very inefficient one, to serve Macmillan's main ends, i.e. money-making'. 'The main effect of the agreement between Macmillan and the Tanzania Publishing House', he said, 'was to secure extortionate potential profits for Macmillan at virtually no risk to themselves, for ill-defined services to the TPH.' Hutchison further points out that several titles produced and sold by Macmillan through TPH were unsuitable for Tanzania. According to the agreement, he adds, Macmillan was responsible for training local staff. However, he continues, 'in the five and a half years that TPH was managed by Macmillan men, precisely one Tanzanian was sent for training'. In 1970 the managers of TPH, Hutchison laments, 'spent more than six times as much money on entertainment (mostly themselves and visiting Macmillan staff) as on training staff'.

The firm was originally founded to publish primary- and secondary-school textbooks for Tanzania in Kiswahili and mathematics for the Ministry of National Education. Later on, it produced supplementary readers in Kiswahili for schools as well as general books for more advanced readership. As the firm became well established it embarked on publishing creative literature in the national language and serious political, social and economic works in English. In 1972, for example, a total of thirty-six new books and reprints were published.

In 1974 negotiations with Macmillan Publishing House over the National Development Corporation (TPH's parent body) to acquire all the shares in the company were started and successfully concluded.

THE MINISTRY OF NATIONAL EDUCATION

The Ministry of National Education is, by far, one of the big publishers in the country as well as a big market for books. The ministry also gets a significant share of the government's budget. In 1972/73, of the total government expenditure amounting to 3,179.4 million Tanzanian shillings (about \$475 million) 473.9 million shillings were spent on education, i.e. about 14.9 per cent of the total budget.[3] At the same time there is a grave shortage of books to meet the educational needs.

Primary educational books

Up to 1974 Tanzania was accommodating a little more than 50 per cent of its school-age children in the primary education system of seven grades. With effect from the same year, the Revolutionary Party (Chama cha Mapinduzi) decided that Universal Primary Education (UPE) would be implemented from November 1977. This meant that all children of school-going age (7 years) were to be given places in schools. As a result of this move, the number of children in primary schools increased from 1,874,357 in 1975/76 to 3,414,210 in 1978/79.[4] With the introduction of UPE in 1977, enrolment in Standard 1 has shot up from about 50 per cent to over 90 per cent. This great intake of students brought the Ministry of National Education face to face, among other things, with the problem of school materials, including books. The textbook shortage is currently very acute in primary schools. The problem is aggravated by the fact that there are very few titles in Kiswahili, the national language, which is the principal medium of instruction.

Secondary/technical and vocational education books

The actual number of primary children entering secondary schools is increasing annually, from 4,300 in 1961 to 15,850 in 1977, although the secondary-school intake has been dropping percentagewise.[5] (In the 1960s some 13 per cent of primary-school leavers got into secondary schools; in the late 1960s and early 1970s the figure dropped to 10 per cent, and in the mid 1970s only 6 per cent could be accommodated in the conventional secondary-school system).

Although the number of students at secondary level is smaller than in primary schools, it is here that the qualitative aspects of textbooks are a major concern. Good books are needed for secondary and technical courses that prepare students for higher education as well as for agricultural, industrial or commercial occupations. Also, there is a great need of books for secondary/technical and vocational education teachers and instructors.[6]

Functional literacy books

In 1967 there were over 13 million Tanzanians, and out of these 7 million were adults. Over 75 per cent of the adults could not read or write, i.e. over 5,250,000 were illiterate. Out of the 13 million Tanzanians, 6 million were youths and out of them 3 million were of schooling age, However, 1,5 million of the population did not have a chance to go to school. That meant that apart from 5,250,000 adult illiterates, there were some 1.5 million youths who were in danger of being illiterate. The drive to eradicate illiteracy originated from President Nyerere's New Year's speech of 31 December 1969, followed by another one in 1970 when an Adult Education Year was declared in Tanzania. The National Literacy Campaign started in 1971 with the objective of wiping out illiteracy.[7] On 12 August 1975, nationwide literacy tests were administered. Sixty per cent of the recorded illiterates had become literate, leaving 3,440,000 who could still not read and write.

The National Literacy Campaign was based on the results of the Unesco Literacy Project, which was started around Lake Victoria in 1968. The objectives of the project were:[8]

To teach the people to read, to write and to solve simple problems in arithmetic.

To raise the level of instruction to the equivalent of full primary school.

To help people to apply the new knowledge and skills to solve their basic economic, social and cultural problems.

To prepare them for a more efficient participation in the development of their country.

To integrate the adult-literacy and adult-education programme with the general agricultural and industrial development of the country.

To provide the necessary reading materials, to impart a knowledge of community and personal hygiene, nutrition, child care, etc., which would help improve family and community life, provide an opportunity of continuing education, and avoid relapse into illiteracy.

Many functional literacy primers and teaching guides have been written to cope with the demand for reading material. The literacy materials try to cover most of the economic activities of the rural population. Up to 1975, 26,655,000 primers and 1,375,000 teacher's guides had been prepared and distributed.[9] However, because of an enrolment of 5,184,982 students from 1971 to 1975, there was a shortage of primers. There is still a great need for primers, including general follow-up reading literature to prevent the newly literates from relapsing into illiteracy.

OTHER PUBLISHERS

There are other important publishers who issue many publications in English, Kiswahili and vernacular languages. Some of the active ones are attached to religious organizations, and these include Vuga Press, Ndanda Press and African Inland Press. Their publications are mostly on religion. There are also several institutional publishers. Some of the most important ones are the Bureau of Research Assessment and Land Use Planning (BRALUP), the Economic Research Bureau (ERB), and the Institute of Kiswahili Research (IKR), all of which are attached to the University of Dar es Salaam as well as the Institute of Adult Education (IAE) and the Institute of Education (IE). Their publications are mostly scholarly.

PRINTERS[10]

Since publishing and printing are closely related, a brief look at some of the major printers in Tanzania is necessary.

Government-owned printing establishment

The National Printing Company, a subsidiary of the National Development Corporation, is vested with the responsibility of offering printing services to other national institutions. Incorporated in May 1967, it became a subsidiary of NDC in July 1967. The company prints many books for the Ministry of National Education, the Tanzania Publishing House and the Institute of Adult Education, whose books are published for the adult education programmes. The firm also prints the party papers *Uhuru* and *Mzalendo* and other papers such as *Urusi Leo, Parapanda, Ulinzi.* The firm specializes in the printing of posters, calendars, cheques, Kalamazoo cards and other types of office stationery.

Printpak Tanzania Limited

Printpak Tanzania Limited became a subsidiary of the National Development Corporation in 1971. As the name suggests, the company is concerned primarily with printing and packaging. It is 100 per cent owned by the National Development Corporation. During 1974, UNICEF supplied machinery for the printing and binding of books under an agreement made between the Ministry of National Education, NDC and Printpak. With the installation of such equipment, Printpak prints thousands and thousands of books for the Ministry of National Education. Other major organizations that use Printpak's facilities include the Institute of Adult Education, the Institute of Education, Tanzania Publishing House and the University of Dar es Salaam. The firm prints the two government newspapers, the *Daily News* and *Sunday News,* as well as a number of magazines.

Government Printer

The Government Printer is by far the largest organization in the country in terms of printed material. It publishes official government documents.

Private printing firms

There are also private printers that play a significant role in the book industry in Tanzania. Some of these are the Tanzania Litho, Dar es Salaam Printers, Iringa Printers and TMP Printers. Generally speaking, the existing printing facilities cannot cope with the demand for books and other materials to be printed. For example, since 1977, when universal primary education was introduced, tenders have been offered by the Ministry of Education to various printers in Tanzania to print educational materials for UPE. The quantity of books to be printed has been much too large for the printers to cope with, and many of them have as a result failed to meet the deadlines for the completion of work.

THE MASS MEDIA

Newspapers, magazines and journals

Tanzania has few journals—about twenty—and even fewer scholarly journals. Magazines are also very few. The Ministry of Information Services Division issues a yearly press directory. The *Press Directory 1979* recorded the following circulation figures for the party and government papers: the English-language papers, the *Daily News* and *Sunday News,* 89,000 and 41,000 copies respectively; the party papers (in Kiswahili) *Mzalendo* and *Unuru* had each a circulation of 100,000. A full list of the newspapers and magazines published in 1979, analysed according to frequency, circulation and regional allocation, has been published by the Ministry of Information Services.[11] The present distribution of newspapers and news coverage is not much different from that obtaining in 1967. A look at the 1967 research findings by John C. Condon explains the situation.[12] (See Tables 1 and 2.)

TABLE 1. Distribution of newspapers in the United Republic of Tanzania, 1967

Newspaper	Ownership	Language	Average daily printing	Editor's estimated readership
The Standard	Private	English	17 000	51 000
Ngurumo	Private	Kiswahili	14 000	50 000
Uhuru	TANU	Kiswahili	11 000	100 000
The Nationalist	TANU	English	6 000	22 000

TABLE 2. News coverage of newspapers in the United Republic of Tanzania, 1967

Geographical area	Percentage of total news coverage			
	The Standard	Ngurumo	Uhuru	The Nationalist
Dar es Salaam	41.0	37.0	62.0	52.5
Up-country	8.0	5.5	23.5	27.0
Zanzibar	1.0	2.5	2.0	1.0
Whole of United Republic of Tanzania	50.0	45.0	87.5	80.5
Outside (rest of Africa, United Kingdom, the Americas, etc.)	50.0	55.0	12.5	19.5

Each newspaper sent about half of its copies up-country and distributed the other half in the capital. Because of poor roads and transportation systems, the regions received the papers irregularly and very late. As far as news coverage is concerned Tanzania, as would be expected, dominated the news of the Tanzanian press. News about Dar es Salaam accounted for nearly 85 per cent of the Tanzanian news in the English-language papers (or about 40 per cent of the total news coverage). In the Swahili papers, 65 to 70 per cent of the national news coverage was from Dar es Salaam, that is 50 to 60 per cent of the total news. Zanzibar news accounted for only 1 to 2 per cent of all the news in all the papers. The English-language papers emphasized international news and the Swahili press local news. The Standard, particularly, was regarded as the 'international paper', and Uhuru or Ngurumo as 'local newspapers'.

RECORDING TANZANIAN PUBLISHING OUTPUT:
THE TANZANIA NATIONAL BIBLIOGRAPHY

The Tanzania Library Service publishes the Tanzania National Bibliography, a list of publications printed in Tanzania and deposited with the National Central Library and the Library of the University of Dar es Salaam. The Libraries (Deposit of Books) Act of 1962 requires printers on the Tanzanian mainland to deposit one copy of all books printed by them with the University Library, and in 1963, following the establishment of the Tanzania Library Service, the Minister for National Education issued the Libraries (Deposit of Books) Order of 1963, which extended the 1962 act by requiring printers to deposit a further copy with the Tanzania Library Service. However, with the enaction of the Tanzania Library Services Act of 1975, the Libraries (Deposit of Books) Act of 1962 was repealed. The 1975 act stipulates that it shall be the duty of every person who prints or produces or causes to be printed or produced in mainland Tanzania any book or other literary work intended for sale or public distribution or exhibition, to supply to the Board, free of charge, not less than two copies of such book or literary work. The definition of a book includes, among other things, documents, periodicals, magazines, newspapers, pamphlets, music scores, picture prints, photographs, maps, plans and manuscripts. Since 1969, Tanzania Library Service has published the *Tanzania National Bibliography*. Efforts are now being made to publish a retrospective bibliography for the period from 1964 to 1968. Detailed statistics of book production in Tanzania for the years 1972 to 1975 are appended to this publication.

The problems regarding the collection of statistics on book production were dealt with in detail at the International Conference on African Bibliography, held in Nairobi from 4 to 8 December 1967. Regarding the acquisition and recording of current Tanzanian materials, Harold Holdsworth, former librarian of the University of Dar es Salaam, had this to say:

Deposit libraries are naturally in the most favourable position to collect, yet even they find breakdowns in supply through failures in the mechanics of distribution, through the absence of trade lists and regular publishers' and printers' lists, through the fact that printings tend to be small and are soon sold, and the reprintings are few, through the existence of so much material which is not available through the trade and therefore not supplied on deposit by printers, who in Tanzania are responsible for delivery, through the failure of many printers and publishers to hold stocks for long periods, particularly of newspapers and magazines. There are failures also on the part of libraries which do not have the staff to claim missing parts promptly or to devote the necessary time to becoming informed about all local publications.[13]

IMPORT AND EXPORT OF BOOKS

To meet the great demand for books a considerable number, mostly in English, have to be imported from abroad, mainly from the United Kingdom. Very few books are exported from Tanzania to other countries. Table 3 shows the situation for the years 1967 to 1970.[14]

TABLE 3. Import and export of books (in thousands of Tanzanian shillings), 1967–70

Year	Imports			Exports		
	Kenya and Uganda	Outside East Africa	Total	Kenya and Uganda	Outside East Africa	Total
1967	885	6 353	7 328	652	185	837
1968	902	4 525	5 427	751	96	847
1969	717	3 672	4 389	588	190	778
1970	1 442	4 365	5 807	1 268	211	1 479

Since Tanzania relies so heavily on imported books from the rest of Africa and overseas, there are various formalities that have to be followed to ensure that genuine payments are made and that the scarce money in the form of foreign exchange is used efficiently. *Exchange Control Circular No. 12* governs payments for books, periodicals, etc., and subscriptions to societies and clubs. Under this regulation, a specific import licence has to be obtained and original invoices or letters of demand for advance payment should be produced to support the application for the licence. The importation of books and periodicals and other cultural materials is also subject to the general *Exchange Control Circular No. 10.* Payment for imports may be made only after goods have been cleared through customs. Where the goods to be imported have not been shipped, sent by rail, etc., and the importer wishes to make advance payment, prior approval of the Bank of Tanzania is required. Importers are advised to try as much as possible to buy goods directly from the suppliers or manufacturers, thus avoiding the use of intermediaries. The Bank of Tanzania also requires that there should be a pre-shipment inspection of goods to ascertain their quality and quantity and price comparison by the General Superintendent Company Limited, the Inspection Agency for the government. Upon completion of inspection, the Inspection Agency issues a Report of Findings. Only after a Clean Report of Findings has been made can goods be transported. Consignments with a value in *pro forma* invoice of less than 10,000 Tanzanian shillings are not subject to preshipment inspection. The Tanzania Library Service is exempt from paying customs duties under the Customs Tariff (Remission of Customs Duties) (Tanganyika Library Services Board) (Order 1966) as amended by the Customs Tariff (Tanganyika Library Services Board) (No. 2) Order 1966. The order stipulates that 'the whole of the import of any goods imported or purchased prior to clearance through the customs by or on behalf of Tanganyika Library Services Board which the Commissioner of Customs and Excise is satisfied are for the exclusive use of the Tanganyika Library Service in the performance of its functions, are hereby remitted'. Tanzania is a signatory to the Unesco Agreement on the Importation of Educational, Scientific and Cultural Materials, which eliminates duties on books and provides that foreign exchange shall be granted for the importation of books for public libraries.[15]

PROMOTION AND DISTRIBUTION OF BOOKS

A prerequisite to book development is the inculcation of the reading habit. One of the most important factors in book promotion is the holding of book festivals, book weeks, exhibitions, etc. The development of libraries is probably by far the best way of promoting book distribution and reading. In this instance public libraries play a vital role. In a developing and poor country like Tanzania, a nation-wide public library service is essential in view of the small per capita income and the inability for the average person to buy books.

Realizing the important role books can play in national development, Tanzania established the Tanzania Library Service in 1963 with the responsibility of promoting, establishing, equipping and developing libraries all over the country. In 1975, documentation services, book production and training were added to the Board's responsibilities. As a national service, Tanzania Library Service has been preoccupied with ways and means of extending library facilities throughout the country in an effort to bring books to the people. The various services below have been and are being provided.

Urban library service

The National Central Library in Dar es Salaam acts as the headquarters of a nationwide library service. It has a fully organized public reference and lending service for both adults and children, a central book-processing and supply unit and a central advisory service. The National Central Library is also responsible for producing the *Tanzania National Bibliography*. Twelve regional libraries have been built in regional towns up-country; the thirteenth and fourteenth libraries are being built. More regional libraries will be built in the remaining six regions before the board embarks on plans to extend libraries to districts.

Rural library service

As about 95 per cent of the population in Tanzania live in rural areas, every effort is being made to provide rural library services using village libraries and mobile libraries.

Postal library service

Books are sent by mail to people who live in places without library facilities. The service is offered free of charge, in that the postage of books both ways is paid for by the Tanzania Library Service, and the reader has only to pay a deposit of 20 Tanzanian shillings for each book borrowed. This money is refunded to him if he ceases to use the service or if he moves to a place where there are library facilities available.

The book-box exchange service

Collections of books are offered free of charge on loan to various institutions such as community centres, clubs and the like which do not have library facilities.

Library service for schools and teachers' college

The Education Libraries Department at the National Central Library provides service to schools and teacher-training colleges. The services given are in the form of advice on the selection of books, design and planning of library buildings, library seminars and actual visits to schools and teachers' colleges. There is also a school mobile-library service—a van that visits secondary schools and distributes books on loan to libraries to supplement their educational needs.

Bookshops

Bookshops are important for the distribution of books. There are just over twenty in Tanzania. Perhaps one of the greatest problems facing bookshops is that the majority are small by international standards and therefore do not have the resources to enable them to stock large numbers of publications, in the absence of firm orders, and in most cases they are incapable of locating, purchasing and forwarding publications for which there is no consistent or substantial demand. Whatever items are kept in bookshops, most of them are sold at exorbitant prices (see Appendix on page 190).

Tanzania Elimu Supplies Ltd (TES)

Tanzania Elimu Supplies Ltd is a commercial enterprise under the aegis of the Ministry of National Education. According to the Memorandum of Association of the Company the following are its objectives:[16]

To carry on the business of dealers in the supplies of stationery, writing materials, teaching aids, sporting materials and other equipment and materials of all kinds for use in schools, colleges and other educational establishments and as agents for the sale of such equipment and materials.
To carry on the business of publishers, booksellers, newspaper and journal proprietors, advertising agents, printers, bookbinders, designers and draftsmen and as agents for the sale of books, journals and other publications of all kinds.

The company has been made the sole official distributor for the Ministry of National Education of textbooks, exercise books, writing material, office supplies and related supplies, to all primary and secondary schools, colleges and the University of Dar es Salaam. The company's operations have now been expanded to include distribution of similar supplies to the general public. TES is establishing branches all over Tanzania to facilitate the distribution of materials to customers.

THE TANZANIA COPYRIGHT ACT, 1966:
ITS EFFECT ON AUTHORSHIP AND PUBLISHING

For about forty years (1919–61) when Tanzania was a British dependency, the British Copyright Law was part of the laws of Tanzania. The United Kingdom Copyright Act, 1911, was extended to Tanzania in 1924 as the Copyright Act, 1911 (Extension to Tanganyika Territory) Order, 1924. However, after independence, and following the enactment of the Tanzania Copyright Legislation, the United Kingdom Copyright Act, 1911, ceased to have effect in Tanzania. The Copyright Act, 1966, makes provision for the copyright of literary, musical and artistic works, cinematograph films, sound recordings and broadcasts. As the law protects only works published in Tanzania, all works published in other countries, whether authored by Tanzanians or by foreigners are not protected by the Tanzania Copyright Act. Tanzania is neither a member of the Berne Copyright Convention (BCC) nor the Universal Copyright Convention (UCC). It does not even have reciprocity arrangements with individual countries. However, before independence and until 1962, Tanzania was automatically a member of the BCC and UCC because the United Kingdom was a member of the two conventions.

According to the Tanzanian Copyright Law, the 'owner of the copyright' means the first owner, an assignee, or an exclusive licensee. The law defines an author as one who is commissioned to write a book or produce a work by a person who is not the author's employer. If he is not commissioned but creates a work or writes a book in the course of employment, the authorship of work may, subject to express agreement, be transferred to the employer. (The term 'work' includes translations, adaptations, new versions, or arrangement of pre-existing works and anthologies or collections of works which by reason of the selection and arrangement, appear to be original in character.) This stems from the fact that public employees are employed full time and may in the course of writing use facts and experience gained in the course of their duties. The enforcement of this clause may lead to greater shortage of books and other literary works as public employees are capable and are in a good position to write authoritative works.

The term of copyright protection for literary works is the life of the author plus twenty-five years. This is apparently twenty-five years short of the international standard, which is 'life of the author plus fifty years'. In the case of anonymous works, government and other organizations' works, protection extends over a period of twenty-five years from the end of the year in which publication occurs. In the event of authors of anonymous works being discovered, the life of author plus twenty-five years formula applies. As for joint authors, the life of the person who survives the others, plus twenty-five years, applies irrespective of his nationality. In the final analysis, the copyright law in Tanzania would appear to have failed to 'reconcile the interest of authors, who give expression to ideas; publishers who disseminate ideas and the members of the public who use ideas'.

BOOK DEVELOPMENT COUNCIL

Despite the various efforts being made by the Tanzanian Government and other organizations for the publication of books, there is an urgent need to have a National Book Development Council as recommended by the 1968 Accra Conference. A National Book Development Council should bring together all those involved with books—authors, printers, booksellers, librarians and other institutions. Although the actual form and statutes of book-development councils differ from country to country, the statement of objects of the Malaysian National Book Development Council could be a model to others, as indicated below:

To bring together the different groups concerned in the production and distribution of reading materials with a view to ensuring efficiency and effective co-operation in the provision and use of reading materials.

To encourage the formation of professional associations relating to reading materials where these do not exist and the strengthening of such associations where they already exist.

To encourage the maintenance of high professional and technical standards in book production and distribution in the country.

To encourage and promote the provision of adequate library services in the country.

To create by suitable means public interest in books and encourage discriminate reading habits among all sections of the community.

To organize and provide training facilities in all matters relating to reading
materials.

To foster and co-ordinate research and investigation into problems in the field of
reading materials.

To do whatever is possible towards the attainment of the above and any other
objectives that will promote the activities of the council.

The establishment of a National Book Development Council in Tanzania will go
a long way towards improving the book industry in the country. There is, at the
moment, an urgent need to do a more thorough study of the book need, and the
problems to be solved. The national Book Development Council, if set up, will
provide the much-needed forum for all those involved with books.

BOOKSHOPS: INVESTIGATION INTO BOOK PRICES IN DAR ES SALAAM

Aims and objective

The professional staff meeting of the Tanzania Library Service Acquisitions
Department in February 1976 passed a resolution to investigate book prices in
Dar es Salaam. The aim of this investigation was twofold: (a) to find out the prices
which bookshops in Dar es Salaam charge to members of the public, in particular
to look into their profit margins and into the consistency of prices as between
bookshops; and (b) to find out the prices which bookshops in Dar es Salaam
charge to the Tanzania Library Service.

Method

The main problem was to ensure that the results of the investigation were
meaningful. Because of inflation, book prices and transport costs are continuously
rising. At the same time the value of the British pound sterling compared to the
Tanzanian shilling has been decreasing. The bookshops, on the whole, were not
happy to reveal their method of pricing but merely declared they charged
'according to the invoice'. (It is interesting to note that all bookshops, except the
university, cut off the United Kingdom price from the dustjacket, thereby
preventing the buyer from making his own conversion.)

   In the United Kingdom a system of retail price maintenance is in force for
books. This means that all bookshops must charge the price printed on the book.
The bookshops purchase books from the publishers at 33.3 per cent discount.
Bookshops therefore make a third profit on each sale to cover their overheads.
Taking the above considerations into account, the TLS method of investigation
was to visit each major bookshop in Dar es Salaam, find recent purchases of
United Kingdom books that had their prices printed on the covers and then find
out for what price the books were being sold. In addition, TLS surveyed books
being currently catalogued in the Acquisitions Department to discover what prices
local bookshops were charging TLS. Cataloguers were asked to identify books
whose prices seemed excessively high.

Results

The detailed results of the investigation appear in Appendix 1, which contains a comparative table of current book prices as related to the United Kingdom price. Appendix 2 contains a list of books bought by TLS from local bookshops at an excessive price.

Conversion rates and profit margins

The University Bookshop, for the past two and a half years, has consistently arrived at the Tanzanian price by converting at 20 shillings to the pound (£) sterling. (Very recently it has begun to convert at a slightly higher rate for specific publishers, e.g. Longmans.) The other bookshops in Dar es Salaam convert on average at 25 shillings to the pound sterling. Over the past three years, the official exchange rate has dropped from 18 shillings to 16 shillings to the pound. The profit margin per book could be calculated as follows:

A book cost £1 in the United Kingdom (i.e. 17/-). The bookshop in Dar es Salaam buys it for £0.66 (i.e. 11/-). The University Bookshop sells it for 20/-. Other bookshops sell it for 24/- or 25/-. Even allowing for transport and overheads, these 100 per cent and higher profit rates would seem excessive.

Inconsistencies

There are inconsistencies in converting from pounds sterling to Tanzanian shillings both between different bookshops and even in the same bookshop. The differences between bookshops are illustrated in Appendix 1. An example of inconsistency within a bookshop is illustrated by the following: in ESA Bookshop, a book priced at £0.40. in United Kingdom was charged variously at 9/95, 11/40, 12/7, 12/40 and 12/50.

Prices charged to TLS

In the majority of cases, the prices charged to TLS are the same as those charged to individual buyers. However, some cases came to light where the price charged seemed excessive. These cases are listed in the Appendix. It is interesting to note that in the United Kingdom bookshops that gain library custom offer those libraries a 10 per cent discount on the retail price of a book.

Recommendations

That, for the time being, TLS order all its foreign books from the country of origin.
That TLS pressure bookshops to reduce their profit margin. If possible, the National Prices Commission should be asked to fix a rate of conversion.
That if TLS gives its custom to a bookshop in Tanzania, it should request special terms.
That TLS question with the relevant bookshops the cases listed in the Appendix and, if due, claim rebates.

APPENDIX 1

Comparative book prices in Dar es Salaam bookshops

British price in pounds sterling	University	Dar es Salaam	Cathedral	ESA	International	Standard	National Supplies Co.
£0.20	4/-	—	5/-	7/50	—	—	6/-
£0.25	5/-	6/25	8/-	—	—	—	—
£0.30	6/-	—	—	8/-	—	—	—
£0.30	6/-	—	—	9/-	7/50	7/50	—
£0.35	7/-	8/75	8/50	10/50	8/50	—	8/50
£0.40	8/-	10/-	—	12/50	10/00	—	—
£0.45	9/-	11/25	—	—	11/-	—	—
£0.50	10/-	12/50	12/50	15/10	12/-	12/-	—
£0.55	11/-	—	13/50	—	—	—	—
£0.60	12/-	15/-	—	—	14/50	—	14/50
£0.65	13/-	—	15/70	—	15/50	—	—
£0.70	14/-	—	—	18/-	17/-	—	—
£0.75	15/-	18/80	19/-	—	18/-	—	—
£0.80	16/-	—	—	—	—	—	—
£0.85	17/-	—	—	—	—	—	—
£0.90	18/-	—	—	21/60	—	21/50	—
£0.95	19/-	—	—	22/80	22/50	—	—
£1.00	20/-	—	25/-	24/-	—	24/-	—
£1.15	23/-	28/75	—	—	—	—	—
£1.20	24/-	—	30/-	31/-	—	—	—
£1.25	25/-	30/-	—	—	—	31/25	29/-
£1.40	28/-	—	35/-	—	—	—	—
£1.50	30/-	—	—	34/-	36/-	36/-	—
£1.60	32/-	—	—	40/-	—	38/-	—
£1.75	35/-	—	43/75	42/-	—	40/-	—
£1.80	36/-	—	—	45/-	—	—	—
£1.90	38/-	—	—	48/50	—	—	—
£1.95	39/-	—	55/-	—	46/50	48/-	—
£2.00	40/-	—	56/-	—	—	—	—
£2.10	42/-	—	—	—	—	55/-	—
£2.25	45/-	59/20	—	—	—	54/-	64/-
£2.50	50/-	62/50	—	—	59/50	—	—
£2.75	55/-	—	—	62/50	—	—	—
£2.95	59/-	—	74/-	—	—	—	—
£3.00	60/-	—	—	—	—	66/-	—
£3.20	64/-	—	—	85/-	—	—	—
£3.75	75/-	—	—	—	84/-	—	—
£4.50	90/-	—	—	109/80	—	—	—
£4.75	95/-	—	105/-	—	—	—	—
£5.50	110/-	132/-	—	—	132/-	—	—
£5.95	119/-	—	—	—	142/50	—	145/-
£15.00	300/-	360/-	—	—	—	—	—

APPENDIX 2

TLS purchases

TLS has made the following purchases from Dar es Salaam bookshops. Even allowing for the normal exchange-rate used by those shops, it would appear that an excess profit has been made.

1. G. Borgstrom, *Fish as Food*. Vol. E. Part 1. Price in United Kingdom: £12.20. Purchase price from Dar es Salaam Bookshop: 413/75.
2. A. Morrison, *Storage and Stock Control*. 2nd rev. ed. 1974. Price in United Kingdom: £2.95. Purchase price from Dar es Salaam Bookshop: 81/25.
3. J. Horsfall, *Teaching the Cello to Groups*. 1974. Price in United Kingdom: £2.75. Purchase price from Cathedral Bookshop: 67/70.
4. F. C. Raphael, *Electric Wiring of Buildings*. Price in United Kingdom: £1.25. Purchase price from Dar es Salaam Bookshop: 41/30.
5. Pax and Urwick, *Dynamic Administration*. 2nd ed. 1973. Price in United Kingdom: £2.50. Purchase price from Dar es Salaam Bookshop: 81/25.
6. Jones, *The International Yearbook of Foreign Policy Analysis 1974*. Price in United Kingdom: £5.50. Purchase price from Dar es Salaam Bookshop: 132/- and 137/50.

APPENDIX 3

*A list of the more important bookshops in Tanzania**

Christian Bookshop,
P.O. Box 301,
Moshi

Tanga Bookshop,
P.O. Box 262,
Tanga

Church Bookshop,
P.O. Box 277,
Bukoba

Tanganyika Mission Press,
Private Bag,
Tabora

Africa Inland Mission Bookshop,
P.O. Box 905,
Mwanza

Cathedral Bookshop,
P.O. Box 2381,
Dar es Salaam

ELCT Lutheran Church Bookshop,
P.O. Box 157,
Singida

City Bookshop,
P.O. Box 442,
Dar es Salaam

Hymil Import Bookshop,
P.O. Box 753,
Dar es Salaam

Dar es Salaam Bookshop,
P.O. Box 2126,
Dar es Salaam

Iringa Bookshop,
P.O. Box 240,
Iringa

ESA Bookshop,
P.O. Box 2126,
Dar es Salaam

Morogoro Bookshop,
P.O. Box 351,
Morogoro

Ndanda Mission Press,
Ndanda

Swedish Free Mission Bookshop,
P.O. Box 222,
Tabora

Standard Bookshop,
P.O. Box 9402, DSM

Catholic Bookshop,
P.O. Box 47,
Songea

Inland Bookshop,
P.O. Box 1402,
Mwanza

Msimbazi Bookshop,
P.O. Box 2428,
DSM

Njombe Bookshop,
P.O. Box 40,
Njombe

Peramiho Bookshop,
P.O. Box 41
Peramiho

* From Tanzania Elimu Supplies, circular to its educational materials distribution agents, 1975.

NOTES

1. J. Ndegwa, *Printing and Publishing in Kenya: An Outline of Development*, pp. 15–26, London, School of Library, Archive and Information Studies, 1971.
2. R. Hutchison, 'Neo-colonial Tactics' *Africa*, No. 23, July 1973, pp. 74–9.
3. N. A. Kuhanga, 'Education and Self-reliance in Tanzania; A National Perspective', *Development Dialogue*, Vol. 2. 1978, p. 38.
4. N. A. Kuhanga, *Hotuba ya Waziri wa Elimu ya Taifa kuhusu Makadirio ya fedha kwa mwaka 1979–1980* (speech of Minister of National Education on 1979/80 estimates), Dar es Salaam, p. 6.
5. Ibid., p. 38.
6. S. Malya, 'Books by the People', *Adult Education and Development in Tanzania*, Vol. I, pp. 114–15, Dar es Salaam, The National Adult Education Association of Tanzania, 1975.
7. *Resolutions of 15th TANU General Conference, 1971*, p. 45.
8. United Republic of Tanzania, Ministry of Community and National Culture, *Tanzania Literacy and Adult Education Project; An Application for Assistance from the U.N. Special Fund*, n.d.
9. K. Laubjerg, *Development of Literacy Education in Jamaica and Tanzania, A Case-study of the Impact of Literacy on the Formation Development Attitudes Among Literacy Participants in two Rural Districts*, Copenhagen, Lirkerod, 1979.
10. National Development Corporation, *Annual Reports*. 1972, 1974.
11. United Republic of Tanzania, Ministry of Information Services, *Press Directory 1979*, pp. 13–15.
12. J. C. Condon, 'Nation and building in the Tanzania Press', *Journal of Modern African Studies*, No. 53, 1967, pp. 335–54.
13. J. D. Pearson and R. Jones, *The Bibliography of Africa: Proceedings and Papers of the International Conference on African Bibliography; Nairobi, 4–8 December 1967*, pp. 50–1, London, Frank Cass, 1970.
14. E. E. Haungamno and C. S. Ilomo, *Books Build Nations*, Vol. II: *Library Services in Tanzania*, London, n.d.
15. Unesco, *Book Development in Africa; Problems and Perspectives*, p. 16, Paris, Unesco, 1969 (COM/69 XVII.56A). (Reports and Papers on Mass Communication, 56.)
16. Tanzania Elimu Supplies, *Six Years of Progress; A Short Report on 6 Years of Rapid Development*, p. 4, D.S.M., n.d.

13 Strategy for cultural industries in a socialist country: cultural policy and audio-visual media in Cuba

Enrique Gonzalez-Manet

Editor, *Cuban National Commission for Unesco Magazine*

A CULTURAL INDUSTRY WITHIN A DEVELOPMENT STRATEGY

Whose culture, what for and with what purpose?

Cuba used to be a country that was invaded by foreign models induced by commercial publicity. The semantic pollution and adulteration of language unleashed public campaigns in 1950 without much effect, but nevertheless significant, due to the opposition by certain sectors to the eroding ideological-cultural penetration.

In the neo-colonial republic, especially after the introduction of television in 1950, a subcultural industry started to develop driven by advertising agencies and transnational corporations. The large mass media became generators of cultural forms, fashion, styles, habits of consumption and social behaviour, the main goal of which was to promote social and commercial competitiveness, the status quo, and individual values based on 'free flow' and 'free market' theories.

The process was in conformity with unequal trade terms and market dependence, and reflected international tendencies through its relations of domination. After 1959 changes in the search for our own identity, within the scope of a general development strategy, were not born without strong resistance from private commercial enterprises, advertising agencies and transnational corporations.

During the first years of the process of social transformation in Cuba, two radically different concepts clashed: (a) the commercializing of culture, with a distorting image governed by the quest for maximum profits and projected as an agent of foreign models, and (b) the diffusion of a culture of a humanist and universal nature, capable of reflecting the people's own idiosyncrasy and of contributing to its development in a new society.

The general features of this approach, oriented more towards education than towards entertainment, more towards the basic necessities than towards consumer habits only accessible to privileged élites, laid the basis for a new cultural structure, soundly consolidated as a result of an ever-growing relationship with the education and communication sectors.

THE CULTURAL INDUSTRY IN CUBA: FACTS AND FIGURES

Cultural development in Cuba is based mainly on sustained progress in education. Four out of ten of the population are engaged in education at different levels. The national budget for education has grown twelvefold; there are more than 650,000 scholarship holders, and a 98 per cent attendance of school-age children, with a negligible drop-out rate. This effort is designed to guarantee the right to knowledge and culture of the people at large, and especially the younger generation.

The institutional bases of the Cuban cultural complex were established in the four-year period from 1959 to 1963, in the midst of an arduous class struggle and an escalation of foreign pressure and aggression. In this short time were created: the House of the Americas, addressed to cultural relations within the continent; the Cuban Institute of Art and Motion Picture Industry; the National Council of Culture; the Cuban Artists' and Writers' Union; the National Commission of Museums and Monuments; the Musical Editing and Records Enterprise; the National Lyrical Theatre; the Cuban National Ballet; the National Dance Ensemble and the National Folklore Ensemble. The National Symphonic Orchestra was reorganized and the National Chorus and the Movement of New Troubadours were created. Lastly, in 1976, the Ministry of Culture was instituted in order to ensure the co-ordination of most of these institutions, and implement cultural policy.

The cinema industry started from zero. With its own solutions, enriched by universal currents, this industry became an important cultural factor. By 1978 it had already produced 100 full-length films, 650 medium-length films, 950 weekly newsreels and 150 cartoons, winning over 200 awards at international festivals. Annual cinema attendance stands at more than 30 million seats for a population of 10 million, not considering the mobile service which reaches the farthest rural areas. The film industry also has a film library, with one of the most complete collections in Latin America.

The publishing industry hardly existed before 1958; printing was dedicated to commercial advertising. About a million books a year were published, especially official documents and primary-school textbooks. Significant novelists and poets, such as the late Alejo Carpentier and the current president of the Writer's Union, Nicolás Guillén, used to publish works at their own expense, of no move than 150 copies. Today, 800 titles are published yearly—25 per cent of which are literature—totalling 30 million copies at prices that can be considered derisory according to world standards, which turn books more and more into a luxury item out of reach of the vast majority.

The country has 130 major libraries, besides 714 minor ones, not counting

10,000 mini-libraries in factories and work centres having a minimum of fifty books of general interest. A national network reaches the farthermost rural zones.

Cuba had six museums in precarious condition in 1958, without any scientific organization and mostly ignored by the people since they were not culturally motivated. Today it has seventy-four institutions of this type, each of a different character, which offer public training and participation programmes for all ages. Forty of these specialize in history, arts and sciences. The Museum of the City of Havana, for instance, receives around 200,000 visitors annually.

There are six nationwide theatrical groups with cultural-extension programmes in factories, farms and schools, and twenty-six°groups of children's theatre that carry on the same activity, especially in rural areas, for the purpose of entertaining, teaching and developing cultural sensitiveness.

One of the initiatives of higher repercussion in this field of activity was the early creation of the National Amateur Movement, to universalize artistic creation and to foster the propensity for art, especially among workers, peasants and students. Teachers and instructors came from the Higher School of Fine Arts, which also trains skilled professionals. Another important project, started in 1977, is the organization of Houses of Culture, of which there are over 100 throughout the country.

The National Amateur Movement represents 20,000 artistic groups, with more than 700,000 children dedicated to music, theatre, dance, visual arts and literature, all of which receive from the Ministry of Culture the necessary means for their activities. The Movement includes some 17,000 reading circles, with an average of ten participants who analyse and debate outstanding national and universal literacy works.

House of Culture promote cultural activities within the communities through lectures, seminars, concerts, festivals, exhibitions, music classes, film debates and recreational programmes. They do not pretend to turn out professionals, but rather to bring people together and develop their cultural inclinations, stimulate creativity and promote artistic enjoyment. The House of Culture of one of the municipal areas in the province of Havana organized hundreds of activities in 1979 with more than 250,000 people attending.

Mass media and telecommunication systems, besides their specific functions, have as an outstanding goal that of complementing the social and cultural development of the people. Investments made and development fullfilled in this sector can be measured through the World Communication Survey, edited by Unesco in 1977, which indicates that Cuba is the only country within the so-called Third World that has national coverage in press, radio and television.

The radio system has fifty-two transmitters—three national, fourteen provincial and thirty-five regional—with a capacity of over 900 kilowatts, 30 per cent of which is in the capital city. They transmit a total of about 1,000 programme hours daily through a modern microwave network.

These stations have different profiles, with informative, cultural, artistic and entertainment programmes. Fifteen new programmes have been created for national transmission within the last three years. Total transmitting hours in 1979 reached a peak of 326,000, 50 per cent of them broadcast by municipal stations.

Programmes are 99 per cent nationally produced, 12 per cent live and 88 per cent recorded.

Musical programmes represent 39 per cent of the total, followed by 22 per cent of an informative kind, 7 per cent juvenile, 4.5 per cent educational and 2.5 per cent children's programmes. Drama, historical and humorous programmes stand at 1 per cent each. Broadcasting power has tripled within the last twenty years. The number of radios, mostly transistor sets, is 250 for every 1,000 inhabitants. A new factory is now being built near Havana and will produce 300,000 radios and 100,000 television sets starting in 1981.

Before 1958 television broadcasts could be received solely by urban viewers, excluding vast rural areas, among which was the Isle of Pines and the whole province of Pinar del Rio. A very high proportion of programmes were imported and the rest imitated those that were successful in the United States. The principal sponsors were North American transnational corporations.

At the present time there are two national and one provincial channel, with a power of 1,200 kilowatts. There are 120 television sets per 1,000 inhabitants, and out of a total of 600,000 rural workers, 80 per cent own radios and 26 per cent television sets.

There still are limitations and deficiencies in connection with both media. Long- and short-term measures are contemplated, among them greater public participation, more technical and scientific programmes, youth debates on different subjects, broader economic information, increased dramatic production based on national events, betterment of the variety and quality of children's programmes and a further effort to guide the population in its use of leisure time.

Twenty-eight microwave stations throughout the country ensure the development of broadcasting and their 5,280 channels also help to provide automatic telephone connections. Most of these resources have been used to promote the urbanization of rural areas by being set up in places that never had these services.

A new project now under way will complement this system, making Cuba one of the first countries in the world to operate a national coaxial cable network. It should be totally installed by 1986, with an extension of 1,800 km. This project, planned in collaboration with the USSR, will satisfy every kind of long-wire requirement, including facsimile. The system has a capacity of 10,000 simultaneous channels, with a duplex channel for television.

Five computerized data-bank networks will be connected to the system. They have been operating on a national scale since the end of 1979 using Cuban-made minicomputers and displays, built and installed by the National Institute of Automatized Systems and Computer Techniques. Already in 1976, the country had more than 300 solid-state physicists, forming the core of progress in this field.

The press has one of the most significant roles in the cultural sector. Before 1958 there were fifteen daily newspapers with a total circulation of 300,000 copies. At present there are two national newspapers—*Granma* and *Juventud Rebelde*—and fourteen with a provincial range. There are also eight weekly and monthly magazines which publish 1.18 million copies and four weekly tabloids with 550,000 copies. The daily press issues 1.1 million copies, which still do not suffice. Distribution to remote areas of the countryside is made by agricultural aviation and even by mule trains.

Cuba's social and cultural awakening has been analysed by Professor Herbert Schiller, of California University, who visited Cuba at the end of 1977. He stated on that occasion that 'the daily behaviour of people, their work ties and their way of life—that is, their mutual relations—constitute a medium in itself and a very deep and consistent form of communication'.

He added that shared motivations and the meeting of social needs turn into solidarity, which is the basis for real communication and went on to affirm:

This process of transmission, based on social reciprocity, is stronger than mass media themselves, which come to have a supporting function in regard to the aims of the community. It may be said that, when such solid ties are developed, mass media acquire a complementary function.

Among other things, he stated that the mass media have such an overriding role in the United States because of the life-style of an alienated society lacking in solidarity. He went on to say that

to the extent that Cubans share common goals and aims, that all participate in a single social effort and relate with one another, there is a powerful cohesion.

This, probably, is their best protection against the powerful system of US broadcasting, which seeks ideological penetration and control. Cuba's experience is very useful and important: it could set an example for those who fear the social implications of the United States informational system.[1]

NOTE

1. Herbert I. Schiller, 'Media and Imperialism', Paris, extract, Centre National de la Recherche Scientifique, No. 6, 1978, p. 269–81.

Part Five

Towards an integrated government strategy for cultural industries

Cultural industries are no doubt the most striking example of the far-reaching changes brought about in society in the past forty years or so by the widespread influence of industrial growth as the dominant cultural pattern the world over, although naturally in different forms and varying degrees.

In terms of *scientific analysis,* the devising of a genuinely integrated approach to all the issues involved means that both the micro- and the macro-economic aspects of the question must be considered, as well as the 'distortions' introduced by cultural industries and the new prospects they open up in the production of messages or what might be called the terms of cultural exchange for an entire population and the individuals comprising it—whatever type of society is being considered—and for the balance of cultures across the globe.

In terms of *decision-making,* the need for integrated strategies is no less important. Of course, the circumstances will be very different according to whether a country has a market, a mixed or a planned economy, but in all of them, the public authorities must have a clear idea of the means of action at their disposal and of the economic, cultural and social consequences of any measures they might adopt. They must also assess as precisely as possible the relative weight of their action among all the initiatives taken by the various categories of agents involved in the growth of cultural industries and of cultural development in general. An accurate assessment of state action from these two angles, important at all stages of economic and social development, is even more decisive in the developing countries, where the practicability of government strategy *vis-à-vis* the private sector, especially where external economic interests are concerned, must be assessed rationally if it is to have any chance of succeeding.

Similarly, the strategy of the *economic decision-makers,* firms or branches of industry, can be effective only if goals, constraints and means are all taken into account so that no essential parameter is overlooked. The only difference here is that it is inconceivable for such a strategy not to be based primarily on economic considerations. Hence the need for commercial executives to be constantly reminded by the public authorities of the ultimate social and cultural purposes of economic growth and more specifically of industrial expansion in the crucial sector of message production, in other words of the substance as well as the form. The following two articles can be best appreciated when seen in this perspective.

Professor Heiskanen of the University of Helsinki has undertaken to analyse the past and foreseeable future balance between state intervention and continuing private sector autonomy in Finland, a country in which there is a fairly substantial degree of state control and one in which the public sector is relatively important. It is particularly interesting to note that Professor Heiskanen concludes his study by saying that it is not the actual balance that counts but the way public intervention and private sector autonomy are combined.

The most important point Augustin Girard makes in his consideration of the role of the public authorities in developing cultural industries would seem to be the need to link up the specific problems of direct or indirect state support at any particular stage of the process of production and distribution of industrialized cultural goods or services in any branch, with the major objectives of a modern cultural policy. Only by adopting an integrated approach to both ends and means can a valid solution be found, not only in economic and technical terms, but also in social and cultural terms, to the different problems posed by the massive-scale development of cultural industries and the imbalance it has engendered on a worldwide scale.

There is no denying that standardization and production on a massive scale threaten one of the foundations of mankind's cultural heritage, namely the diversity of the conceptions, values and behaviour patterns comprising it. It is therefore more than ever necessary to examine the impact of cultural industries on all social practices, taking into account the different types of society. This should be a step towards helping government authorities in the Member States of Unesco to take decisions and work out strategies.

Once again, however, it is not enough to point out the negative aspect of cultural industries as against conventional forms of activity. What seems more important and more realistic is to analyse their positive interactions so as to determine to what extent and on what basis they might support one another at the creative as well as at the promotion and distribution stages, and particularly as regards participation and training. The conclusions that might emerge from studies of this kind would be worth bringing to the attention of officials and decision-makers responsible for cultural industries and conventional cultural activities, and also planning bodies.

In this connection, the recommendation adopted at the meeting held in Montreal in June 1980 offer valuable guidelines both for Unesco's activities and for new topics for investigation by national research agencies. The need for an operational definition of cultural industries, the 'practicability' of cultural industries in developing countries, the occupational breakdown and employment situation in cultural industries, consumer profile by socio-economic group, the creative worker's share in firms' profits, forms of direct or indirect state aid, interrelationships between information, communication and culture, participation by young people in cultural industries, consistent application of new technologies, how cultural industries can make a constructive contribution to creative work, the possibility of developing tourism of a genuinely cultural nature: such are the paths along which research on cultural industries may be both ambitiously and realistically directed. Whether or not the challenge that cultural industries so often represent can be transformed into a new opportunity for world cultural development will depend largely on the results of such research.

14 Public intervention and private-sector autonomy in cultural industries in Finland

Ilkka Heiskanen

University of Helsinki, Department of Political Science

PRIVATE-SECTOR AUTONOMY AND PUBLIC AND COLLECTIVE INTERVENTION IN CULTURAL INDUSTRIES

In order to approach more systematically the problem of public intervention in cultural industries, we can introduce a new concept of 'quasi-governments', i.e. organizations which perform the tasks, usually assigned to central and local governments, of representing the public interest in developing important sectors of society. Usually the concept has been used to refer to voluntary organizations and strong interest groups and their representation on different public bodies (commissions, boards, etc.). We can naturally also include among these 'quasi-governments' trade associations and industrial federations, trade unions, etc., where they are explicitly or implicitly given responsibility for certain social tasks which are of wider public interest but which, for one reason or another, it is preferred to entrust to non-governmental actors. Such delegation of responsibility to business enterprises in the software production of cultural industries has also been rather common. They have—at least in Western market-economy countries—been left with certain tasks which may be labelled 'national cultural policies', i.e. they are given the right to determine important areas of cultural development. We must, however, emphasize that it is not a question of allowing the market mechanism to function but rather just the opposite. It is generally assumed that the enterprises involved in cultural industries will weigh economic and cultural interests against each other, determine the right balance and give cultural considerations if not primacy at least some kind of preferential or protected status *vis-à-vis* strict profit-making interests. We may list many examples: (a) book publishing, where publishing houses subsidize high-quality fiction and poetry with profits made from popular fiction and non-fiction; (b) the record industry, where record companies subsidize classical and experimental music with the profits earned from light classical and popular music; and

(c) newspaper and magazine publishing, when publishing houses subsidize quality journals and magazines with the profits made from popular ones. As we shall see later, this 'self-assumed responsibility' is expected less from film and radio/television companies than from publishing houses and record companies.

The above discussion has actually bi-polarized the very idea of shaping cultural development via cultural industries. On the one hand, we can emphasize the autonomy of cultural industries and the role of their business enterprises as 'quasi-governments' having the capacity and expertise to determine the cultural aspects of development. On the other hand, we can stress the public-good characteristics of cultural-industry products and advocate public intervention, in all branches or in the important ones, either by milder regulation via subsidies or legislation, or by stricter direction via public ownership and legislative control. We must also take note, however, that this bi-polarization is rather artificial and there is also a whole range of other alternatives. Thus in the case of public intervention we must not fall into the trap of 'statism', that is to say, assume that public ownership or legislative control is and must necessarily be in the hands of government and central state administration. First, we can just as well have lower-level public administration and autonomous units to take charge of public intervention. We may mention as examples radio stations or cinemas owned by local or regional self-government units (municipalities, provinces). Secondly, the word 'public' may refer not only to the state and lower-level public authorities but also to other collective units acting clearly on the behalf of collective interests of society or a part thereof. That is, some collective organizations or associations may participate in the activities of cultural industries and represent more or less broadly defined 'collective interests' in shaping such activities, and consequently also national cultural policies. We should, however, make a distinction between 'partial collective intervention' aimed at improving the position of specific groups within cultural industries (for example, intervention by professional or trade associations, industrial federations and labour market organizations), and the 'global collective intervention' which aims at changing the position and functions of cultural industries *vis-à-vis* the population at large (consumers' movements, private foundations, or organizations for the advancement of the arts or high quality cultural products).

We can list the following types of public or collective intervention in the market-based activities of cultural industries (their firms and enterprises): (a) intervention by the central state administration; (b) intervention by public lower-level administrative units, self-government units, autonomous public corporation or boards; (c) intervention by voluntary associations, foundations or consumers' co-operatives advocating 'global collective interests'; (d) intervention by professional or trade associations, employers' or labour organizations; and (e) intervention by business firms themselves, acting in a 'quasi-government' capacity which autonomously balances the economic business interests and professional and societal cultural interests.

These different types of public or collective intervention may also appear in different combinations in different countries and different branches and phases of cultural industries. This can be easily seen by comparing radio and television

systems, public support to the film industry or copyright legislation in different
countries. We shall discuss below the reasons for different types and degrees of
intervention. It is important to point out here that these combinations are not
solely sums of their component parts, i.e. we cannot simply say that a
radio/television system of a given country is owned 60 per cent by the state and
40 per cent by private organizations. The matter is more complex because in any
given combination the different elements (government control, lower-level public
intervention, organizational/associational intervention, etc.) can penetrate each
other on ideological and interpersonal levels and be differentially penetrated by
pure business interests. Thus, for example, public communication commissions or
boards set up to monitor government or audience interests may be manned by
business or labour interests that change their original functions; the bookselling
consumers' co-operative may join the very price-fixing cartel it was established to
oppose; and an originally autonomous television corporation may become a tool
of a government coalition or dominant parties. An analysis of this intertwining and
penetration is a *sine qua non* for understanding the functioning of any given system
of public or collective intervention.

CULTURAL INDUSTRIES, CULTURAL DEVELOPMENT AND REASONS FOR PUBLIC OR COLLECTIVE INTERVENTION

There seems to be a wide variety of reasons which favour, or give justification to,
increased public or collective intervention in cultural industries. The following list
of reasons has been extracted from documents, where researchers, planners,
decision-makers and representatives of interest groups have advocated increased
public or collective intervention. For each item we also give examples of the type
of intervention advocated. Thus public or collective intervention has been
advocated by suggesting that there is a need:

1. To provide public or collective subsidies for economically weak but culturally important branches, phases of production/distribution, or business enterprises.
2. To protect weak national branches, phases or enterprises against foreign competition.
3. To control such branches, phases or enterprises that are considered to be of special national interest. These interests may be technological (effective use of national R&D, observance of agreements stipulating international co-operative use of technology), economic (a need for large national investments in order to build up new infrastructures), or ideological (a need to control the media, which can be used to educate—or manipulate—large segments of society).
4. To maintain 'fair' international competition by preventing the raising of national barriers to trade in cultural-industry products.
5. To utilize effectively national R&D and to encourage related national economic development.
6. To protect the rights of the owners of intellectual property (authors, artists,

adapters, performers) upon whose ideas and works cultural-industry products are based.

7. To control potentially controversial contents of cultural-industry products.
8. To counteract a certain structural development, especially business concentration and cartel formation, which may prevent competition and the rise of new small- and medium-size firms and lead to too great a dominance of large corporations.
9. To counteract such trends as increased preponderance of foreign products, increased importance of best-sellers and top products, and increased homogenization and standardization of the content of products.
10. To safeguard creativity and secure the position of lesser-known authors/ artists, and quality products.
11. To safeguard easy and equal access of all potential consumers to the products of cultural industries; and also to ensure sufficient information about the quality of the products.

We can from our list spell out some major issues that will arise in connection with the organizing and synchronizing of public and collective interventions. Such issues include:

The potential conflict between different types of economic objectives. Such conflicts can be especially seen to arise between national economic interests (Points 1, 2, 3, 5) and those of international economic co-operation (Point 4). Conflicts can also ensue between the economic interest of encouraging business (Points 2, 4 and 5) and that of defending the rights of intellectual property owners (Point 6).

The problem of potential conflict between economic and cultural objectives. This controversy can be found, for example, in Point 8 where the prevention of business concentration may lead to a less effective and internationally less competitive organization of business. The same controversy may appear in Point 9 where public and collective intervention against 'best-sellerism', top-product dominance and homogenization and standardization may lead to diminished economic efficiency.

The problem of potential conflict between ideological, ethical and moral objectives and economic and/or cultural objectives. It goes without saying that ideological, moral and ethical restraints may prevent economic efficiency and suppress cultural creativity.

The problem of potential conflict between economically effective technology and culturally effective technology. This issue is embodied in Points 3, 5, 8 and 11 above. Economically efficient adoption of new technology may, when favoured by public intervention, require effective management and large-firm size, but this in turn may lead to monopolization, cartel formation and 'mass product' orientation. This in turn may conflict with the desired cultural objectives, and also prevent the use of new technology to improve citizens' access to 'quality culture'.

The problem of potential conflict between the observance of consumers' subjective needs (assumed to be guaranteed by free competition, free distribution and free price formation) and long-range objectives of diversity and quality of products. This issue is found in Points 10 and 11. Free competition and new channels of distribution lead to increased best-sellerism and homogenization and standardization of products.

The problem of the potential conflict between the interests of creators and consumers. This issue appears in Points 6 and 11. The protection of intellectual property may prevent the use of new media and distribution channels which would make products more easily accessible to consumers.

The problem of potential conflict between bureaucratic interests of creators and consumers. It goes without saying that the bureaucracy's protection of national interests (Point 3) and its general interest in predictability and stability may conflict with the demands of diversity, creativity and consumers' easy access to cultural industry products.

HISTORICAL BACKGROUND AND RECENT ECONOMIC AND INSTITUTIONAL DEVELOPMENT OF FINNISH CULTURAL INDUSTRIES

The early twentieth century

At the beginning of the century the graphic industries were rather well established in Finland and expanded during the whole second period; for example, the number of book titles published rose from 880 in 1900 to 1,337 in 1937. The most popular magazine had, at the beginning of the century, a circulation of 20,000 and the titles of magazines and journals published rose from 131 in 1900 to 429 in 1930. The public library system was established around the turn of the century and by 1930 had a combined collection of 1.3 million volumes.

The arrival of new mechanical/electronic cultural industries to Finland was remarkably fast. Films were first shown in Finland by the famous French cinematographer, Louis Lumière, in 1896. The first permanent cinema was founded in 1901. The first Finnish feature film *(The Secret Distillers)* was completed in 1907 and in 1930 the number of feature films made in Finland came to seventy-four. There were 100 cinemas by 1915 and over 200 by 1930. The biggest company throughout the years, Suomi-Filmi Ltd, alone produced twenty-three feature films in the 1920s. The large American distribution firms arrived in Finland at the end of the 1920s and at the beginning of the 1930s. The first Finnish gramophone record was made in 1901 (by Will Gaisberg of the Gramophone Company). A real 'gramophone fever' raged at the end of the 1920s when local record production really got under way. In 1929 nearly a million domestic records were sold. These records were, however, pressed and often also recorded abroad (mainly in Stockholm, Copenhagen, Berlin and London).

The first period also marked the arrival of the radio. The first broadcasts for larger audiences began in 1923 and the first (voluntary) association for this purpose was founded in the same year. A joint-stock company for radio broadcasting was established in 1925 and it became a government joint-stock company in 1934, but the density (radios per household) remained rather low until the mid-1930s. Journals and magazines developed steadily, mainly on the basis of subscriptions.

The mid-1930s to the late 1950s

This second period was a turbulent time which comprised the aftermath of depression, preparations for a war economy, two wars, and reconstruction after the lost wars. War-time temporarily boosted all the cultural industries (excluding the record industries—even though the recording and pressing of records was first initiated in Finland around 1938). Book sales and cinema attendances reached their peak and radio density more than doubled from that of the mid-1930s.

The boom levelled off after the wars in the case of the graphic industries, but film production and cinema attendances, although somewhat decreased, still remained high. The record industry started to recover slowly and by the late 1950s was approaching the same figures as at the end of the 1920s. Journals and magazines developed steadily, mainly on the basis of subscriptions, although the traditional general magazines received competition from new 'news and photo' journals and women's magazines.

The period from 1950 to 1975

The rapid expansion and the developmental features of the Finnish cultural industries during the last period is understandable against this background of passivity during the second period. The organizational inertia delayed the start of television broadcasts but development, once started, advanced rapidly. Television broadcasts were started on a commercial basis by a private company in 1956, and the government-owned Finnish Broadcasting Company (FBC) began its own broadcasts a year later. A commercial television company, the MTV, operating on the licence and using the channels of the Finnish Broadcasting Company, was founded in 1957. Regular television broadcasts by the FBC in January 1958 also meant the adoption of an obligatory television licence fee. Links with international networks (Eurovision) were established, and the receiving area expanded fast. By 1962, 92 per cent of the population was within the receiving area and the number of television sets increased exponentially.

Another direction where cultural industries also started to expand was the radio and record industry. Radio broadcasting time increased in the early 1960s, and music programmes, especially the popular daytime ones, had a greater share. But the record industry did not begin to move until the 1970s when the sales of records and cassettes expanded exponentially. Although television temporarily halted the development of journal and magazine publishing, the latter too received a new lease of life in the 1960s and expanded until 1974. Book publishing maintained its old traditions, relying on the production of reference books, encyclopedias and school- and textbooks for its profits. However, the first signs of resorting to international best-seller appeal could be perceived. The traditional pulp-fiction industry, too (based mainly on romance type of appeal), begot its modern counterpart in expanding sex, thriller, crime and general comic-book industry. The only branch that definitely fared ill in the cultural-industry explosion in the 1960s and early 1970s was the film industry, where ticket sales during the worst period went down by 10 million per annum and domestic production came to a standstill.

A more detailed account of the economic and institutional state of the Finnish cultural industries in the mid-1970s confirms, first, that the traditional graphic branch, book publishing, is still the most important economically.[1] However, the modern electronic branch, radio/television, has obviously developed rapidly and the growth of the record/cassette industry has been astounding. The only stagnant branch in the period 1970–76 is the film industry, which shows no real growth.

Some reasons for the varying economic performance of the four branches are rather obvious and well known. Thus the rapid growth of the record industry is usually explained by the rise of popular music, which, in turn, is seen as a result of the development of youth culture and the increased purchasing power of young people. The impact of this development hit the Finnish record industry belatedly in the early 1970s. The stagnation of the film industry is usually explained by the arrival and expansion of television and the effect of its substitution for cinema-going. The Finnish film industry was already in trouble before, but television is, of course, the main cause of the sharp fall in the number of cinemas in the 1960s. The healthy economic state of radio/television in the mid-1970s can be explained by the increased income from the colour-television licence fee, and advertising money from MTV. This sound state of affairs was further consolidated in the 1970s by increased economizing and austerity policies adopted after the first economic crises of the 1960s.

There is still, however, a lot left to be explained. First of all, the long-lasting depression of the film industry cannot be explained solely by the competition from television. In the latter half of the 1970s the Finnish film industry began to show some signs of revival, which now seem to be fading away. Secondly, the television companies have not been able to develop much national production despite the relatively good economic conditions. And, thirdly, the boom of the record industry levelled off and practically faded out in the latter half of the 1970s despite the rise of an indigenous Finnish youth culture. Only book publishing has been stable and economically rather sound throughout the 1970s.

There may be some further, more structural explanations for the varying economic performance of the four branches. Although the information concerning maximum audiences and break-even points is no doubt inexact and rather unreliable, it suggests some reasons for economic successes and failures. The break-even points are, or were in 1975/76, rather low for books (fiction) and (pop) records. On the contrary, the break-even point for the film industry is rather high, especially when the audience must be gained solely from the home market. The break-even point for Finnish television-programme production—which cannot be estimated in any quantitative figures—can be conceived analogously as high. The production costs for television drama are the same as those for feature films, but audience responses and ratings (and, of course, also transmission costs) limit the freedom to produce programmes for small audiences only. Thus a maximum audience of 250,000 for a film would be still satisfactory for a television drama in Finland, but one could not go much under this figure without special reasons (critical acclaim, potential foreign markets, etc.).

The above cost and audience factors also explain the economic fluctuations in the latter half of the 1970s. The development of costs (especially royalty, copyright and promotion costs) and prices in the record industry have been a major factor in the levelling off of the boom. But not alone, because there are two other factors, piracy and home recording, which also interfere and do not allow for price increases without audience losses. In the Finnish film industry the long period of stagnation created suppressed cost pressures, which seem to erupt as soon as the signs of revival, or increased public subsidies, appear, and then dampen the recovery. The same problem appears in another form in the operations of the Finnish public radio/television monopoly company, FBC. The economizing and austerity of the first half of the 1970s probably created suppressed pressures for technological investments and bureaucratic expansion, and these needs, and not those of national programme production, are served first.

The differences in the economic state of the four branches can be further understood by examining the relative share of the different phases of production/distribution in the formation of the final consumer price. Although the data are again rather inexact and unreliable, one can notice some interesting differences. First, the two branches of 'divisible products', i.e. book publishing and the record industry, differ from each other in two respects. The record industry has the additional cost factor of studio rental and musicians' fees, which increase the 'pre-production' costs. Secondly, the wholesale costs of book production are heavier because of more cumbersome stocking and transportation. With the popular-music boom and its hits, the record industry has its own problems. The hits are unpredictable and remain popular for only a short period of time, and consequently demand frequent updating of stocks. Stocking problems—together with the good economic situation and the appearance of new distribution channels—has, in both branches, led to the dominance of production over wholesale. The breakdown figures also indicate the modest position of creators in the Finnish record industry. Royalties and copyrights amount to only 12 per cent, which means that records are made to promote the performers, while in countries with a large record business the performers perform to promote records. On the other hand, low royalties and copyright payments make national production cheap and profitable.

Although the retail price breakdown for the film industry is less detailed, two interesting observations may be made from its figures. First, one can notice the importance of retail distribution, i.e. exhibition, which is reflected in its prominent share. Secondly, one can compare here the differences between the 'income distribution' of domestic and foreign films. It is clear that the production phase of national films is much more favoured than that of foreign films.[2] On the other hand, foreign products are usually those meant for worldwide distribution and therefore they reap profits from a much wider audience than do Finnish products. It seems that national exhibition—by a higher leasing share of foreign films—subsidizes national production and thus acts as a 'quasi-government'. The coin has, however, two sides. On one side, national products draw large audiences and broaden the circle of active cinemagoers; they are thus advantageous in that sense. On the other, the top foreign products and cheap low-quality films, which are used to make profits, also push aside less successful films, for example experimental national ones. Thus there are inherent problems in the role of exhibition as a 'quasi-government'. It may also be pointed out that the money earned by the independent exhibition of foreign products does not as a rule return to production as it most likely would if the domestic production were stronger and in control of exhibition. This is of course true also with respect to the programming-oriented television companies: there is no 'moral obligation' to use money which is not earned by the sale of national products for national production.

Reference may be made here to the first indicator of public intervention, i.e. taxation, as a cost factor. The 'divisible products'—books, records and cassettes—are treated as consumer goods and carry normal sales tax (Finland has not adopted a value-added tax). On the other hand, taxation is used, in the case of the film industry, as a means of supporting national production and exhibition, both in general and in order to subsidize quality production according to grade and to enhance more effective and regionally balanced distribution. We shall return to this and to the economics of radio and television below.

Indicators of business concentration seem to suggest that there is no significant correlation between economic success and business concentration. The figures are, however, somewhat deceptive. At present, two big firms in book publishing (Otava, WSOY), and one large company in the record industry (Fazer), form the backbone of these two branches. On the other hand, film production is taken care of by small, often transient and amateurishly run firms—especially since the older and bigger firms turned to distribution and exhibition—and it is generally admitted that this is one weakness of Finnish film production. It may be argued that the two above-mentioned book-publishing houses, one vertically integrated record company (production, music publishing/ wholesale distribution, ownership of music shops), together with three newspaper/journal publishers and one retail-distribution firm (Railroad Books Ltd), form an 'élite' group of Finnish cultural-industry firms. And they, if any, also function—alongside the producers' and distributors' cartels—as 'quasi-governments' within the Finnish cultural industries.

The dominant phases of the different branches are: production in book publishing, integrated production/distribution in the record industry, and wholesale distribution and exhibition (separately) in the film industry. We have indicated above the reasons for this dominance, and the dominance is further reflected in the degree and direction of vertical integration (the controlling ownership across the phase border). Dominance and vertical integration can be conceived as having both positive and negative consequences. On the one hand they create strong competitive business units, which can also act as 'quasi-governments' and subsidize weak products and production. They may, however, also lead to profit-seeking and expansionism to the neglect of the cultural aspects of development (diversity of products, equal access to distribution); or they may lead to bureaucratization and risk-avoidance, which may also be hostile to creativity and versatility.

Finnish anti-trust legislation is very lenient and allows for rather free cartel formation. Surprisingly, the cartels in the cultural industries have, however, been more often than in other sectors targets for anti-trust action. An example of this is abolition of the fixed-price system in book publishing and the liberalization of general retail trade, which made the rack sale of books and records possible in supermarkets, groceries and other general-purpose shops. The cartels lost some of their importance in the 1970s and they have turned more into bargaining organs of the industries *vis-à-vis* the government, especially in price matters. The cartels are probably more important as 'quasi-governments' in the film industry, where there are no major firms to take over this role.

Two important economic institutional aspects of cultural industries deserve attention. First, the development of retail sale has proved to be an important factor in determining the role of culture industries in cultural development. There are several new modes of retail distribution, which bring the products more efficiently to the public: department-store and rack sales, and book clubs in book production; rack jobbing and special sale spots in the record industry; cinema complexes in the film industry; and local radio and cable television in broadcasting. It has been pointed out that some forms of this 'modernization' (rack sales, book and record clubs) favour cheap popular products and best-sellers and other types favour diversity and audience orientation (cinema complexes, local radio). In Finland modernization has mainly produced the former type of consequences.

The next, and final, aspect is the internationalization of national cultural industries. In Finland the penetration of foreign capital into national cultural industries has been very limited and it existed originally only as import companies of foreign firms in the film and record industries. In the record industry the foreign companies turned to production in the 1970s and—alongside some book clubs and comic-book firms—they constitute the only economic and institutional signs of foreign economic presence. 'Cultural penetration' by way of foreign products, or their translation or imitation, is another story, which will be examined below.

THE IMPACT OF ECONOMIC AND INSTITUTIONAL FACTORS ON CULTURAL DEVELOPMENT OF FINNISH CULTURAL INDUSTRIES

Book production

In the case of book production the importance of the arts-based products (fiction, children's books, poetry, art books) slowly decreased in the 1970s. The volume and number of titles has slowly increased, but the major publishing houses have increasingly concentrated on the profitable large-public school-books and textbooks. One probably cannot speak about an actual 'crisis of fiction', but none the less, non-fiction seems to be the main production line, which is then supposedly used to support arts-based products. Similarly the number of new titles in fiction categories has decreased.

As to the types of product, one might speak of a 'trifurcation' into quality fiction and poetry, standard entertainment fiction and romance, and pulp fiction. The relative importance of the latter two categories has increased and the 'romance and pulp' has expanded within the publishing houses specializing in this category and surprisingly also within the 'more respectable' major publishing houses. The relative importance of top products and best-sellers has increased especially because of the international best-sellers. There is some indication of increased homogenization and standardization in all three categories of arts-based books: the same authors of 'quality books', the same sources and topics of standard entertainment and romance, and pulp fiction seem to maintain their position from year to year. The importance of foreign products (translations) has increased in all categories.

What are then the reasons for the above trends in development? Although the causal relations are difficult to prove by rather flimsy and soft empirical data, the following explanations suggest themselves:

The new managerial generation which ascended to leadership in the 1960s and 1970s is more business-trained and business-oriented and takes the traditional 'cultural mission' of editors less seriously; this is obviously true as regards production companies, but the same change of orientation has probably spread via vertical integration to the levels of distribution.

There has been some change in the gate-keeping system; the most obvious change is the increased importance of international book fairs, where international best-sellers are picked out by the staff members of the publishing houses.

Liberalization of the domestic retail sale legislation which made department-store and rack sale possible.

The new distribution channels (see the previous point; which, together with the book clubs, favour best-sellers).

Increases in advertising costs have made publishers focus on promoting top products and best-sellers; multimedia promotion has also increased and favours foreign multimedia products (by authors such as Alistair McLean, Desmond Bagley, Ian Fleming, etc.); this is especially true because the Finnish film and television industries are not sufficiently able to create their own multimedia products.

The record industry

In the record industry one cannot of course speak about any significant products which are not arts-based (reproduction of classic or popular music). The onslaught of popular music has, of course, increased its share of sales, but the number of titles of other types of music (especially classical music) has remained high according to international standards. There is a definite subsidizing of classical music from the profits of popular music both at the company level and via the copyright organization (Teosto, the Finnish Composers' Copyright Bureau controlled by the interests of 'serious' music). The bifurcation into 'serious', classical music and popular music is, of course, traditional and strong, and intermediate music (jazz, big-band music, light classical music, traditional music and ballads) has had a rather insignificant position in the Finnish record industry. The best-sellers—and the very idea of 'top pop'—became increasingly important in Finland in the 1970s, but probably less so than in the leading countries of the record industry.

Naturally the very fact that even in Finland only 10 per cent of records make a profit and subsidize the losses of 80 per cent, together with increasing costs, has caused pressures towards favouring top products and best-sellers. Although some trends of homogenization and standardization are noticeable (especially in the latter half of the 1970s—disco music!) there have been also some counterforces. First is the low cost of cutting national records. Consequently there have been independent producers who have tried to enrich the production and favour records of domestic origin. Secondly, Finnish radio (FBC) has forbidden programmes based on popularity charts and has also tried to act on the behalf of less-popular and less-well-known music. The latter factors together with special features of Finnish culture have also favoured records of domestic origin. Thus about half of the records and cassettes sold in Finland have been produced in Finland, but those of original Finnish music (neither translations nor adaptations) are, of course, fewer (30-40 per cent of all the titles).

If we take into consideration the strong international pressures and the greater 'openness' of the record industry to these pressures, this industry has probably fared better culturally than book publishing, at least in the first half of the 1970s. If we examine the same set of potential causes as in the case of book publishing we can probably say that:

There has been an increase in the business orientation of the new managers (mainly in the major companies), but there has been also some 'counter-culture' orientation among small independent entrepreneurs.

The gate-keeping system, especially in small companies and the radio, has tried to maintain diversity and favour records of Finnish origin.

The modernization of the distribution channels (especially rack jobbing) has favoured best-sellers and standardization, but there has been, at the same time, some increase in the demands of, and also channels for, more diversified music (special music shops, mail-order sales).

Multimedia promotion has increased, however, and it has favoured foreign best-sellers and homogenization (also, as indicated above, disco music came in strongly in the latter half of the 1970s to Finland); there has been, however, a renewal of Finnish popular music (for example, Finnish rock, punk) and the other Finnish media have promoted them rather efficiently.

The film industry

The goal of the film industry is, of course, to produce feature films, though Finnish film-makers usually acquire their skills in documentaries, short films and advertising films, but the last-mentioned can bring in money for attempts at feature film production. The bifurcation of Finnish film production into 'serious' and 'entertaining' was from the mid-1960s until the mid-1970s very deep. On the one hand, there were thrillers, folksy dramas and especially more modern comedies (the last category being mainly produced and directed by one person, the Louis de Funès of the Finnish cinema). On the other hand, there were very intellectual attempts at 'arty' or 'socially significant' films produced by small and transient companies under combined producer/director leadership (usually the same person). The former categories of film usually drew the audiences by their Finnishness, the latter drew mainly some critical acclaim as 'promising'. This situation was, of course, precipitated by the very fact that the old companies had either folded up or turned solely to distribution and exhibition. There was little consensus or willingness to co-operate, and the system was more or less divided into two establishments, where the money from exhibition went only to a very limited extent to national production. The crucial step in public support, the establishing of the Finnish Film Foundation, was the adoption of the patent solution of 'forcing' the exhibition money into production by tax arrangements. During the late 1970s the situation improved somewhat, and not solely because of public intervention. Some of the 'intellectual' producers/directors started to operate in new areas and began to make 'quality' films with sufficient audience appeal: and some of the old firms have turned back to production.

The above description answers the questions concerning best-seller appeal and the homogenization and standardization of the domestic film. The situation is more complex with foreign films. More than 200 films are imported annually into Finland, and for a break-even return they need an audience of 100,000. This is not very difficult for an internationally known film but still only about 5 per cent can be called successes and money-makers. The concentration of popularity on a few top products has probably increased in the latter half of the 1970s, and the international best-sellers (expensive gigantic films) top the pop list even in Finland. On the other hand, the renovation of old theatre networks and the rise of new cinema complexes have also somewhat increased the variety of films, and at least the number of spectators which rose by about a million from 1976 to 1978. As to internationalization, the share of foreign films has been steadily over 90 per cent (92–95 per cent) of all the films shown. Still, from 1972 to 1978, for example, the audience share of Finnish films rose from 8 to 18.2 per cent. In the latter half of the 1970s, Finnish film-makers also started to co-operate with foreign film-makers to obtain better financing and to facilitate foreign distribution. The closest neighbours (Sweden, the USSR) are the most common partners and it has been estimated that a recent joint Finnish-Soviet product will reach 70 million spectators in the socialist countries.

Radio and television

The functions of radio and television lie, of course, to a large extent outside the actual arts-based culture: in the transmission of information (news), social analysis and criticism, sports, religion, etc. About a third of the programmes of the Finnish Broadcasting Company (in the 1970s) can be counted as 'arts-based' and this share is probably still higher in the case of the commercial MTV, because it does not have the right to broadcast news. The bifurcation into 'serious' and 'light' programmes within the sphere of arts-based programmes is at least as deep and as much discussed as in the film industry although the dividing line in the case of individual programmes is probably even more difficult to draw than in the film industry.

In a small country with very limited programme production of its own, the dividing line is more often that between domestic arts-based programmes (drama, feature films, classical music, ballet, etc.) and foreign cheap entertainment (standard series and serials, old feature films). It may safely be said that whichever way we draw the line, the bifurcation deepened in the 1970s. It has become an accepted commonplace that the lengthened broadcasting time must be filled to a large extent with cheap foreign programmes, and that quality domestic programmes (including good-quality entertainment) are a luxury. On the other hand, the concentration of popularity and programming on best-sellers and top products has scarcely increased, if we omit song contests and old Finnish movies, which have proved to be real attractions in the latter half of the 1970s. Complaints that homogenization and standardization have increased in all categories of programme are frequent and diversity, in terms of new and varied programmes and innovative programming, has been rather rare. As to the internationalization of programmes, the two major companies maintain the magical line of 50 per cent: that is, more than half the programmes are domestic. This policy does not, however, rest on a natural basis of domestic production. The FBC maintains the line with news and current affairs programmes, the MTV with old domestic feature films. On the other hand, audience ratings show that Finnish dramas and feature films are the most popular programmes—as they still are in the cinemas.

The arrival of television also pushed radio in Finland to the secondary position of a news and music medium, and a medium of horizontal programming. With the boom of the record industry, radio became all over the world the most powerful promoter of recorded music and radio programmers and disc-jockeys (DJs) became the most powerful gate-keepers of the record industry. This happened also in Finland, but, as we indicated earlier, there have been conscious attempts to control the gate-keeping role of radio and diminish its effects as the promoter of top hits and best-sellers. This has even succeeded to a considerable degree. In general, audience attitudes towards radio, its programmes and news functions have been more favourable than those towards television, although this may also be due to the difference in visibility of the two media.

Mediation of the effects from economic and institutional development to cultural development has, in the field of radio and television, some peculiarities owing to the strong monopolistic position of the public radio and television company. In order to understand the development in the 1970s we must point out the following facts and events:

Although the Finnish Broadcasting Company has since 1948 been under the rather strict control of Parliament, managerial and political problems have played a central role in its development during the 1960s and 1970s.

The company experienced a period of 'radical renewal' from 1965 to 1971; led by the director-general of that period, its objective was to make radio and television a leading force for social and cultural change and reform; this experiment led to political battles, the dismissal of the director, and to 'normalization' under increased party-political control.

Since 1971, the board of supervisors and the programme councils (that is, the organs of parliamentary control) have increasingly emphasized impartiality and politically and socially 'balanced' programming; and the new director-general has focused mainly on the managerial tasks. Consequently the 1970s was a period of uneventful development—or even stagnation; but it was also a period of increased political appointments even for the operative tasks of the FBC, and it has also been a period of increased trade unionism among its employees.

All the above events have left their imprint on management, programme production and programming: management has been that of austerity and economic efficiency, programme production has become more of a routine with little encouragement to innovations, and the programming has become standardized by the rules concerning impartiality, division of labour between the two channels (TV1 and TV2), and the relative share of different types of programme.

The above description pertains only to the FBC, but the same events have also influenced the commercial company; the MTV's role has been strengthened by the 'normalization' and increased inertia of the FBC. This and economic success have increased its appetite, and it has aspired to broaden its activities: to get more broadcasting time, to secure the right to broadcast news, to become an active partner in the development of new technology and media. The MTV's problem, however, is that the implementation of most of its aspirations require political decision-making and blessing from Parliament and the political parties; and to obtain this, the MTV must also be politically cautious and also careful about its programmes in order to maintain a good public image and audience support (this, of course, gives a new dimension to the importance of audience polls and ratings); and it goes without saying that all this cannot lead to innovative programme production and programming.

But in another way the two television companies are also prisoners of each other; the tax from the MTV should actually liberate the FBC to operate over and above the imperative constraints of the public licence fee, that is, from the need to be popular to justify the use of the viewers' money. This advantage has been cancelled, however, by the very existence of the MTV. The latter gives the audience a comparison basis and forces the FBC into a popularity contest, in general and on the level of the acquisition of international popular programmes.

There is no need for much discussion about the promotion of radio and television programmes; there is a steady information system which expanded strongly in the first half of the 1970s: it comprises the radio/television sections of newspapers and journals, special bulletins and journals, and especially gossip about the programmes and their stars in the general journals and magazines. However, special mention should be made of audience ratings which maintain the 'market mechanism' within radio/television activities: they are important both for the FBC (justification of spending) and the MTV (competition with the FBC, information for advertising).

One can, however, elaborate further on the role of radio and television in creating and magnifying multimedia promotion. Especially in the 1960s and the first half of the 1970s television was the major promoter of all performing artists and the creator of new celebrities, and as such, a major promoter in all the branches of cultural industry, though radio has become the real 'gatekeeper' for the record industry. However, in contrast to the radio, television has been less conscious of its multimedia effects and it has, to a larger extent, promoted best-sellerism, top products and transient fashions.

PRIVATE-SECTOR AUTONOMY AND PUBLIC AND COLLECTIVE INTERVENTION IN THE FINNISH CULTURAL INDUSTRIES: OVERVIEWS AND FURTHER ELABORATION

Book publishing

The major measures of the public sector which have influenced substantially the economic, institutional and cultural development of the book-publishing industry are as follows:
Sales tax, which was introduced in 1964 after thirteen years of suspension, and is as severe as that of average consumption goods (now 14 per cent).
The abolition of the fixed-price system (the right of publishers to determine the retail price) and the liberalization of retail (that is, the right to sell all books in department stores, supermarkets, stands, kiosks, etc.).
The continued delegation of school-book production to the private sector (the approval of the National Board of Schools and the National Board of Vocational Education is, however, needed for regular textbook use).
The purchase of books by the public library system.
The above measures of public intervention have mainly grown up out of general economic and cultural policies without conscious considerations. There are, however, more direct measures aimed at controlling and guiding the branch. One can find such measures as:
The system of state grants and other forms of public aid to authors.
The regulation of the freedom of publishing in order to enforce ethical and social responsibility of authors and publishers (legislation concerning rules of printing and distributing printed material, free copy deposits, libel).
The regulation of publishing from the moral point of view (prevention of the violation of moral standards, religious convictions, privacy).
The first system expanded considerably during the 1960s and 1970s and now includes several different subsystems, such as library loan, compensations, prizes, actual grants, fellowships and pensions given by the Ministry of Education, the Central Arts Council, the Arts Council for Literature, provincial arts councils and some special boards and committees. The second of these systems is upheld by the Constitution and a special law (Act of Freedom of Printed Reproduction). The third one is upheld by the criminal code and a special law (Act of Distributing Obscene Literature).

The first of these measures can provide rather flexible policy means for developing the branch. The system has, however, been directed more towards improving the conditions of authors than to guiding the system as a whole. The other two sets of measures create the stable (and sometimes even rather conservative) institutional environment for the branch. They are mostly dormant and have nowadays cultural or economic significance only in certain extreme cases and situations. This happens usually when a vigilance movement tries to revive some old statutes or their interpretations (for example, accusations of blasphemy, curbing of pornography). All in all, the 'modernization' of these measures (in practice, if not in the letter of the law) has been generally accepted.

As to the collective intervention exercised by professional organizations, voluntary organizations and trade associations, two of which were mentioned earlier in this report, may be cited:

Measures for the protection of authors' rights (copyright regulations).

Measures taken by the publishers' association to regulate the activities of its members and to influence public policies.

The copyright system

The Finnish system of copyright follows the outlines of the Berne Convention. Although the system has a definite national legal basis (Copyright Act), it can be at least partly considered as a collective non-public system of intervention. The owners of the right must themselves, either individually or via their organizations, secure their rights and implement the legislation. In book publishing the monitoring of the rights is on an individual basis, although the Finnish Writers' Association acts sometimes as a pressure group in copyright matters. In Finland, as anywhere else, the copyright legislation has become a central problem for the arts and cultural industries. This is mainly due to the new technological development, and in the case of book publishing, to illegal copying. To help solve this problem, an association to defend the interests of publishers and authors was founded in Finland in 1979. The whole copyright legislation is also up for reform, but because of the huge new problems, the results can scarcely be expected before the latter half of the 1980s. Until now, the impact of copyright legislation on economic and cultural development has been much smaller in book publishing than in the record industry. This is partly due to the semi-professional status of most Finnish authors: there are few full-time writers. The problems of secondary rights have been also less acute than in the major book-publishing countries.

We have already referred to the status and activities of the most important trade association of the branch, the Finnish Publishers' Association. It has, however, lost some of its importance, and from an economic point of view the new cartelling of the retail trade (bookshops) into co-operative chains of joint purchasing and distribution is much more important. These chains are usually co-ordinated by a special firm, organized as a consumers' co-operative. This formation of the co-operative chains has become rather common in the retail trade of special products, which must combat the increasing control of the markets by the general wholesale business.

The other organs of collective interest (e.g. the Finnish Authors' Association, the Finnish chapter of PEN) are less visible in the collective control and guidance of the branch. Separate mention may, however, be made of the Finnish Association of Libraries, which co-ordinates the activities of public libraries and represents their economic interest *vis-à-vis* the publishers and the state.

The record industry

Private autonomy is still greater in this branch than in that of book production. The sales tax for records has been always taken for granted, and there is no acquisition of records for 'public purposes' (as educational aids, library stock, although there are now a few public libraries with record sections). As we mentioned earlier, one can, of course, interpret increased importance of rack jobbing as a consequence of the general liberalization of the domestic retail trade. A special case of public intervention, however, is:

The liberalization of foreign trade (starting with FINNEFTA) which lowered the prices of the hardware and accelerated the boom of the record industry in the 1970s. Now the same factor is turning to the disadvantage of the branch, because of the home-recording of the music by the audience (Finns have, from the very beginning of the boom, used more tape recorders and cassette recorders than record players).

Another type of public intervention which we have not listed in our overview is:

Public promotion of records and the whole industry by radio and by the juke boxes of the publicly controlled Slot Machine Association. We have indicated above the active role of radio; the Slot Machine Association has made a similar—though more business-oriented—promotion of national 'single' records. The association is also an important purchaser of singles.

As to collective intervention, this branch is more developed than book publishing. First of all, there are two established and active organizations, which monitor the observance of copyright legislation, collect the payments and distribute them to the property-owners. They are Teosto, the Composers' Copyright Bureau, and Gramex, the Performing Artists' Copyright Organization. The former is a part of the international copyright system, the latter is still only national, because Finland has not signed the Rome Convention. Secondly, we have already indicated the rather central role of the Finnish National Group of the IFPI, which has co-ordinated the price negotiations and import policies of the producers. We have also indicated that the cartel-type activities of the group are now probably waning because of the increase in 'wild' importing.

The film industry

The film industry has probably attracted most attention among planners and reformers committed to cultural development. From the perspective of this interest—often amounting to zeal—the choice of the measures suggested and implemented is rather narrow. The major measure, used also in Finland, is:

The re-allocation of the resources within the branch by maintaining a special tax and 'recycling' its revenues.

The technical aspects of the tax and the recycling of its revenues in Finland are complex. In short, there is a 'quality graded' admission tax of 10–30 per cent (highest for low-quality entertainment, violence and sex), a 10 per cent point discount for socially or culturally important types of film (documentaries, children's films, etc.) and for small cinemas and cinemas in small communities; and a further 10 per cent point discount if the cinema pays a 4 per cent levy to the Finnish Film Foundation. The economic consequences of this arrangement at firm level are again complex. We can in this context spell out the general logic and concrete form of realization.

First of all, why should there be a tax at all with its complex manipulation? After the 'discounts', the tax brings in very little money to the government (for instance, in 1980, the production subsidies from the foundation were estimated to be 5 million markkas, while the government's gains from the tax were estimated at 2 million markkas). The tax is not levied, however, because of greediness or bureaucratic inertia on the part of the Ministry of Finance, but has several functions. First of all, it has a censorship function: it can be used to punish 'morally dubious' films. It is this type of film which still brings in the above-mentioned 2 million markkas. Secondly, the tax and the foundation levy help to wring some money from foreign producers and importers, which the Finnish distributors and cinema-owners could probably not get through direct negotiations. Thirdly, the system at least formally observes the rules of the international agreements concerning the liberalization of international trade, which the Finnish Government has signed (FINNEFTA, EEC, OECD'S regulations concerning invisible operations). Fourthly, the arrangement stipulates clearly the 'rules of redistribution' of the money for the long-range development of the branch ('if 4 per cent via Foundation mainly for production, then 6 per cent directly to the exhibition'). Some of these functions could be maintained if the tax were to be abolished and the levy maintained, but not all.

The Finnish Film Foundation was originally controlled by the interest groups of the branch, but it is now under political control (the board and management are politically appointed). A Finnish film will automatically get back the 4 per cent levy paid by cinemas from its revenues. The main function of the foundation is to subsidize quality production. The support must be applied and the foundation decides project by project. About 60–70 per cent of the foundation's annual aid is used for this purpose. In addition, the foundation supports the other phases of the branch from the rest of its annual resources: it gives guarantees against the losses of importing quality films, loans and interest subventions for the renovation of cinemas, and subsidies for public relations and advertising of the Finnish cinema.[3]

There are mainly two types of criticism directed against the foundation solution. First, the money is not considered sufficient. It has been calculated that between 1970 and 1976 the average cost of making a feature film was 441,000 markkas and the average loss 174,000 markkas. It is open to question, however, whether the increased direct-production support would solve the financial problems. We have indicated above that the suppressed cost pressures might make this solution much more expensive than the figures now show. Secondly, some experts have criticized the system where a politically elected body decides in detail and project by project which film-makers and projects will get subsidies, and how much. It has been suggested that the subsidies should go to financially sound companies and to film-makers who can prove their qualifications, and not to individual projects or ideas.

In film production we encounter another form of production support that has not yet been discussed. This is the functioning of the other branches of cultural industries as 'quasi-governments'. Thus we have:

The support of film production by television companies which at the same time agree with the producers about the later broadcasting of the subsidized film. In Finland the active company in this area has been the MTV. For example, between 1974 and 1977 it gave financial or service support to thirteen films. The FBC has also increased its support to film production and nowadays both companies support at least one film production a year. It may also be mentioned that one of the major publishing houses bought a film company and some cinemas. This is still a curiosity, but may be an indication of future trends, because the rights for books, filming and exhibition are increasingly sold together and by the one and the same international integrated corporation.

In the field of financial support we also find the same system of public support to the arts and artists as in film publishing: state prizes, grants, fellowships and pensions financed by the state budget and distributed by the Ministry of Education, Central Arts Council, Arts Council for Film Art, provincial arts councils and some boards and committees. Furthermore, the Ministry of Education has also helped to finance experiments in establishing municipal cinemas, and it has also subsidized the operations of the Finnish Film Archives.

If we move from financial aid to moral uplifting we encounter in the film branch a new system, namely:

Public *ex ante* moral control of the contents of all films: i.e. film censorship. The control is carried out by the National Board of Film Censorship appointed by the government. Finnish film censorship is concerned mainly with the social and ethical content of films, but a few films have been also rejected by the National Board of Film Censorship because of their political content (usually they have been deemed to offend other countries, which is an offence even according to the Finnish criminal code). But the board does not punish by banning only: it also decides the tax category for the films, and it is thus important in the implementation of the much discussed tax law. Finnish film censorship is rather strict, because Finland has ratified the resolutions of the pre-war Geneva Convention concerning the distribution of pornographic material.

As to collective intervention in the film industry, we have mentioned above the cartel-type associations on different levels: the Film Producers' Association (or actually two of them), the Finnish Film Chamber, the Distributors' Association and the Theatre Owners' Association. All of these function co-ordinatedly and form a 'quasi-government', although it has been somewhat removed from the major battlefield, production and its public support. These associations have, however, been important in day-to-day arrangements of the branch and in organizing the relations *vis-à-vis* the state administration. There is another group of 'more radical' organizations comprising the Federation of Film Societies, the Association for Television and Film Education, Film Contact and several other educational associations and information centres. The grouping here into two separate categories reflects to a certain extent the above-mentioned bifurcation of production, and the political battles of the 1960s and the early 1970s.

As to copyright legislation in the film industry, special mention may be made of the stipulations of the Copyright Act concerning the use of literary material and music in films. Music payments are collected by the Composers' Copyright Bureau.

Radio and television

Our second branch of rather limited private sector autonomy is that of radio and television. In this field, we may describe public intervention as:

The control and guidance of the radio/television branch by state ownership of the Finnish Broadcasting Company; the control is made effective by licensing the company in a monopoly position as the only company having the right to radio and television broadcasting. This control expands to include the MTV, which does not have its own operating licence, but operates under the FBC's licence and on its network. The FBC is under parliamentary control through its politically appointed board, and this control also covers the FBC's 'lease-holder', the MTV. Political control is reinforced with the programme content control by the politically appointed programme councils, the technical and administrative control by the Ministry of Transportation and by the technical and administrative control of co-operation with the National Board of Post and Telegraph. The legislative basis for this political and administrative system is provided by the old Radio Act and Radio Company Act.

The arrangements described above provide only the political and administrative framework for radio and television activities. In addition there is a jungle of normative regulations laying down the actual concrete rules for activities and functions to be carried out daily. Thus for the whole system of radio and television activities there are:

Regulative norms of the Operation Licence (given by the government) which stipulate how to observe the assigned channels and frequencies, how to maintain impartiality, how to carry out *ex ante* programme control and the relations between the FBC and the MTV.

The special *Rules of Programme Activities* give more detailed regulations concerning the basic objectives of programme policies, impartiality and the procedures of the programme councils. Furthermore, there are special regulations for the responsibility of radio/television employees. These are incorporated in the Radio Responsibility Act, and in the Correction Norms, which stipulate the rights of audiences and individual citizens *vis-à-vis* radio and television programmes, in case they should violate citizens' reputation, privacy or career. There is a special correction board which hears complaints. However, the Council for the Mass Media mentioned above can also deal with the complaints against radio/television programmes and their producers.

Television films are not affected by *ex ante* censorship but they are naturally subject to the stipulations of the Radio Responsibility Act.

There is no doubt that the above thicket of rules and regulations is partly of political origin; and that these rules and regulations may entail strong constraints over activities. The economic oddities of the present radio and television organization were discussed above; and it seems that the internal normative control and guidance system may have characteristics (multiplicity, bureaucratic inflexibility) which prevent the efficient use of radio/television in general and for cultural purposes.

Finally, in the case of the radio/television branch the international context of activities also provides a special system of control and guidance. Finnish membership in the ITU and the participation of the Finnish Broadcasting Company in the activities of the EBU, the OIRT and the CEPT are examples of this. All these organizations may be sources of regulative binding norms and have considerable effects on national radio/television activities. The 1965 Montreux Convention constitutes another example.

PUBLIC AND COLLECTIVE INTERVENTION AND PRIVATE-SECTOR AUTONOMY: CONCLUSIONS AND RECOMMENDATIONS

We can start by asking what precipitates public intervention. Let us first consider political and ideological aspects. It seems that we can very easily find examples of the following vicious circle: (a) political and ideological reasons for intervention; (b) control and change of economic and institutional factors; (c) disynchronization with general economic and institutional development; (d) increased economic and institutional problems; and (e) need for more public economic and institutional intervention. A similar vicious circle can start with economic reason: (a) economic reasons (usually the felt need to rescue a branch or some firms from a financial slump and imminent bankruptcy); (b) control and change of financial and institutional factors; (c) isolation from the general economic and institutional development; (d) increased economic and institutional problems; and (e) need for more public economic and institutional intervention.

We can also point to a similar vicious circle for a collective intervention based on partial (i.e. special group) interests. This could be: (a) fast economic development of the branch; (b) increased motives of a group or some groups to increase their share of the development; (c) strong collective intervention; (d) economic and institutional changes; (d) disynchronization with the general economic and institutional development; (e) increased economic and institutional problems; (f) increased collective intervention; and (g) increased economic and institutional problems.

The same vicious circles can also be started by interventions which are motivated by cultural, moral or ethical reasons: (a) financial and institutional intervention; (b) disynchronization with, or isolation from, the general economic and institutional development; (c) increased economic and institutional problems; and (d) increased need for public economic and institutional intervention.

We can next ask, what is, then, the relationship between economic and institutional development and cultural development? To this we can give again a simple answer: cultural development fares ill when economic and institutional development fares ill, but cultural development does not necessarily fare well when economic and institutional development fares well. And furthermore: public and collective interventions which make economic and cultural development fare ill also cause cultural development to fare ill but public and institutional interventions which make economic and institutional developments fare well do not necessarily make cultural development fare well.

The above vicious circles and commonplaces are not meant to be directed against public and collective intervention in general. We may condense them into the following recommendations:

There are legitimate economic and institutional reasons for public intervention in cultural industries, but these must not isolate or disynchronize the development of cultural industries from the general economic and institutional development.

There are legitimate cultural, moral and ethical reasons for public intervention in cultural industries, but these must not isolate the development of cultural industries from the general economic and institutional development.

There are legitimate collective interests to start collective intervention, but this intervention must not isolate the development of cultural industries from the general economic and institutional development.

There are legitimate reasons for public and collective interventions to curtail economic and institutional development, if it runs counter to cultural development.

There are also reasons to abstain from public economic and institutional development, if it runs counter to cultural development, and reasons to abstain from public economic and institutional intervention when it would favour such economic and institutional development if detrimental to cultural development.

One may agree with all these recommendations, but still argue that it is in practice difficult to decide what are 'sufficient and legitimate reasons' to intervene and what constitutes 'development'; and it is also difficult to weigh cultural and other priorities in decision-making. Despite these arguments we can try to use the above recommendations for a rough overall evaluation of the public and collective intervention in Finnish cultural industries in the 1960s and 1970s.

In the first place, there is, all in all, a rather average amount of public intervention within Finnish cultural industries, when compared with the other sectors of the Finnish economy. Finland has a rather long tradition of state-owned industry and a somewhat shorter one in subsidies to, and direct regulative control of, private business. From this perspective, the public radio and television company and subsidies to the film industry are by no means anomalous, nor can any of the less extensive and intensive types of intervention be counted as such. Our first criticism is, however, directed against the strongest forms of public intervention, namely the radio/television monopoly and the special film subsidies. This does not, however, depend on the degree and intensity of the intervention, but the disynchronization of the development of these branches in relation to the general economic and institutional development. There is the danger of the above-mentioned vicious circles in these branches, and the description and analysis presented above should substantiate this argument.

Our second general criticism pertains to public interventions which focus on social and economic development irrespective of the cultural consequences. We have pointed out in our description such measures as the sales tax on books, abolition of fixed prices for books and liberation of international trade. It is difficult to believe that all these measures were economic necessities, but if they were, one may still criticize most of them for neglecting the cultural consequences and not providing 'soft transfers' and compensations for the industries. There are possibilities of doing so, even in the case of the liberalization of international trade, as the foundation system in the film industry indicates.

One cannot direct much criticism from our general perspective towards the rest of the measures. The ethical and moral regulations have lost a lot of their repressive nature, and can be opposed at best on ethical and moral grounds (that is, it is not 'right' to have such regulations). Some of the allocative measures (like the school-book 'contracts' of book publishing) may divert firms from arts-based products. However, the rest of the measures are mainly of a limited allocative kind, which can scarcely be criticized from other perspectives than that of adequacy. The lack of adequacy does not pertain only to the amount of money or control. Some measures are inadequate because their functions have not been sufficiently considered and they have not been sufficiently focused. Thus, for example, grants to the arts and to artists are mainly given as social services, and the diversity of creation or the need to educate new generations of artists are not sufficiently considered. Similarly, the financial and technical aid of television to film production may be short-sighted from the same perspective. One could also probably worry about the development of copyright legislation and its implementation: when further developed, it may give rise to some major barriers both for the economic and cultural development of cultural industries.

We have discussed above the sins of commission. When we turn to the sins of omission, that is, begin to enumerate the insufficiencies and the lack of intervention, we have naturally much more to criticize. One might, of course, suggest more money, more technologies and more rational regulations for all branches. As to economic and institutional interventions, on the basis of our previous analysis the following areas call for urgent reform: (a) copyright legislation (with a potential compensatory tax for the book-publishing and record industry); (b) a sales tax reform (to alleviate the problems of the book-publishing and record industry and make them equal with the film industry); (c) radio/television legislation (for greater economic efficiency, decentralized companies, less bureaucracy, and better protection against political pressures); and (d) improvement of the position of national cultural industries in international competition (export subsidies, promotion services, compensation for the consequences of the liberalization of trade, better regional co-operation—in a Scandinavian and European context—with other countries as regards production, financing and distribution). Some of these reforms (copyright legislation, radio/television legislation) are already under preparation, but one cannot expect much in terms of speediness or results in these two controversial areas. The other wishes are still more utopian.

We can draw up a less utopian and more concrete list when we turn to more specific cultural problems. Our suggestions are based on our analysis of the cultural consequences of economic and institutional development, and the mechanism mediating between economic and institutional and cultural development.

Thus we shall first recommend the enhancing of the status of arts-based products in the cultural industries. This could be done in several ways: through public contracts and purchases (within the public library or educational system); by developing gate-keeping systems (especially radio/television promotion and cultural programmes, providing new distribution channels, the training of managers and critics, encouraging and subsidizing small business enterprises specializing in arts-based products).

Secondly, we might recommend such measures as would diminish the bifurcation of cultural industry products into 'high' culture and 'popular' or 'mass' culture. Here one should focus on measures enhancing and encouraging the 'lower part', that is popular culture within cultural industries. The measures set forth in the previous point could apply here as well, but the education of the creators, mediators (writers, translators, DJs, radio/television programmers, journalists), and consumers would be of major importance.

Thirdly, we could recommend measures which would curb best-sellerism and over-emphasis of the top products. In this area regulation of the gate-keeping and promotional systems (radio, television, journals/magazines) via subsidies, training and alternative channels should be given priority.

Fourthly, we would recommend measures that would prevent the homogenization and standardization of the products. In this area measures could be planned to encourage creators (both in 'high' and 'popular' culture), facilitate the career of young artists, make their access to production easier and in general provide 'talent nurseries' for cultural industries. The same problem can, of course, be approached from the other end by improving consumer education and thus creating a more diversified demand.

Fifthly, one could recommend improvement of the competitive position of domestic products *vis-à-vis* international imports. Nearly all the measures recommended in the previous points could be used for this purpose. Special attention should be paid, however, to the positive use of the multimedia effect in promoting domestic production.

NOTES

1. Actually the other graphic branch, journal/magazine publishing, is the second or maybe even the first. In 1976, this branch published 250 commercial and more than 750 non-commercial titles, and the sales income of the leading twenty commercial journals was more than 400 million markkas.
2. The distribution of income may vary considerably as regards the production of films, depending on whether they are worldwide successes or cheap, old, low-quality material.
3. The functions of the foundation have been expanded to cover decision-making concerning some of the quality-film subsidies and grants financed by the state budget.

15   The role of the public authorities

Augustin Girard

The government authorities, the natural protectors of creative artists at the input stage of the industrial process, and of the general public (consumers and practitioners) at the receiving end of that process, will implement strategies very much their own, not necessarily opposed to those of private business, but very often designed to offset them. Care must be taken to ensure that the greatest possible number of creative artists are given every possible chance, that the wide range of tastes, ideologies, traditions and forms of expression is respected, and at the same time that a culture of quality, a living, creative culture conducive to genuine awareness and learning is accessible in practice to all sectors of the population. Support must therefore be given judiciously to the branches of industry that are necessary for modern cultural life and responsible for extending a country's influence abroad, maintaining its cultural independence and modernizing antiquated cultural institutions. What must also be done is to promote the quality of cultural life, one that is now shared by all, and counteract the natural trend towards the baser forms of entertainment—a sign of the degradation of a people and the decadence of a nation.

The main criterion to be borne in mind by the public authorities when singling out one or another stage in the production and marketing process that may require attention in any particular branch of cultural industries will therefore be one or more of the six major objectives a modern cultural policy may set itself:

Broadening access to culture; democratizing, decentralizing and stimulating the cultural life of the people.

Improving the quality in the mass media and developing community and individual media.

Fostering creative work, offering scope for many skills, making better use of talent and raising the standard of living of artists and those professionally engaged in cultural activities.

Modernizing traditional cultural institutions.

Strengthening national potential for cultural production.

Ensuring a country's cultural influence abroad and safeguarding its cultural independence.

Means available to the public authorities

There are five ways in which the public authorities can achieve the major objectives concerning cultural industries:

Direct aid, consisting mainly of subsidies or purchases of goods and services out of the state budget; such assistance should be kept to a minimum because the inevitable bureaucratic, centralizing mechanism of state systems are detrimental to creative cultural work.

Indirect aid in the form of tax relief, varying a great deal from one country to another. It includes special tax rebates, reduced VAT rates and straight-forward exemptions, but there are also more sophisticated arrangements involving special or added taxes levied when a rebate is granted; the revenues they bring in return to the branch of industry concerned in the shape of a special, extra-budgetary support fund. Indirect aid of this kind is preferable for it is conducive to decentralized decision-making and an increase in the number of decision-making authorities.

Regulations (specifications, programme contracts, etc.) which compel certain branches to comply with rules governing public service, such as for example the maximum percentage of foreign films on television, the number of channels reserved for local television, and so on.

International conventions, especially concerning copyright (authors and artists).

Other incentives like festivals, prizes, lotteries, etc.

Lastly, extending to cultural industries bank guarantee arrangements and export loans which exist for other branches of industry in difficulty.

A double-entry table can thus be drawn up for each category of cultural industry in which the purposes of cultural policy are set against possible types of public aid (Table 1). When a particular branch is being investigated for aid purposes, it is necessary to determine which stage in the production-marketing process will bring in the highest returns on the assistance provided, taking into account the cultural policy objective to be attained.

TABLE 1. The role of the state in cultural industries

Objectives of a modern cultural policy	Role of the public authorities					
	Direct aid	Tax-relief measures		Regulations	International conventions	Other incentives
		rebates	added taxes			
1. Broadening access to culture: democratizing, decentralizing, stimulating the cultural life of the people						
2. Improving quality in the mass media and developing community and individual media						
3. Fostering creative work offering scope for many skills and making better use of artistic and professional talent						
4. Modernizing traditional cultural institutions						
5. Strengthening national potential for cultural production						
6. Ensuring the country's influence abroad and safeguarding its cultural influence						

Conclusion

This work demonstrates that thinking during the past decade has had the merit of seeking to implant the cultural debate in the material context of its subject, particularly when it has deliberately focused on the problems of cultural production (how cultural products are thought up, selected, designed, manufactured, distributed, promoted and consumed), even though some authorities still refuse to concede the importance of the 'leisure industries'.

The products of the cultural industries are tending to invade the general human cultural environment and most leisure activities. The very fact of promoting the consumption of such products as opposed to other types of cultural attitudes and practices (creation, participation, long, reflective learning processes) is leading to radical changes in the cultural development of societies and seems to be affecting the very values upon which the different cultural identities are based. Whether one likes it or not, the tendency towards uniformity and mass culture is undermining one of the foundations of the cultural heritage of mankind, namely, the very diversity of the conceptions, values and customs of which it is composed.

It is therefore more than ever necessary to examine the effects of cultural industries on social practices as a whole, taking into account the diversity of social models. This should assist public authorities in the Member States of Unesco in taking decisions and framing strategies in this field.

It is not sufficient, however, to stress the negative effects of the cultural industries in relation to more traditional activities. It is more important and more realistic to analyse their positive interactions so as to determine to what extent and under what conditions each could support the other, both at the stage of creation and at that of promotion and distribution, particularly in activities involving participation and training. The conclusions that might be drawn from these analyses deserve to be brought to the attention of policy-makers and decision-makers in the cultural industries, as well as those involved in traditional cultural and planning bodies.

Economic analyses should nevertheless, in the future, remain central to any comprehensive consideration of this subject. They should, in particular, bring into sharper focus the general problems and sectoral aspects of the cultural industries. It is also clearly on the basis of such analyses that the public authorities and private sectors will set up or develop national cultural industries.

In any case, what is at stake is the establishment or resumption of a dialogue between cultures which would no longer take place only between producers and consumers but would foster conditions for collective and truly diversified creative effort in which the receiver would become a transmitter in his turn, while guaranteeing that the transmitter, even when institutionalized, would learn to become a receiver once again. What is at stake is harmonious development in diversity and mutual respect. This development cannot be reduced to 'economic growth accompanied by social change'. This indeed is essential, 'if development is to be worth anything, but this change should be in a certain direction, for the better, that it should neither condemn man to even harsher conditions nor reduce him to the status of a slave or a robot within a disorganized, soulless community; that far from constricting man, it should set him free'.[1]

---

1. *Thinking Ahead: Unesco and the Challenges of Today and Tomorrow*, Paris, Unesco, 1977, p. 95.